Reappraisals in History

Reappraisals
in HISTORY

*New Views on History and Society
in Early Modern Europe*

by J. H. Hexter

HARPER TORCHBOOKS ♦ *The Academy Library*

HARPER & ROW, PUBLISHERS, NEW YORK AND EVANSTON

8352 14

To Ruth
and the Memory of Fan

Acknowledgment is gratefully made for permission to reproduce essays by Professor Hexter which originally appeared in the following journals: The Editors of *The American Historical Review* for 'The Problem of the Presbyterian Independents'; *Encounter* (London) for 'Storm Over the Gentry'; *Explorations in Entrepreneurial History* for 'The Myth of the Middle Class in Tudor England'; *Journal of Economic History* for 'A New Framework for Social History'; *Political Science Quarterly* for 'The Historian and His Day'; and The University of Chicago for 'The Education of the Aristocracy in the Renaissance' from *Journal of Modern History*, © The University of Chicago.

CONTENTS

		Page
Acknowledgments		vi
Foreword *by Peter Laslett*		vii
Preface		xvii

I IN GENERAL

1.	The Historian and His Day	1
2.	A New Framework for Social History	14
3.	'Factors in Modern History'	26

II IN PARTICULAR

4.	The Education of the Aristocracy in the Renaissance	45
5.	The Myth of the Middle Class in Tudor England	71
6.	Storm Over the Gentry	117
	Appendix A: Bibliographical Note	149
	B: The 'Contemporary Witnesses'	153
	C: An Individual Case: Sir Thomas Tresham	160
	D: Professor Tawney's Statistics	162
7.	The Problem of the Presbyterian Independents	163

III PERSONAL

| 8. | Personal Retrospect and Postscript | 185 |

ACKNOWLEDGMENTS

I AM GRATEFUL to the *American Historical Review, Encounter*, the *Journal of Economic History*, the *Journal of Modern History, Explorations in Entrepreneurial History*, and the *Political Science Quarterly* for permission to reprint essays which in their first and unrevised form appeared in those publications.

To acknowledge in detail the excellent advice given me by many academic friends, whose wisdom I hope rather than expect may be reflected in this book, would make a very long list of names. Moreover, it might lead friends with tender consciences to disqualify themselves from reviewing the book, a consummation devoutly to be avoided. To one most helpful scholar I am free here to attempt to express, however inadequately, my gratitude. My friend Peter Laslett has not only given time on which there are many other heavy demands to write a foreword to *Reappraisals in History*; he also proposed the collection in the first place and unselfishly undertook all the effort needed to find a publisher for it.

To my wife, Ruth Mullin Hexter, and my grandmother, the late Fannie Marks, to whom this book is dedicated, my debt is beyond measure and beyond words. Those who know me well may gain some sense of its dimensions when I say that my grandmother put up with me for almost thirty years and my wife has done so for almost twenty.

FOREWORD

' HISTORICAL REVOLUTION', writes Professor Hexter, 'comparable to the scientific revolution of the seventeenth century seems desirable (and may indeed be under way).' This is perhaps the most important point which a historian could make about his study, and it is put forward half in parenthesis, almost as an aside. In the work he has done on our history, it would seem, this American scholar has come to relish the English liking for understatement.

He goes on to assure us that this fundamental change in historical attitude will be no heroic matter, for one of its characteristics will be to abandon the hope of a historians' Galileo, Newton or Einstein. It will not consist in the creation of ambitious general theories, but in 'piecemeal advances', historian after historian will re-examine 'the place and time with which he is mainly concerned, and [will seek] to contrive, for telling about what went on in that bounded time and place, a vocabulary of conceptions better suited to bring out its character'. Karl Popper's 'piecemeal social engineering' comes to mind, with all its explosive energy. In the intellectual world of our day the force of an idea does not vary with its grandiosity.

These essays in historical revision, then, will be read in the knowledge that their author is concerned with general and fundamental things as well as with particular problems. They will be judged for their critical penetration and for their suggestive fertility, their success in disposing of established conventions of historical opinion and in propounding new ones. But they will also be read for the information they contain. In 'The Education of the Aristocracy in the Renaissance', for example, will be found a juxtaposition of facts about the training, reading habits and attitudes of noblemen over most of Western Europe of a kind which would be hard to find in the writings of British scholars of any period. Hexter brings us face to face with a failing peculiar to our country and lamentably characteristic of our generation, our inveterate insularity.

In this he is an example of the advantages possessed by the American tradition of historical criticism, advantages in diversity of intellectual ancestry and in distance from the scene of recurrent entanglement, advantages which are too often overlooked in the discussion of its failings. From a boyhood in the Middle Western state of Ohio when immigration from the wide world was at its height, he proceeded through a succession of university organizations unlike any in our country, until he reached the graduate school at Harvard, again an institution for which we have no counterpart. There he became a student of the *Renaissance period*, a phrase which he criticizes in this book. It did at least compel him to address his attention to all the countries of Western Europe between the fifteenth and eighteenth centuries, as well as to England which was to be his particular province.

His first work, *The Reign of King Pym*, was published at Harvard in 1941. In this, it must be said, there was little enough to mark him as the original amongst his contemporaries, useful and illuminating as it is as a historical monograph. Eleven years later, however, he published *More's* Utopia, *the Biography of an Idea* (Princeton, 1952). This book is a remarkable *tour de force* of literary biography, literary detection and historical insight, showing to the full the versatility and cosmopolitanism which had come to characterize his maturer writings. There are also several occasional pieces in the intellectual history of his chosen centuries, and Hexter is as much of an authority on Machiavelli's use of his sources as he is on the social and religious texture of Stuart Parliaments. He is at present at work on an introduction to 'Utopia' for the definitive edition of More's *Works*. Meanwhile his plan of revision for the set of assumptions made by the historians of the periods and subjects which concern him has been taking shape little by little.

It was not until 1958 that he became known as the most formidable of all American critics of English historians writing on English subjects. An address to the American Historical Association was published in London in the monthly magazine *Encounter*. 'Storm Over the Gentry' now appears here for the first time in full academic dress.

No more modest revolutionary can be imagined, and his achievement might easily be underestimated. More than any other historian of the present day he must be held responsible for the breaking of a circle of explanation, one which had prevailed for three or four generations and which had come to constrict imagination and intellect alike. This was the convention which demanded that all historical change must be referred to the rise and fall of social classes, and most of English history to the rise of the middle classes, especially what happened in Tudor and Stuart times. His critical work severs the stalk at the point where it springs out of the ground. Not only is the factual support of such an attitude shown to be illusory, but it is also demonstrated that its propositions simply do not explain: social causation of historical events is

ıot like that. What goes for the exponents of the middle-class hypothe-
is goes also for those who have used national sentiment in a similar way,
ıs Pollard did to explain the career of Tudor England. It must be
tressed that it is the manner in which explanations are formulated
which comes under the scythe, as well as their content. Down go the
tunnel historians', the 'factor analysts', the unaware, uncritical users
ıf such obvious historians' words as *development*, *tendency*, or *trend*.

What was a gentle breeze when Hexter first talked of the myth of
he middle class in Tudor England in 1948 has now become a strong
wind, the wind which may well end, as he suggests it will, in turning
ıur attitude to historical change right about. Already it seems difficult
ıo believe that so meticulous and illuminating a scholar of the Tudor
cene as Dr. Louis Wright can have committed himself to the state-
nents quoted here out of his *Middle Class Culture in Elizabethan Eng-
and*, or that he can ever have been satisfied with such a title, even in
[935. Equally odd, today, is to see how a historian of the subtlety and
ınsight of Professor Trevor-Roper was content to adopt a trivial varia-
ion on the rise-and-fall-of-a-class theme as his explanation of the
Civil War in 1953: if a rise of the gentry would not do, then it must
ıave been a fall, not of all but of some of them. It is most unlikely that
ıxplanation of this sort would be felt to be persuasive now, for the
:limate has changed and is changing, drastically. Nevertheless it is
;oing to be so long before all traces of the rise of the middle class and
he rise of the gentry disappear from the school textbook and the
ıniversity lecture that Professor Hexter might well have taken us
ürther along the way towards abandoning them altogether in their
.ccepted form. Perhaps, therefore, I may be permitted here to sketch
n the lines of one of the further arguments which his position implies.

The question which I wish to raise is whether the whole enterprise
ıf accounting for the dramatic events of the middle of the seventeenth
:entury in England is not to some extent misconceived. Is it right to
.ssume, as always seems to be assumed, that a long-term, overall ex-
ılanation is necessarily called for?

Now it is natural, though it may not be justifiable, to suppose that
;reat events have great causes. Anything as conspicuous, as interesting
.nd as influential as the only civil war in our history, with all its implica-
ions for our liberties and the liberties of the rest of the world, must
urely, we feel, have been a cataclysm, the climax of a process going
leep down into the social fabric and extending over many generations,
ıackwards and forwards in time. This attitude is the more to be expec-

ted in the English, because they pride themselves upon the continuity of their political life, which is otherwise unbroken, and upon their perennial ability to solve their differences without violence and without war. What could be more understandable than that we should have come to set aside a whole century, from 1540 to 1640, for the causes of the Civil War? and the whole period 1640-88, or even 1625-1714, for the English Revolution?

But in so far as it is true that what happened when the revolt began was causally connected with large numbers of things which had gone before, 'economic' and 'social' as well as 'political' and 'constitutional', it may also be trivial. For the same thing is equally true of any event, happening at any time or place, however slight in itself and however unimportant in its consequence. All societies, even English society at its stablest, are liable to break down into conflict, even armed conflict. Conflict is a common enough form of social interaction: there is nothing special about the things which bring it about. Since nearly everybody has an obvious interest in preventing differences from becoming collisions all parties will take strenuous avoiding action when collisions threaten. But collisions sometimes take place nevertheless, just as car collisions do, and there is a logical resemblance. Accidents on the road are rare because every driver does all he can to avoid them, but they happen, at a statistically understandable frequency. When they do happen, it makes sense to look for long-term, even 'deep-seated', causes, as well as for the errors of the drivers concerned, for such things as the continued growth of traffic, and the increase in its speed, or the progressive inadequacy of the roads. The more disastrous the accident, the more elaborate the examination will probably be, of all its circumstances and causes. But it does not follow that the more dramatic and important the crash and its consequences, the more profound the causes and the more likely it is that we are faced with the climax of some perennial 'process'.

This consideration should help us to restore to the events of the middle of the seventeenth century in England 'a sense of a future' as Raymond Aron puts it. A great deal of the argument of these essays insists upon the obvious point that all we can expect of a study of social movement is an explanation of increasing liability to conflict and civil war, never of its actual occasion. Confusion between what might be called secular and particular causes has been one of the reasons for the inconclusiveness and sterility of the lengthy controversy over the rise of the gentry. Perhaps it will be shown that the emergence and rise to political effectiveness of this particular social type did have a great deal to do with the emergence of those acute political differences which ended in war. But it does not therefore follow that a historian's duty is done if he examines this cause only. The differences between man, and groups of men, which give rise to insoluble conflict are always multiple and complex.

Nor does it follow that the gentry were a party—one side—in the conflict, the conflict in Parliament or on the battlefield. This elementary correction of error was made early in the controversy, the egregious error, for example, which turns the battles of the Civil War into engagements between the *rising bourgeoisie* (the gentry, and the town notables) and the *feudal remnant* (the Crown, nobility, Church and traditionalists). Statements of such crudity are fortunately difficult to find nowadays in the works of responsible historians writing in English. But we must not forget that they are accepted dogma over much of the rest of the world, as amongst the historians of south-east Europe who wish to trace in the development of their own countries equivalents to the *bourgeois revolution* which they are convinced must have happened in Stuart England: for them the English Revolution is a classic case.

If a man wishes to go on supposing that the 'real' cause of all these events was the rise of a class and its conflict with another class, because he believes on general grounds that the motive power of historical change is only to be sought in this particular direction, then he is unlikely to be convinced out of it by the present argument. His conviction may well survive the change in the historian's climate which we have referred to, even the consummate tunnel and boring work which is contained in these essays. We may assert with Hexter that the only proper historian's approach to the problem of conflict and breakdown is in the exact study of all the sources of disagreement and discontinuity, of every opposition and interest, which can be found in early Stuart Society. We may set out, with him, to give its proper weight to what the men themselves said they were quarrelling about, which was first and foremost religion and then the Constitution. But we shall reach the stage where satisfactory explanation becomes possible only when we have worked out some general critique which can relate political with religious differences, economic growth with such things as changes in literacy, in population, in the position and function of the family.

The controversy over the rise of the gentry, then, and the causes of the Civil War, is being ended by facing historians with a challenge which they have ignored for far too long, the challenge to learn from sociologists, to become sociological historians. The present writer is engaged in working out some small part of the factual content of such a sociological historian's view, attempting to recover the texture of Stuart society, and the ways in which any action, any change had to come about within it. In that study scepticism about terms drawn from outmoded historical criticism is taken even further than Hexter takes it, even to the point of dispensing with *class* altogether, and excluding *revolution* from the Stuart era. It contains, moreover, two points arising directly out of the work Hexter publishes here, points which perhaps should be mentioned.

In his 'New Framework for Social History' Hexter insists that the period of the rise of the middle classes cannot be pushed backwards to the seventeenth century, and must be referred to the nineteenth. A process which has often been extended to cover seven centuries is thus confined to a century and a half. Attention is exclusively directed for the first time where it properly belongs, to the land, where was sited that ruling segment which dominated English society, and was indeed for most purposes English society *tout court*. Hexter is surely right to insist on the versatility of that social segment, on its secular success in ensuring that it was the goal of social ascent. In fact to call it 'uppermost' or even 'ruling' is tautologous: it was these things and did these things by definition.

But he falls short of asserting, what seems also to be the truth, that the so-called middle classes never in fact displaced the ruling segment, rapid as was social mobility in the early industrial era. It does not strictly make sense to put it like this, because the ruling segment exercised a function as much as it occupied a position. And it went on exercising this function, in spite of increasing loss of homogeneity and identity in face of the rapidity with which owners of wealth were thrown up, until the beginnings of class politics in 1900. The middle class never rose, at least it never rose to the top: and it never ruled.

This extension of Hexter's position belongs as much to the history of the nineteenth and twentieth centuries in England as it does to the seventeenth. It can be studied in such contexts as the work of Professor Aydelotte, in his paper read at the meeting of the American Historical Association in December 1960, for example. But it cannot be carried further here. We must end with a more detailed application of one of Hexter's suggestions in the period which is more properly his concern.

Sir John Neale has made us familiar with the penetration of country gentry into the House of Commons in the reign of Elizabeth. The ease with which they were able to push the townsfolk out of the way, was perhaps in part responsible for the twist given to Marxian and Fabian interpretations of the Stuart period. It demonstrated at the outset that the townsfolk, the bourgeoisie proper, could never have been powerful enough to challenge royal authority at any time, therefore it had to be assumed that the gentry themselves could be identified with the rising capitalist. This or something like it may well have been the original occasion of the trend of interpretation which ended in Tawney's work on the subject.

Another lesson which Neale taught us is taken further by Hexter in his 'Education of the Aristocracy', as well as by Curtis and other historians of the universities. The gentry who got themselves into Parliament were increasingly educated gentry and representative of county communities, family communities, which were displaying an increasing intellectual awareness. Higher education in fact was refounded in England in Elizabeth's reign, and refounded in such a way that the intelligentsia was henceforth contained within the ruling segment. It was not, as it had been in the Middle Ages, a column apart—the clerisy. The consequences of this for the political life of succeeding generations have yet to be recognized.

The political stability of English society depended on two things, on the maintenance of ordered responsibility within each community of gentry, and on the interplay between these county communities and the central organization, the Crown and its institutions. The occasional meetings of Parliament were opportunities for local political awareness to be merged for a short period with national political awareness, and the politics of Parliament when it was in session were national politics, the stuff of constitutional development. Far greater in extent, and absolutely unbroken in their continuity, were the politics played within each county community, and it was there that the collective memory of Parliament was to be found between sessions. There local offices were intrigued over, seats in Parliament were lost and won, family rivalries were maintained: continuity was kept up because differences were resolved, resolved that is to the extent that was necessary to ensure that there was a county community at the end of each line of connection with central government.

This is only a partial anatomy of political consciousness at that time, though it must suffice for our present purpose. As the Tudors gave way to the Stuarts politics, national and local, began increasingly to include the politics of intellectual difference, of arguments about theory, or something approaching theory. This may be recognized as the traditional story of the beginnings of constitutionalism, told however without supposing that the occasional and intermittent life of the Commons was the whole political life of the English gentry. In the counties from day to day, as well as at Westminster once in five years, men differed volubly over issues which were issues for discussion, as well as over prestige and office, economic interest and family aggrandizement. Above all they were being torn apart, family from family and man from man, by religious differences, differences which they argued about, and which some of them preached about, wrote and published about. For they were not content to leave even publication to the clergy, so little did the Church retain her function as the official intelligentsia.

Of course it was only a small number within every community which took to argumentation in this way, but politics is always a matter of the vigorous, articulate, able few at work among an inert majority. Anyone who resented the activities of the proselytizing Puritan gentleman, or the fanatical defender of the Ancient Constitution, found himself drawn into argument too. Under such circumstances each county community, and the ruling segment as a whole, found it increasingly difficult to maintain political continuity, to contain their frictions, to keep contact in such a way that government could go on. Even the men who wished to be loyal, and for the most part everyone did, became exceedingly difficult to manage. Even if they agreed on fundamentals, as they perpetually claimed, what now interested them was their differences, and there were always arguers on hand to exacerbate. The royal task of maintaining spontaneous assent to policy became hazardous, and in the crisis of the 1640s it became impossible. What wonder that the Stuarts wished to dispense with Parliament, and so added to the turbulence by giving the gentry reason to believe that their liberties were indeed in jeopardy. Government by discussion is not a correct way to describe what went on in Tudor, Stuart or Hanoverian times. But it may be quite accurate and very important to lay it down that government, agreement, civil peace in England over this whole period did involve the resolution of intellectual differences, that it was maintained in spite of such differences, that political breakdown was also an intellectual event.

It may perhaps seem tempting to try to give this revised meaning to the phrase 'Rise of the Gentry'. Certainly the rise to intellectual awareness of political issues which marked the history of the English gentry in late Tudor and early Stuart times may turn out to be the crucial development for the conduct of political life. But to translate the rise of the gentry into something like this leaves out of account the many other changes which have been associated with it and which must have their roles assigned to them. Moreover to keep the phrase at all might tempt the unwary into the mistakes we have tried to identify, to think of it as the one-final-social cause of a cataclysm, even as the occasion of the Civil War. It would be far better to lay 'The Rise of the Gentry' carefully alongside 'The Rise of the Middle Classes', and to place them reverently together in a prominent position within the great and growing collection of outmoded historical expressions. There may they long exercise the ingenuity and delight the heart of our newest type of scholar, the historian of historiography.

Professor Hexter was at the University of Edinburgh for the year 1959 to 1960, and he lectured at other universities. From Oxford he came to Cambridge and delivered 'Factors in Modern History' to us. This is the latest of his historical reappraisals and it may well be that he will have nothing to add on this theme after what he has now said in the postscript at the end of this book.

He hints there at the reasons. They are also the reasons why he now publishes a collection of occasional essays rather than the full-length book which they all imply. When he was in Britain he met almost everyone affected by the prolonged controversy over the gentry. In spite of the reputation for acrimony which this interchange has earned for Tudor and Stuart historians, it must be said that no harsh word was spoken, not a hint of recrimination. But then, for all his outrageousness, Jack Hexter is one of the very popular figures in the huge community of historians in the United States of America. It was not to be expected that the British would be able to resist him.

February 1961 PETER LASLETT

PREFACE

Reappraisal in history does not necessarily result in dissent from the views reappraised; but in fact most of the reappraisals in this book are of the dissenting kind. One should not have to point out that dissent from another historian's views does not imply personal animus toward him or contempt for his abilities. Indeed, reappraisal of the views of a historian whose efforts one regards as contemptible is hardly worth the trouble. Specifically, as to the historians whose work is reappraised in this book, I hold my seniors among them in very high respect; and my contemporaries among them I hold both in sincere esteem and in warm affection.

I have not tried to bring all the footnotes up to date; but where a recent work seemed to bear specifically on the main thesis of one of the essays that work has received mention. The exception to the rule is 'Storm Over the Gentry', to which is appended an up-to-date bibliography. The storm has perhaps somewhat abated since that essay first appeared, but a gentle drizzle of studies more or less germane has continued to fall; and it is only too likely that my bibliographical appendix has failed to note one or two of them. To their authors, my apologies. Circumstances have prevented my retracing a few lost references in 'The Myth of the Middle Class in Tudor England'. For this, my apologies to the reader.

The rejection of their early efforts sometimes unduly discourages young historians. They may perhaps be raised from unwarranted despair by the contents of this book and by its publication. Three of the essays in it were rejected by scholarly journals in good standing—'The Myth of the Middle Class in Tudor England' by the *Journal of Economic History*, 'The Historian and His Day' and 'Storm Over the Gentry' by the *American Historical Review*. All of the rejections came when the author was over forty. A letter of rejection is not a divine decree; it is neither an immutable nor an eternal judgment, but the decision of one or two fallible men, subject to reversal by other men equally fallible. So let young historians take heart; and in this matter may all historians be young at heart.

St. Louis,
January 1961

I

The Historian and His Day *

FOR A GOOD while now a fairly strenuous contest has been in progress between two opposed schools of historical thought. Accepting a classification suggested by Professor R. L. Schuyler, one of the keenest though most courteous of the riders in the lists, the division lies roughly between the 'present-minded' and the 'history-minded' historians. In the course of time many historians have joined one side or the other in the controversy with the natural consequence that there has been some sense and a good deal of nonsense talked on both sides. In general, for subtle psychological reasons that I am unable to fathom, the kind of scholar who, distrustful of ideas and theories, believes that history is all facts has tended to take the side of the history-minded historians. For more obvious reasons the chronic do-gooder, who believes that knowledge justifies itself only by a capacity to solve current problems, lines up with the present-minded position.

This peculiar alignment has frequently obscured the issues at stake. It is easy to expose the feebleness and absurdity of those who want only facts and of those who want only current problem-solving; and it is fun, too. Consequently the attacks on both sides have often been directed mainly against these vulnerable positions, and it has sometimes seemed as if the main bodies were too busy assaulting their opponents' camp followers to come to grips with one another. For, of course, there is nothing intrinsic to the history-minded position that precludes ideas or theories or, if you prefer, generalization. Nor is there anything in present-mindedness that demands an optimism as to the efficacy of history as a panacea for current social ills.

Obviously it is not fair to judge either the history-minded or the present-minded historians by the vagaries of their respective lunatic fringes. Casting off the eccentric on both sides, there remains a real and

* An earlier version of this essay appeared in the *Political Science Quarterly* in June 1954.

serious divergence of opinion, as yet apparently irreconcilable, maintained on both sides by scholars whose achievements entitle their views to respectful consideration. The divergence is connected at least ostensibly with a fundamental difference in general outlook between the two parties to the argument. In a sense the present-minded are realists with respect to the study of history, the history-minded are idealists.

The approach of the latter to the problem is essentially apodictic. They say we *ought* not to intrude our contemporary value systems and preconceptions and notions into our reconstruction of the past. They insist that it is our *duty* as historians to understand the past in its terms, not in our own; and they document their thesis with some undeniably horrible examples of what has happened in the last century to historians who looked at the past with the dubious prepossessions, current in their own day, but since invalidated or replaced by other prepossessions equally dubious. Truly there is nothing quite so *passé* as the intellectual fashions of yesteryear. We find them at once especially ludicrous and especially disturbing when they are worn by men of high talents. We do not like to see the nineteenth-century present-mindedness of so perceptive a man as J. R. Green transforming the roughneck barons of Runnymede into harbingers of nineteenth-century democracy and nationalism. Our embarrassment is even more acute when the victim of present-mindedness is a great historian. We are unhappy when we watch Bishop Stubbs adding Victorian liberalism to the cargo that the Anglo-Saxons brought with them to England from their North German forests. And as the conviction of sin is brought home to us we are warned, 'There but for the grace of history-mindedness go you'.

Convinced by the dreadful examples arrayed before us we resolve to eschew the wickedness of modernism and thenceforth hew to our obligation to be history-minded. And then a clear and chilly voice says: 'But my dear fellows, you can't be history-minded. It might be nice if you could, or it might not, but in any case it is impossible. So all this pother about the obligation to be history-minded is rather silly. Only a particularly repulsive sort of Deity would bind men to do what in the very nature of things they are unable to do.' So an almost medieval emphasis on the duty to be history-minded is deflected by a rather Machiavellian observation as to the facts of life. Medieval assertions about what statesmen ought to do Machiavelli met with assertions about what statesmen—the human animal being what it is—are sure to do. History-minded assertions about what historians ought to do are met with present-minded assertions of what—the history-writing animal being what he is—the historian is certain to do. The harsh fact of life is that, willy-nilly, the present-day historian lives not in the past but in the present, and this fact cannot be altered by any pious resolve to be history-minded.

What we say about any historical epoch in some ways reflects our experience; and that experience was accumulated not in the fifteenth, in the sixteenth, or in any other century than the twentieth. When we look back on the past, we do so from the present. We are present-minded just as all earlier historians were present-minded in their day because for better or worse we happen to live in our own day. Indeed the very horrid examples cited by the proponents of history-mindedness afford irrefutable evidence that the best of former historians were in their day present-minded, and we can hardly hope to be different. So the best thing for us to do is to recognize that every generation reinterprets the past in terms of the exigencies of its own day. We can then cast aside our futile history-minded yearnings and qualms and deal with the past in terms of our day, only mildly regretting that, like all the words of man, our own words will be writ on water. By this intellectual stratagem the present-minded turn—or seek to turn—the flank of the history-minded.

We must admit that some points in the argument of the present-minded are true beyond dispute. It is certainly true, for example, that all that we think is related to our experience somehow, and that all our experience is of our own day. But though this be true, it is also trivial. It is a plea in avoidance dressed up as an argument. Granting that we can have no experience beyond what we have acquired in the course of our own lives, the question is, does anything in that experience enable us to understand the past in its own terms rather than in terms of the pre-possessions of our own day? Banal statements about the origin of our ideas in our own experience do not answer this question; they merely beg it.

In the second place, we must admit that in some respects all historians are present-minded, even the most determined proponents of history-mindedness. All historians are indeed engaged in rewriting past history in the light of at least one aspect of present experience, that aspect which has to do with the increments to our positive knowledge that are the fruit of scientific investigation. Consider a single example. Up to a few decades ago the Dark Ages before the twelfth century were considered an era of total regression, technological as well as political, social and cultural. Then Lefebvre de Noëttes described results of certain experiments he had made with animal power. He had reproduced antique harnesses for draft horses. In such harness the pulling power of the horse proved to be less than a quarter of what it is in modern harness. But 'modern' harness, involving the use of a rigid horse collar, makes its appearance in Europe in the tenth century. So in the Dark Ages a horse could deliver about four times the tractive force that it could in antiquity. Now no historian would suggest that we disregard Lefebvre de Noëttes's experiments in our consideration of medieval agrarian history; a fourfold increase in the efficiency of a very important source of power is something that no economic historian can afford to overlook. Yet when we do apply the results of Lefebvre's experiments to medieval agriculture we are being present-minded in at least two ways. In the first and more simple way we are rewriting the history of the Middle Ages in the light of the present because until the present the particular bit of light that was the work of Lefebvre did not exist. But we must go further. It was not pure accident that such work had not been done in earlier ages. Historians in earlier ages would not have thought of going about the investigation of medieval agriculture as Lefebvre did. In making his historical investigations by the method of experiment and measurement, Lefebvre was distinctly reflecting the preoccupations of his own age and of no earlier one. In this particular area of study at any rate, scientific-mindedness is present-mindedness.

It seems to me that the proponents of history-mindedness must, and in most cases probably do, concede the validity of this kind of present-mindedness in the writing of history; and if this is all that present-mindedness means, then every historian worth his salt is present-minded. No sane contemporary scientist in his investigations of the physical world would disregard nineteenth-century advances in field theory, and no sane historian in his work would rule out of consideration insights achieved in the past century concerning the connection of class conflict with historical occurrences. But this is only to say that all men who are professionally committed to the quest of that elusive entity—the Truth —use all the tracking devices available to them at the time, and in the nature of things cannot use any device before it exists. And of course the adequacy of the historical search at any time is in some degree limited by the adequacy of the tracking devices. In this, too, the historian's situation is no different from that of the scientist. Adequate investigation of optical isomers in organic chemistry, for example, had to wait on the development of the techniques of spectroscopy. If this is what present-mindedness means, then present-mindedness is not just the condition of historical knowledge. For all knowledge at any time is obviously limited by the limits of the means of gaining knowledge at that time; and historians are simply in the same boat as all others whose business it is to know.

Now I do not believe that the proponents of present-mindedness mean anything as bland and innocuous as this. On the contrary I am fairly sure they mean that the historian's boat is different from, and a great deal more leaky than, let us say, the physicist's or the geologist's boat. What then is supposed to be the specific trouble with the historian's boat? The trouble, as the present-minded see it, can be described fairly simply. The present-minded contend that in writing history no historian can free himself of his total experience and that that experience is inextricably involved not only in the limits of knowledge but also in the passions, prejudices, assumptions and prepossessions, in the events, crises and tensions of his own day. Therefore those passions, prejudices, assumptions, prepossessions, events, crises and tensions of the historian's own day inevitably permeate what he writes about the past. This is the crucial allegation of the present-minded, and if it is wholly correct, the issue must be settled in their favor and the history-minded pack up their apodictic and categorical-imperative baggage and depart in silence. Frequently discussions of this crucial issue have got bogged down because the history-minded keep trying to prove that the historian can counteract the influence of his own day, while the present-minded keep saying that this is utterly impossible. And of course on this question the latter are quite right. A historian has no day but his own, so what is he going to counteract it with? He is in the situation of Archimedes who could find no fulcrum for the lever with which to move the Earth. Clearly if the historian is to be history-minded rather than present-minded he must find the means of being so in his own day, not outside it. And thus at last we come up against the crucial question—what *is* the historian's own day?

As soon as we put the question this way we realize that there is no ideal Historian's Day; there are many days, all different, and each with a particular historian attached to it. Now since in actuality there is no such thing as The Historian's Day, no one can be qualified to say what it actually consists of. Indeed, although I know a good number of individual historians on terms of greater or less intimacy, I would feel ill-qualified to describe with certainty what any of their days are.

There is, however, one historian about whose day I can speak with assurance. For I myself am a historian at least in the technical sense of the word; I have possessed for a considerable time the parchment inscribed with the appropriate phrases to indicate that I have served my apprenticeship and am out of my indentures. So I will describe as briefly as I can my own day. I do so out of no appetite for self-revelation or self-expression, but simply because the subject is germane to our inquiry and because it is the one matter on which I happen to be the world's leading authority. Let us then hurry through this dreary journal.

I rise early and have breakfast. While eating, I glance through the morning paper and read the editorial page. I then go to the college that employs me and teach for two to four hours five days a week.[1] Most of the time the subject matter I deal with in class is cobwebbed with age. Three fourths of it dates back from a century and a quarter to three millennia; all of it happened at least thirty years ago. Then comes lunch with a few of my colleagues. Conversation at lunch ranges widely through professional shoptalk, politics, high and ghostly matters like religion, the nature of art or the universe, and the problems of child rearing, and finally academic scuttlebutt. At present there is considerable discussion of the peculiar incongruence between the social importance of the academic and his economic reward. This topic has the merit of revealing the profound like-mindedness, transcending all occasional conflicts, of our little community. From lunch to bedtime my day is grimly uniform. There are of course occasional and casual variations—preparation of the ancient material above mentioned for the next day's classes, a ride in the country with the family, a committee meeting at college, a movie, a play, a novel, or a book by some self-anointed Deep Thinker. Still by and large from one in the afternoon to midnight, with time out for dinner and domestic matters, I read things written between 1450 and 1650 or books written by historians on the basis of things written between 1450 and 1650. I vary the routine on certain days by writing about what I have read on the other days. On Saturdays and in the summer I start my reading or writing at nine instead of noon. It is only fair to add that most days I turn on a news broadcast or two at dinnertime, and that I spend an hour or two with the Sunday paper.

Now I am sure that many people will consider so many days so spent to be a frightful waste of precious time; and indeed, as most of

[1] A change in place of employment since the above sentence was written has resulted in a reduction in the number of hours I spend in teaching.

he days of most men, it does seem a bit trivial. Be that as it may, t remains one historian's own day. It is his own day in the only sense n which that phrase can be used without its being pretentious, pompous nd meaningless. For a man's own days are not everything that happens n the world while he lives and breathes. As I write, portentous and momentous things are no doubt being done in Peiping, Teheran, Bonn, nd Jakarta. But these things are no part of my day; they are outside of ny experience, and though one or two of them may faintly impinge on ny consciousness tomorrow via the headlines in the morning paper, hat is probably as far as they will get. At best they are likely to remain luttering fragments on the fringe of my experience, not well-ordered arts of it. I must insist emphatically that the history I write is, as the resent-minded say, intimately connected with my own day and nextricably linked with my own experience; but I must insist with even stronger emphasis that my day is not someone else's day, or the deal Day of Contemporary Man; it is just the way I happen to dispose f twenty-four hours. By the same token the experience that is inex- ricably linked to any history I may happen to write is not the ideal xperience of Twentieth-Century Man in World Chaos, but just the vay I happen to put in my time over the series of my days.

Now it may seem immodest or perhaps simply fantastic to take lays spent as are mine—days so little attuned to the great harmonies, liscords and issues of the present—and hold them up for contemplation. Yet I will dare to suggest that in this historian's own humdrum days here is one peculiarity that merits thought. The peculiarity lies in the urious relation that days so squandered seem to establish between the resent and a rather remote sector of the past. I do not pretend that am wholly unconcerned by the larger public issues and catastrophes f the present; nor am I without opinions on a large number of con- emporary issues. On some of them I am vigorously dogmatic as, ndeed, are most of the historians I know. Yet my knowledge about uch issues, although occasionally fairly extensive, tends to be hap- azard, vague, unsystematic and disorderly. And the brute fact of the natter is that even if I had the inclination, I do not have the time to traighten that knowledge out except at the cost of alterations in the rdering of my days that I am not in the least inclined to undertake.

So for a small part of my day I live under a comfortable rule of land intellectual irresponsibility vis-à-vis the Great Issues of the Con- emporary World, a rule that permits me to go off half-cocked with nly slight and occasional compunction. But during most of my day

—that portion of it that I spend in dealing with the Great and Not-So Great Issues of the World between 1450 and 1650—I live under an altogether different rule. The commandments of that rule are:

1. Do not go off half-cocked.
2. Get the story straight.
3. Keep prejudices about present-day issues out of this area.

The commandments are counsels of perfection, but they are not merely that; they are enforced by sanctions, both external and internal. The serried array of historical trade journals equipped with extensive book-review columns provides the most powerful external sanction. The columns are often at the disposal of cantankerous cranks ever ready to expose to obloquy 'pamphleteers' who think that Clio is an 'easy bought mistress bound to suit her ways to the intellectual appetites of the current customer'.[1] On more than one occasion I have been a cantankerous crank. When I write about the period between 1450 and 1650 I am well aware of a desire to give unto others no occasion to do unto me as I have done unto some of them.

The reviewing host seems largely to have lined up with the history-minded. This seems to be a consequence of their training. Whatever the theoretical biases of their individual members, the better departments of graduate study in history do not encourage those undergoing their novitiate to resolve research problems by reference to current ideological conflicts. Consequently most of us have been conditioned to feel that it is not quite proper to characterize John Pym as a liberal, or Thomas More as a socialist, or Niccolò Machiavelli as a proto-Fascist, and we tend to regard this sort of characterization as at best a risky pedagogic device. Not only the characterization but the thought process that leads to it lie under a psychological ban; and thus to the external sanction of the review columns is added the internal sanction of the still small voice that keeps saying, 'One really shouldn't do it that way.'[2]

The austere rule we live under as historians has some curious consequences. In my case one of the consequences is that my knowledge of the period around the sixteenth century in Europe is of a rather

[1] *American Historical Review*, 51 (1946), 487.
[2] I do not for a moment intend to imply that current dilemmas have no suggested *problems* for historical investigation. It is obvious that such dilemmas are among the numerous and entirely legitimate points of origin of historical study. The actual issue, however, has nothing to do with the point of origin of historical studies, but with the mode of treatment of historical problems.

different order than my knowledge about current happenings. Those preponderant segments of my own day spent in the discussion, investigation and contemplation of that remote era may not be profitably spent but at least they are spent in an orderly, systematic, purposeful way. The contrast can be pointed up by a few details. I have never read the Social Security Act, but I have read the Elizabethan Poor Law in all its successive versions and moreover I have made some study of its application. I have never read the work of a single existentialist but I have read Calvin's *Institutes of the Christian Religion* from cover to cover. I know practically nothing for sure about the relation of the institutions of higher education in America to the social structure, but I know a fair bit about the relation between the two in France, England and the Netherlands in the fifteenth and sixteenth centuries. I have never studied the Economic Reports to the President that would enable me to appraise the state of the American nation in the 1950s, but I have studied closely the *Discourse of the Commonwealth of England* and derived from it some reasonably coherent notions about the condition of England in the 1550s. Now the consequence of all this is inevitable. Instead of the passions, prejudices, assumptions and prepossessions, the events, crises and tensions of the present dominating my view of the past, *it is the other way about*. The passions, prejudices, assumptions and prepossessions, the events, crises and tensions of early modern Europe to a very considerable extent lend precision to my rather haphazard notions about the present. I make sense of present-day welfare-state policy by thinking of it in connection with the 'commonwealth' policies of Elizabeth. I do the like with respect to the contemporary struggle for power and conflict of ideologies by throwing on them such light as I find in the Catholic-Calvinist struggle of the sixteenth century.

Teaching makes me aware of the peculiarities of my perspective. The days of my students are very different from mine. They have spent little time indeed in contemplating the events of the sixteenth century. So when I tell them that the Christian Humanists, in their optimistic aspiration to reform the world by means of education, were rather like our own progressive educators, I help them understand the Christian Humanists. But my teaching strategy moves in the opposite direction from my own intellectual experience. The comparison first suggested itself to me as a means for understanding not Christian Humanism but progressive education. There is no need to labor this point. After all, ordinarily the process of thought is from the better known to the worse known, and my knowledge of the sixteenth century is a good bit more precise than my knowledge of the twentieth. Perhaps there is nothing to be said for this peculiar way of thinking; it may be altogether silly; but in the immediate context I am not obliged to defend it. I present it simply as one of those brute facts of life dear to the heart of the present-minded. It is in fact one way that one historian's day affects his judgment.

In the controversy that provided the starting point of this rambling essay, the essential question is sometimes posed with respect to the relation of the historian to his own *day*. In other instances it is posed with respect to his relation to his own *time*. Having discovered how idiosyncratic was the day of one historian we may inquire whether his time is also peculiar. The answer is, 'Yes, his time *is* a bit odd.' And here it is possible to take a welcome leave of the first person singular. For, although my day is peculiar to me, my time, as a historian, is like the time of other historians.

For our purposes the crucial fact about the ordinary time of all men, even of historians in their personal as against their professional capacity, is that in no man's time is he *really* sure what is going to happen next. This is true, obviously, not only of men of the present time but also of all men of all past times. Of course there are large routine areas of existence in which we can make pretty good guesses; and if this were not so, life would be unbearable. Thus, my guess, five evenings a week in term time, that I will be getting up the following morning to teach classes at my place of employment provides me with a useful operating rule; yet it has been wrong occasionally, and will be wrong again. With respect to many matters more important, all is uncertain. Will there be war or peace next year? Will my children turn out well or ill? Will I be alive or dead thirty years hence? three years hence? tomorrow?

The saddest words of tongue or pen may be, 'It might have been.' The most human are, 'If I had only known.' But it is precisely characteristic of the historian that he does know. He is really sure what is going to happen next, not in his time as a pilgrim here below, but in his own time as a historian. The public servant Conyers Read, for example, when he worked high in the councils of the Office of Strategic Services did not know what the outcome of the maneuvers he helped plan would be. But for all the years from 1568 during which he painstakingly investigated the public career of Francis Walsingham, the eminent Tudor historian Conyers Read knew that the Spanish Armada would come against England and that the diplomatic maneuvers of Mr

Secretary Walsingham would assist in its defeat. Somewhat inaccurately we might say that while man's time ordinarily is oriented to the future, the historian's time is oriented to the past. It might be better to say that while men are ordinarily trying to connect the present with a future that is to be, the historian connects his present with a future that has already been.

The professional historian does not have a monopoly of his peculiar time, or rather, as Carl Becker once put it, every man is on occasion his own historian. But the historian alone lives systematically in the historian's own time. And from what we have been saying it is clear that this time has a unique dimension. Each man in his own time tries to discover the motives and the causes of the actions of those people he has to deal with; and the historian does the like with varying degrees of success. But, as other men do not and cannot, the historian knows something of the results of the acts of those he deals with: this is the unique dimension of the historian's time. If, in saying that the historian cannot escape his own time, the present-minded meant this peculiarly historical time—which they do not—they would be on solid ground. For the circumstances are rare indeed in which the historian has no notion whatever of the outcome of the events with which he is dealing. The very fact that he is a historian and that he has interested himself in a particular set of events fairly assures that at the outset he will have some knowledge of what happened afterward.

This knowledge makes it impossible for the historian to do merely what the history-minded say he should do—consider the past in its own terms, and envisage events as the men who lived through them did. Surely he should try to do that; just as certainly he must do more than that simply because he knows about those events what none of the men contemporary with them knew; he knows what their consequences were. To see the events surrounding the obscure monk Luther as Leo X saw them—as another 'monks' quarrel' and a possible danger to the perquisites of the Curia—may help us understand the peculiar inefficacy of Papal policy at the time; but that does not preclude the historian from seeing the same events as the decisive step towards the final breach of the religious unity of Western Civilization. We may be quite sure however that nobody at the time, not even Luther himself, saw those events that way. The historian who resolutely refused to use the insight that his own peculiar time gave him would not be superior to his fellows; he would be merely foolish, betraying a singular failure to grasp what history is. For history is a becoming, an ongoing, and it is to be understood not only in terms of what comes before but also of what comes after.

What conclusions can we draw from our cursory examination of the historian's own time and his own day? What of the necessity, alleged by the present-minded, of rewriting history anew each generation? In some respects the estimate is over-generous, in one respect too niggardly. The necessity will in part be a function of the lapsed time between the events written about and the present. The history of the Treaty of Versailles of 1919 may indeed need to be written over a number of times in the next few generations as its consequences more completely unfold. But this is not true of the Treaty of Madrid of 1527. Its consequences for better or worse pretty well finished their unfolding a good while back. The need for rewriting history is also a function of the increase in actual data on the thing to be written about. Obviously any general estimate of the rate of increase of such data would be meaningless. History also must be rewritten as the relevant and usable knowledge about man, about his ways and his waywardness, increases. Here again there has been a tendency to exaggerate the speed with which that knowledge is increasing. The hosannahs that have greeted many master ideas about man during the past fifty years seem more often than not to be a reflection of an urge toward secular salvation in a shaky world rather than a precise estimate of the cognitive value of the ideas in question. Frequently such master ideas have turned out to be plain old notions in new fancy dress, or simply wrong. Perhaps the imperative, felt by the present-minded, to rewrite history every generation is less the fruit of a real necessity than of their own attempts to write it always in conformity with the latest intellectual mode. A little less haste might mean a little more speed. For the person engaged in the operation it is all too easy to mistake for progress a process that only involves skipping from recent to current errors.

If, instead of asking how often history *must* or ought to be rewritten we ask how often it *will* be rewritten, the answer is that it will be rewritten, as it always has been, from day to day. This is so because the rewriting of history is inescapably what each working historian in fact does in his own day. That is precisely how he puts in his time. We seek new data. We re-examine old data to discover in them relations and connections that our honored predecessors may have missed. On these data we seek to bring to bear whatever may seem enlightening and relevant out of our own day. And what may be relevant is as wide as the full range of our own daily experience,

intellectual, aesthetic, political, social, personal. Some current event may, of course, afford a historian an understanding of what men meant five hundred years ago when they said that a prince must rule through *amour et cremeur*, love and fear. But then so might his perusal of a socio-psychological investigation into the ambivalence of authority in Papua. So might his reading of Shakespeare's *Richard II*. And so might his relations with his own children.

For each historian brings to the rewriting of history the full range of the remembered experience of his own days, that unique array that he alone possesses and is. For some historians that sector of their experience which impinges on the Great Crisis of the Contemporary World sets up the vibrations that attune them to the part of the past that is the object of their professional attention. Some of us, however, vibrate less readily to those crises. We feel our way toward the goals of our historic quest by lines of experience having precious little to do with the Great Crises of the Contemporary World. He would be bold indeed who would insist that all historians should follow one and the same line of experience in their quest, or who would venture to say what this single line is that all should follow. He would not only be bold; he would almost certainly be wrong. History thrives in measure as the experience of each historian differs from that of his fellows. It is indeed the wide and varied range of experience covered by all the days of all historians that makes the rewriting of history—not in each generation but for each historian—at once necessary and inevitable.

2

A New Framework for Social History *

THIS PAPER DEALS with historical comparison along a time axis in connection with the problem of a new framework for social history. Lest I be thought to aim at heights of egomania never before scaled, let me hastily add, however, that the full title of my observations would not be 'Comparison along the Time Axis: A New Framework for Social History! Come and Get It!' It might rather be 'Comparison along the Time Axis: A New Framework for Social History? Can Anything Be Done with It?'

By social history, I mean that sort of history-writing that makes social groupings and especially socio-economic classes the focus of its attention. At present scholars concerned with this kind of history seem to make one of two choices, neither altogether happy. They try to operate without a framework, or they operate within a stultifying framework—the Marxist interpretation of history. To choose the former is to choose inaccuracy and incoherence in describing chaos. To choose the latter is to choose intelligibility and coherence in describing a myth, and then to baptize the myth as history. The curious and brute fact is that a good number of historians *say* they choose the first horn of the dilemma; and then firmly impale themselves on the second horn. More historians than I should like to number, much less name, are in their historical practice bad and incompetent Marxists, incompetent because unconscious; Marxists in spite of themselves. They say they have no framework for social history, yet they write the social history of Western civilization for every century up to the nineteenth in terms of the rise of the middle class and the decline of the aristocracy, in those strictly Marxist terms and in no other.

Now why do so many historians in fact write history from a point of view that in theory they sincerely reject? The explanation of this

* An earlier version of this essay appeared in the *Journal of Economic History* in December 1955.

paradox, I believe, might go something like this. With the power of genius Marx drove home the importance for history of the conflict of economic interests organized through social classes aiming at the attainment, retention, and extension of power. But Marx did not merely *raise* the problem of classes. To his own satisfaction he solved it. This solution, based on the observed fact of class conflict, is a complete and coherent theory of social change. It is called dialectical materialism. It conceives of the social process as a regular succession of stages of socio-economic development emerging from one another as antitheses and syntheses. Historians were rightly impressed by Marx's insight into the conflict of classes. It gave them a whole new set of exciting insights into the way things happened. But when they picked up the notion of class conflict, they quite unconsciously picked up with it Marx's theory of social change. They bought themselves a package deal. The trouble is that the concept of class interest and class conflict is sound, one of the consistent patterns of history; but the Marxian theory of social change, dialectical materialism, is only the brilliant product of an overheated, overspeculative, nineteenth-century German imagination. Since any new framework for social history ought to seek to avoid the confusion into which an unwary absorption of the Marxist scheme has hitherto led historians, we had better have clearly in mind the bare essentials of that scheme as it applies to the Western world.

The Marxist scheme derives its explanation of almost a millennium of the history of Western civilization from three indisputable observations of fact and one somewhat gratuitous assumption. The first fact is that before the year 1000 the dominant social class in the Western world was composed of men who derived both their income and their power from the possession of large amounts of land and of enforceable claims on the labor and income of the men who worked the land. The second fact is that between A.D. 1000 and Marx's own day the Western world underwent vast changes, economic, social, political, religious, intellectual. The third fact is that in Marx's own time in the countries most advanced economically the dominant social class was composed of men who derived income and power not from land but from the ownership or control of industrial and trading capital. The gratuitous assumption is that the total history of all the major processes of change —economic, social, political, religious, intellectual—for the whole millennium can be explained in terms of the ceaseless conflict of the two classes, the landed class and the business class, a conflict marked by the gradual, irregular, but uninterrupted decline of the former, and the contrapuntal uninterrupted, irregular, but gradual rise of the latter. For about fifty years these facts and this one gratuitous assumption have served as the effective framework of social history. They have been the stickum with which the specialists have held together whatever particular bits of social history they have happened to be dealing in. Historians who have not used that stickum have simply sold their wares loose, as if to say to the consumer of history, 'Here it is. Put it together if you can. We can't.'

What is wrong with the Marxist theory is fairly clear. The trouble lies with the gratuitous assumption, which is in fact Marx's theory of social change. To the exigencies of Marx's gratuitous assumption the multiplicity and variety of change in a millennium of Western civilization simply cannot be fitted. The course of history from the ninth century to the nineteenth was just not as Marx described it. Indeed, the fruitful part of Marx's vision—the sense of the historical role of economically based social groupings, their inner structure, their interplay and conflicts—has been utterly blasted by its barren aspects, a pitifully narrow and provincial theory of historical change; and the whole Marxist operation has degenerated into sterile pedantry. That historians, by no means Marxist, have joined in the dreary game of 'Button, button, where is the bourgeoisie?' has made that game no more edifying or less dreary.

What can we learn from this sad misadventure? First, that any new framework for social history must not be a prefabricated theory of social change for which historians will forever thereafter be called upon to supply proofs. Second, that it must be a tentative sort of scaffolding, easily extended or torn down and reconstructed to help us in handling our materials, as we learn more about what we can do with those materials. Third, that on the fundamental principle that 'History is what happened to happen', it must take social and economic groupings as it finds them. It must not therefore prostrate itself in unholy worship before the altar of the materialist mystical three—feudal, bourgeois, proletarian.

Now the caveats just entered considerably simplify the task of this essay. They absolve me from attempting to draw up a substitute for Marx's overall theory of social change. The way social change in fact took place is something we may find out about by *using* our framework; it is not and *ought not be* something to be found *in* the framework. Moreover, with no commitment to an overall theory of social change, it becomes possible to propose a framework for a particular time span and for a particular area without feeling bound to warrant its utility at all other times and in all other places. The place my framework for social history is built for is England, the time for which the framework is built is from around 1000 to 1750.

The period of English history we are considering is about a century short of the time span for which the Marxist dialectic was primarily constructed. Moreover we are going to start with a solid fact as Marx did. Indeed we are going to start with the very same fact that Marx started with: around the year 1000 the dominant social class in the Western world was composed of men who derived their income and indirectly their power from the possession of land and of enforceable claims on the labor and income of the men who worked the land. The second fact is very like Marx's second fact: from the year 1000 up to within a hundred years of Marx's prime the Western world underwent vast changes—economic, political, social, religious, intellectual. Our third fact, however, is rather different from Marx's: one century before Marx's time, in the country most advanced economically, England, the dominant social class still derived most of its income and power from the possession of large amounts of land.

This third fact is the one most likely to arouse controversy, and within the compass of this essay adequate evidence to establish it cannot be offered. Indeed it is not easy to state precisely the conditions of proof of the statement that one class or another is dominant. For the case in point I will mention only one special index, the game laws. In the eighteenth century the operation of these laws provided the landed gentry with a charter of hunting privilege that effectively excluded all other classes. This privilege differed from others enjoyed by other groups in that it did not derive its justification from any benefit, real or imagined, that the grant or exercise of the privilege might confer on the country. It was a privilege conferred by a ruling class on itself merely as a perquisite of ruling. It is not without significance that by Marx's day, middle-class action in England had radically altered the structure of the eighteenth-century game laws along with the rule of the landed of which those laws were a symbol.

Of course, if one accepts this third fact as accurate, the whole perspective of social history shifts away from the customary Marxist pattern. That pattern, you will recall, is bound up with the thesis that the vast transformations of seven or eight centuries are wholly intelligible only if viewed as consequences of the rise of the bourgeoisie and the decline of the landed aristocracy. If in fact the aristocracy did continually decline during the period in question, then the hypothesis would merit consideration; if not, not.

But if we take the word *decline* in any common sense, then the landed aristocracy of England did *not* continually decline between 950 and 1750. After the Norman conquest in the eleventh century, England acquired a fully systematic feudal organization with the landed aristocracy, of course, at the top. The foundations of feudalism—its basis in tenure of land, conditional upon the rendering of military service—crumbled in the next two centuries, destroyed by the increased circulation of money and its own inadequacies as a means of raising an army. Commercial farming began to play a significant part in the rural economy. Alongside the rural economy a reasonably consequential urban economy appeared. The local laws under which English communities had hitherto been ruled were shunted toward obsolescence by the law of the king's courts, the common law of England. The waves of the renaissance of the twelfth century lapped against England's shores, and systematic learning acquired a measure of economic, political, and social value for him who possessed it. Still the landed aristocracy sat at the top of the heap. The secular boom of the thirteenth century gave way to the secular bust of the fourteenth. English trade shrank and so did commercial farming. After the 1350s the big operator whether in agriculture or finance was up against it. The efficient, hard-headed, high-handed central administration that England had known from the days of Henry II to those of Edward I gradually fell into decay. England's assembly of estates grew out of its infancy and became Parliament. By the scheme of commissions of array, indenture, and livery the power of the feudal group was replaced by that of 'goodlordship', a new kind of clientage that has been described as 'bastard feudalism'. In any case, at the top of the illegitimate heap there was still a more or less legitimate landed aristocracy.

The Tudors put an end to the violence of the waning Middle Ages, and private armies were no longer *de rigueur* in the best circles. The Tudors also broke with the Roman Church and threw rich nourishing packets of monastic land onto the market. The vogue of humanism put an unheard-of premium on book learning. The House of Lords no longer dominated the House of Commons. But as lord lieutenants, deputy lieutenants, justices of the peace, and outrageously enough after all, as representatives of the very towns of the 'rising bourgeoisie' in the House of Commons, the landed aristocracy still stood at the summit, the ruling class of England. I will not pursue the ponderous progress of the aristocracy any further down the corridor of the centuries. What we are dealing with is not a continuously declining class, but a class that rather successfully maintained its power during all the vicissitudes of three quarters of a millennium during which almost everything else changed quite, quite drastically. Of course the landed class itself changed drastically too. If it had not done so it could not have maintained its power. It is a far cry from Geoffrey de Mandeville's adulterine castles in the reign of King Stephen to the pleasant country mansions of the Whig oligarchs in the reign of George II. Nevertheless a continuity is there and it is substantial. In the history of the English aristocracy from 1066 on, there are bends; but there is no break in the continuity of its existence. Moreover, the roots of the power of Stephen's bad barons and of George's arrogant oligarchs were the same; they lay in the main in the extensive possession of land. But while the roots stood fast, that which grew from them underwent not one but several metamorphoses, fitting itself into societies such as Geoffrey and Stephen never dreamed of. The problem then is one of adaptation. Through seven-odd centuries the English aristocracy deployed their landed wealth in such a way as to retain power in their hands; but the way they deployed that wealth changed as the world they lived in changed around them. How then did they do it?

It seems to me that if historians were systematically to pursue that question down through the centuries they might learn a good deal about the social history of England. But specifically how should historians go about exploring the problem of aristocratic domination and its metamorphoses? To the question of technique there is obviously no one answer. So I will only propose one possible approach, the value of which could be tested only by trying it in practice.

I believe some biologists suggest that the key to the understanding of the nature of health is the study of disease, that the examination of the abnormal provides the clue to the normal. Now the different modes of organizing society seem to be subject each to its own peculiar disease. The characteristic malaise of aristocratic supremacy in English society was what English social diagnosticians were to recognize and describe as 'the overmighty subject'. The disease of course antedates its name, and looking all the way back before the Norman conquest we can discern its etiology in the case of Earl Godwin of Kent, the father of Harold whom William the Conqueror defeated.

As a rough approximation, overmighty subjects were men who in one way or another had acquired enough power in one form or another to be, or to be regarded as, a threat to the official custodians of public authority.

It seems to me that if we were to examine the story of the overmighty subject we might learn a great deal about the way the English magnate transformed his landed wealth into power by successive adaptations to emergent circumstances. Beginning with Earl Godwin in the eleventh century we might follow with Geoffrey de Mandeville in the twelfth, Simon de Montfort in the thirteenth, Thomas of Lancaster in the fourteenth, the king-making Earl of Warwick in the fifteenth, question mark for the sixteenth, a Puritan aristocratic connection in the seventeenth, the Duke of Newcastle in the eighteenth.[1] Perhaps such a series might conclude with a sketch of some actual nineteenth-century equivalent of Anthony Trollope's Duke of Omnium. Then we should be able to understand in detail why the greatest of Victorian landed magnates could not play the role their predecessors had played in previous centuries.

When we seek what underlay the excessive power wielded by these overmighty subjects we discover that it was in all cases similar: all of them used their lands as a base from which to move to a position of command or control over men. Ultimately it is only by means of such a transformation that wealth can become the basis and instrument of domination, since men, not money or land, are the source of power. Precisely what kind of men, precisely how they were organized, how the 'boss' built his 'machine', how he used it, to what collective sentiments (if any) he appealed to gain support and to vindicate his conduct, all these questions and many more would be the object of investigation. As such investigation proceeded we might learn something of the condition of society during the career of each overmighty subject, for in each instance it is the general organization, the habits, the institutions, the state and development of the natural and human resources of the society in which they operate that condition the activities, limit the success, and determine the failure of the overmighty subjects. That Geoffrey de Mandeville supported his position on a string of strategically situated Essex castles, that the Puritan connections aimed at and won initiative in the House of Commons, that the

---

[1] The immediately felt need to put 'question mark for the sixteenth, a Puritan aristocratic connection for the seventeenth' suggests at the outset certain peculiarities of those two centuries.

Duke of Newcastle made himself the almost indispensable man by the busy and judicious management of a tidy cache of rotten and pocket boroughs—this tells us something about Geoffrey, the Puritan connection, and the Duke; but it also tells us something about the nature of the societies in which these particular courses of action provided the lines of access to power.

As I observed before, there are surely other ways to get answers to the question 'How did the landed adapt themselves to changing conditions in such a way as to retain a dominant position in English society during seven centuries of change?' I should like, however, to point out two distinctive merits that inhere in approaching the problem through studying the overmighty subject.

First a simple matter of fact. Reporters like bad news better than good news and purvey it more abundantly; and this is true whether the reporter is a monastic chronicler or an eighteenth-century gossip. Now most overmighty subjects are bad news indeed; one way or another they make a lot of trouble. And consequently we can know a good bit more about them than we can about the less outrageous and therefore less notorious and less amply reported members of their class. The overmighty subjects are easier to document than most of their contemporaries.

The second point is connected with the first. Because we can know a good bit about most of these overmighty subjects we can tell a pretty coherent story about most of them. And telling a story is a good thing for a historian to do. Many of us have got so preoccupied with analysis and argumentation that we are in danger of forgetting how to tell a story and even of forgetting that telling a story is the historian's real business after all. Ultimately we do our best for the succession of human actions in time, which is history, when we tell the most intelligent story we can about it, or about that part of it which we know. So telling the stories of the overmighty subjects might be a reasonably satisfactory way to deal with eight centuries of English social history.

How should such work be done? It seems to me it should be co-operative. I am not beset by a consuming passion for co-operation of a highly organized sort in the field of scholarship. At best co-operative enterprises are the obverse and the confession of our individual limitations and incapacities; and they have often provided a circuitous route to a general mediocrity quite easily and directly attainable without the inconvenience that they involve. In the particular case in point, however, co-operation seems to be the lesser of two evils. The kind of easy familiarity with an era that the man who has devoted a lifetime to studying it enjoys is hard to come by. The amateur will go astray for lack of that firm grasp on the obvious which is the principal asset of the expert. It might be well to have an expert for the selected overmighty subject of each century. But the man dealing with the overmighty subject of any given century after the eleventh and before the nineteenth would have to keep in touch with the men working with the preceding and following centuries. Perhaps it might also be well to have the eleventh-century man keep in close touch with the nineteenth-century man in a chaste academic emulation of *La Ronde*. Such a procedure would keep at least two of the collaborators aware of the social distance between the tenth century and the nineteenth.

So much for the particular advantages of approaching the study of the durability and adaptations of the landed class through the adventures and misadventures of the overmighty. But I should like to point out certain general advantages of a vague framework of the kind I have proposed. All historians, I am sure, have at one time or another run into the rank-or-file dilemma. 'File' history is concerned with what Spengler called the *nacheinanderung*, the 'after-one-anotherness', of events. It deals with events in temporal sequence. It gives us our political histories of this place, and constitutional histories of that place. 'Rank' history is concerned with what Spengler calls the *nebeneinanderung* of events. It deals with the relation of more or less simultaneous events as manifestations of the temper of an age, or, as the anthropologists would have it, the pattern of culture. It gives our era histories —the Renaissance, the Age of Enlightenment. The 'rank-or-file' dilemma is that while both kinds of history are important we can only write one at a time. It is as if Heisenberg's indeterminacy principle were transferred to history. If we deal vigorously with a chain of events in time we lose track of the connectedness of each part of the chain with the other happenings contemporary with it. If we deal with the interrelations of events in a particular time we lose track of the connections of each particular event with its antecedents and consequences.

I am quite sure that if there were any wholly satisfactory way to attain a true marriage of rank history to file history, better men than I would have found it long ago. I am afraid that we will have to settle for a good bit less than a true marriage—a fairly frequent if somewhat casual liaison perhaps. Now it seems to me that for the accomplishment of such a liaison the framework for social history that I have out-lined has rather good possibilities. It follows a chain of circumstances, the destinies of the landed, down the corridors of time. Thus in one of its aspects it is sound 'file' history. But at each major change in the *modus operandi* of the landed in organizing their power structure we would be compelled to halt and to relate that change to the conditions and the characteristics of the whole society to which it was an adapta-tion. This procedure would help minimize the worse defects of 'file' history, its tendency to overlook those forces that exercise a short-run effect on the chain of development under consideration. Thus in the sixteenth century, the period of history that has most preoccupied me, humanism, the New Monarchy, the Reformation, Puritanism, the long Tudor-early Stuart peace, and above all the problem of main-taining a harmonious balance between court interests and country interests—all demanded certain kinds of adaptation on the part of the landed. By the end of the seventeenth century these forces were pretty well played out; at least they were not a serious concern of the landed magnates as such. In most file-history writing, such short-run com-plexes receive rather cavalier treatment. In economic histories, for example, Puritanism is usually dismissed with a nod, or more often a grimace, at Max Weber. Humanism and court and country get even shorter shrift. The framework above proposed should prevent this kind of curt dismissal, and act as a prophylactic against remarks about how *in the long run* such matters did not affect the *basic* realities. It would enable us to observe how the magnates' reaction to short-run realities became a part of the historical character of that class, and were carried right along with it on its trip down the long run.

Nor does the usefulness of the proposed framework end with its capacity to provide a partial resolution of the rank-and-file dilemma and to elucidate the adaptive maneuvers of a single social class. The study of adaptation among living things throws light on the trans-formations both of the species under investigation *and* of its environ-ment. Some species adapt to change in the environment by destroying other species or by forcing on them radical changes in the pattern of their lives. This is as much as to say that some species have adapted to changes in their environment by forcing further changes on their environment. What is true of living things is even more frequently true of human groups and especially of human groups with a dominant position in society such as the landed enjoyed. Thus sometimes as we follow the adaptive actions of the landed we will be able to observe how they impose a new pattern on other sectors of society. Consider the loose-knit but far-reaching fabric of clientage that the fifteenth-century landed magnates organized under the name of 'goodlordship'. It seems to have been the response of the magnates to the decline of their estate revenues and the almost simultaneous enfeeblement of the royal government. But the response itself had wide and deep ramifications. They are manifest, for example, in the advice of a lesser landed gentleman: 'Get yourself lordship, for it is the law and the prophets'. It shows again when old established merchant families like the Celys cast about for a lord to protect their interests. Once more it appears in the reform plans of an eminent judge. The twofold aim of Sir John Fortescue's scheme of reform is to provide the crown with revenues greater than those of any magnate, and to remove the magnates themselves from their dominant position in the royal council. The magnates had used their strategic situation in the council to provide their own household officials with government jobs, and had thus turned the royal service into a supply base for the maintenance of their clientage organizations. Thus their adaptive maneuvers had imposed alterations on the conduct of trade, on central administration, and on the relations of the landed classes. These are but a few examples of the way fifteenth-century society had to reorientate itself in consequence of the course of action pursued by the magnates to meet a crisis in their own affairs. They lie out on the surface of history where the most casual explorer can see them. To make out fully the underlying shifts in the formations of society of which these instances are but the surface outcrops would be difficult work. Clearly this essay is not the place for it. My aim is simply to indicate how a relatively simple framework can be used to open up and deal with some of the most intricate problems of social history.

A major merit of the conception of a framework for social history set forth above is that one cannot make preposterous claims for it. One cannot possibly insist that it is the only viable framework for all social history, since it is explicitly a framework only for a specified time and place. One cannot even claim that it is the only viable framework for the time and place to which it is pertinent. One cannot indeed claim that in working out its central problem one will exhaust the data of English social history. There will remain important aspects of English social history so far out on the periphery of the question of how the aristocracy stayed on top that they will never get built into it. For such data other frameworks would have to be developed and the hope entertained that the structures erected with their help could be brought into intelligible relation with the one I have proposed.

There is another thing to be said for using the question 'How did the aristocracy do it?' as a framework for English social history from the eleventh to the eighteenth century. It is after all a *question*. It does not offer an explanation; it seeks one. It involves a minimum of direction about what to find and a maximum of openness to whatever answers investigation brings to light. To those who regard history as a disordered scrap heap which exists only to be scavenged for usable parts by the constructors of unavowed but predetermined eschatologies this openness will scarcely seem desirable. Working historians, however, who in their slovenly way would rather arrive at conclusions than start with them, may see some small virtue in a work plan that places the conclusion at the end rather than at the beginning of an investigation.

Then, too, although our question does not enfold the whole of social history, an attempt to answer it *will* involve placing a very considerable part of English social history and a great deal of the rest of the history of England in an intelligible and coherent pattern about a center socio-economic in character. Finally, since the whole of Western civilization was socially in much the same condition as England in the tenth century, and since the destinies of other aristocracies were quite different from that of the English, it offers an opening for another kind of comparative study—the study in which the differentiae are not only of time but of place—that remains one of the most promising and least traversed avenues of historical investigation.

3

' Factors in Modern History '*

TO ALLAY ANY perplexity that may have assailed the reader on a hasty reading of the title of this essay, it may be well to point out that that title is not *Factors in Modern History* but *quote Factors in Modern History close-quote*, and that the operative signs are the quotation marks. In this essay, therefore, there will be no effort, doomed to futility at the outset, to deal in a few pages with the factors—whatever they may be—in modern history—whatever that is. This paper is about no such vast subject, but about a rather short book called *Factors in Modern History*. The book was published over half a century ago, in 1907; and its author was Professor A. F. Pollard.

Pollard was a great academic statesman—not an academic who made his way in national politics, but an imaginative builder within the bounds of Academe. Among the historians of his day in England no other left as a legacy so many active and lively institutions for the advancement of historical knowledge. Indeed, if the creation and fostering of such institutions is the best measure of academic statesmanship, then Pollard not only towers above his contemporaries among the historians, but must stand near the top among all the men of learning of his day both in England and elsewhere. As early as 1903 he had envisioned the complex structure of interlacing groups and activities that were needed to make a great history school at the University of London; and what he had envisioned he had the good fortune, the vigor, the courage and the tenacity to bring into being long before he died. The Historical Association, the journal *History*, the Institute of Historical Research, and the *Bulletin* of that Institute are more than inert monuments to Pollard's energy and effectiveness, and they do more than serve as passive memorials of their spiritual father. Rather they continue his creativity by carrying on in their independent existences the work he had nearest his heart.

Professor Pollard was also a notable scholar. There are not many historical surveys of which, fifty years after their publication, one can

* This essay has not been previously published.

say they are still the best things available. But one can say just that of Pollard's volume on the history of England from 1547 to 1603. And of course his biographies of Henry VIII, Cranmer, and Wolsey remain without peer.

Factors in Modern History was no such peerless performance, and certainly Pollard would not have claimed that it was so. Why then, a reader might properly ask, should he have inflicted on him a long disquisition on a book written more than half a century ago, a book which, although it possesses a certain excellence, can hardly be described as a classic of history? One might answer that, classic or not, *Factors in Modern History* is still quite a live book. In America within the past year it has been freed from larval compression between hard covers and metamorphosed, indeed apotheosized, into a paper-back. Moreover, so it has been told me, generations of English schoolmasters have used *Factors in Modern History* to introduce sixth formers to the study of history above the merely infantile level. It has thus become a bit of standard equipment for the initiation rites of the historical phratry.

Yet even were it less gorgeously covered with badges of success, the book would warrant close examination. For the purpose of this study *Factors in Modern History* has a special virtue which results from the quality of A. F. Pollard's mind. It was a mind strong and shrewd, but neither particularly sensitive nor particularly subtle. In *Factors in Modern History* that mind produced a work of broad generalization. The book portrays in primary hues and with little reserve or qualification the best thought of fifty years ago—a good part of it Pollard's own—on the seventeenth century and on that particularly difficult period, the sixteenth century. One would have said the Tudor period, were it not that in this book Pollard casts his glance, somewhat casually and dimly one must confess, at continental Europe. *Factors in Modern History*, therefore, provides us with a sort of color chart. Contrasting it with the views of present-day historians on the sixteenth and seventeenth century, we become aware of some of the changes that have taken place in our understanding of history in the past fifty years.

Before we make such a contrast, however, we ought to render to Pollard the homage that is his due for the assault he made on certain historical idols of his own day. It was a day—before Armageddon—when English liberal Parliamentary democracy was riding high, and when its supposed excellences were frequently ascribed to certain superior national traits putatively inherent in the English race. On the kind of historical thinking that produced pronouncements—solemn, pompous and silly—on the role of race in English history, Pollard wrought a splendid destruction. And of history writing that praised a mythical Lancastrian constitution because it was supposed to have advanced toward Parliamentary supremacy, and damned the Tudors because they were supposed to have inhibited the growth of Parliament, he made short work. If it did not make it impossible for historians to talk such nonsense—nothing seems to prevent a really determined historian from talking nonsense—at least the publication of *Factors in Modern History* made it more difficult, and demanded of the historian a more headlong propensity toward fatuousness. For his holocaust of historical idols we are all still debtors to A. F. Pollard.

Now, having rendered our meed of praise, we must turn to the less congenial, but more essential, task of exploring the deficiencies that the past half-century of historical study has revealed in Pollard's work. In so doing, we in no way belittle the man or his work. He and, with far less skill, we, work in the same craft, the art of history. A certain dialectic requires us to augment, or modify, or partially destroy the work of our predecessors in order to advance that art. Since it is a condition of the proper exercise of our art that we add to, refine, reconstruct and sometimes reject what we have inherited from earlier historians, the fact that we do so does not diminish our admiration of those historians, who in their time did to the work of others what we seek to do to their handiwork.

Ostensibly, the factors in modern history which Pollard deemed most important are revealed by the headings of the early chapters of his book: 'Nationality', 'The Advent of the Middle Class', 'The New Monarchy', 'Henry the Eighth and the Reformation', 'Parliament', and 'The Social Revolution'. A close scrutiny of Pollard's argument, however, reveals that for him the roots cf modernity are not quite so anarchically tangled as those chapter headings seem to indicate. In fact, there are but two interrelated, but not wholly interdependent, factors to consider—the emergence of the sovereign national state and the advent of the middle class. Having isolated these two factors in his first two chapters, in the remaining chapters Pollard describes their impact on the fabric of sixteenth- and seventeenth-century society.

Thus, the chapter on 'The New Monarchy' demonstrates the triumphant political embodiment of the principle of nationality in the persons of the monarchs of the sixteenth century. The chapters on 'Henry the Eighth and the Reformation' and on 'Parliament' show how in that century the concurrent aims and aspirations of the national sovereign and of the middle class combined to break England's links with Rome and to enhance the importance of the House of Commons. And so on. The essence of the matter is that the middle class and the national state destroyed the dominance of the Catholic Church and feudalism, which were the twin pillars of the Middle Ages. Thus, by the operation of these two factors, medieval history ended and modern history began.

Fifty years after the publication of *Factors in Modern History*, few historians would deny that eventually in the Western World the middle-class men of the towns and of trade came to exercise a power in both the economic and the political sphere that surpassed and supplanted that of the landed aristocracy. Few also would deny that in that world a passionate identification with the national state superseded an identification with the universal Church as the center of men's ultimate loyalties. The doubts that Pollard's arguments might encounter today would not be directed toward these two facts, but toward his chronology. Was the middle class quite so important, quite so masterful, *in the sixteenth century*, as Pollard thought it was? Was the national state quite so predominant in power, quite so pre-eminent among the loyalties of men, *in the sixteenth century*, as Pollard supposed? To both these questions the answer of most present-day historians probably would be 'No'.

On the first question, the question of the middle class, it is unnecessary to spend much time here, since a subsequent essay in this volume, 'The Myth of the Middle Class in Tudor England', attempts to set forth some of the grounds for a negative verdict in this case. It may be worth mentioning here, however, that some of the methods by which historians have tried to prove the dominance of men of the town and trade in sixteenth-century England and sixteenth-century Europe have been a trifle peculiar. For example, a gauge which measures the power of a class by the number of its members who bought their way out of it and on to the land, and by the speed with which they did so, is a very ambivalent instrument indeed; and the data that it renders call for great care in interpretation. Although a suspicion that the middle class was not rising in the sixteenth century in quite the way formerly alleged has taken hold among professional specialists, it has scarcely corrupted the sweet and innocent minds of the writers of textbooks, in whose works that class continues to ascend for six centuries or so in a smooth Pollardian way. But in matters of this sort a lag of three or four decades is to be expected among the writers of history textbooks, and we historians are nothing if not patient.

The myth of the national state will probably prove even more durable than the myth of the middle class.

As to the role Pollard ascribed to the national state in the sixteenth century, a role to which he imputed pan-European import, one can but feel that here he was the victim of anachronism, induced by an insular myopia prevalent in his day. It is the myopia most notoriously advertised in the tiresome old story about the English newspaper headline, 'Fog Over Channel. Continent Isolated'. As a consequence of focusing his attention on England, and of generalizing for Europe from what he saw in England, Pollard ascribed to the political nation in the sixteenth century a dynamic force as fact and ideal that it had scarcely acquired in most of Europe until the nineteenth century. Even beyond that, he may well have exaggerated the national element in England itself. If we look at the British Isles from the continent rather than the other way about, we may be inclined to minimize, rather than maximize the role of nationality. Should we emphasize nationality, for example, as Pollard does, in accounting for the Protestant Reformation in England and Germany? In practical effect the religious conflict in Germany was settled in 1555 by leaving the determination of the religion of their own principalities in the hands of scores of sovereign princelings of the Holy Roman Empire. About this settlement there was nothing national. Noting that from 1530 to 1560 England passed from Roman Catholicism to English Catholicism to moderate Protestantism, to radical Protestantism, to Roman Catholicism, and back to moderate Protestantism again, a German observer might draw his own conclusions. Since each of these frequent shifts in the religion of England took place at the command of the current sovereign, our German friend might be pardoned for concluding that things in England were pretty much the way they were at home, that the will of the prince had a good deal to do with the religion of the region, and that nationality had precious little to do with it.

In general, it would seem that at various times and in various regions of Europe in the sixteenth century the sense of belonging to a nation was an element of varying intensity; that the people who in present-day jargon were in positions of decision-making took national sentiment into account and exploited it—as they took into account and exploited other kinds of sentiment—when such exploitation was feasible; but that such people were themselves rarely dominated by national feeling. On the role of national interest in the sixteenth century Professor Garrett Mattingly, whose vast but lightly-worn learning and unfailingly shrewd judgment have earned for his opinions a universal respect, says:

> National interest was still too vague a concept to guide or even to excuse the policies of the monarchies. When the spokesman for the Estates General of 1506 besought Louis XII not to marry his daughter, the heiress of Brittany, to any but the natural heir to France, when an independent member of Parliament grumbled that the last English war across the Channel had cost more than twenty such ungracious dog-holes as its conquest, Thérouanne, would be worth . . . perhaps these citizens were fumbling toward what the nineteenth century would have regarded as a valid idea of the national interest. But their notions were still unformed. Mostly the third estates wanted just peace and lower taxes, and their infrequent murmurings were dismissed by their betters as the petty and short-sighted views of tradesmen unfit to meddle with the affairs of princes (*Renaissance Diplomacy*, p. 162).

In fairness to Pollard, one must add that Elizabeth and some of her advisors may have constituted an exception to Mattingly's rule.

Besides moderating his emphasis on nationalism and the middle class, historians writing fifty years after *Factors in Modern History* might want to stress some aspects of European history from the fifteenth to the seventeenth century that Pollard paid little attention to. Certainly they would say a great deal more about the Price Revolution, the gradual, but cumulatively spectacular, increase in the dearness of things that resulted from the augmentation of Europe's supply of precious metals in the sixteenth century. To the impact of the shift in price structure on the economy of the Western world, and on its social structure, Pollard devotes scarcely a paragraph, whereas that shift has become the framework on which many present-day historians hang their account of economy and society in Europe from about 1500 to 1650. It is not, however, quite sure that this has been all pure gain. There is a growing suspicion that when the historical dust has settled a bit, it will be discovered that the importance recently ascribed to the influx of gold and silver from America has been somewhat excessive.

With respect to another omission in *Factors in Modern History* there would be something close to unanimity among present-day historians. In a book devoted to the discovery of the roots of modernity in the sixteenth and seventeenth centuries they would look for the names of

Copernicus, Kepler, Galileo, and Huygens, of William Gilbert, William Harvey, Robert Boyle and Isaac Newton—and in Pollard's book they would look in vain. Those names do not appear. This omission reveals a decisive change in the content of historical study during the past fifty years. The branch of that study called the history of ideas and the branch of that branch called the history of science have flourished mightily since 1907. This massive development of knowledge has left no doubt that the Scientific Revolution was a decisive turning point in the history of Western thought, possibly *the* decisive turning point in the history of the human mind. Historians today might feel, with Pollard, that to thrust the events of the sixteenth century into the medieval pigeonhole would burst the joints of that already overstuffed repository. Yet most of those historians would probably be reluctant to ascribe modernity to sixteenth-century men, whose world was still the closed hierarchical organic cosmos that medieval schoolmen had constructed by blending scripture, Aristotle, and Ptolemy, and not the infinite, mechanical universe that Kepler, Galileo, and Newton built. And this is but to say that one matter, which seemed fairly settled in the 1900s, has since become quite unsettled—the matter of periods in history, of how best to divide into manageable segments the onward flow of events in time. Pollard was reasonably confident that it made sense to place the divide between medieval and modern history in the sixteenth century. Today doubts about the wisdom of selecting this particular line of division merge with yet graver doubts about the actuality, and even the convenience, of the very concepts, medieval and modern. It may be—and it will not be for the first time—that a loss of certainty stands at the beginning of knowledge.

In the past fifty years, historians have not only broadened our understanding of the sixteenth century; they have also refined it, made it more precise. To describe what has taken place in the refining of our historical analysis is not easy, since it has been a bit-by-bit process, whose general purport has not attracted much attention even from those engaged in it. So if my exposition seems a little shaky at this point, it is because it rests on home-made, and not well-made, foundations. In brief, it seems to me that the historical researches of the last five decades have revealed the sixteenth century to be an era during which the lines of class interest and national interest were traversed and frequently—perhaps more frequently than not—dominated by other lines of allegiance and action. We may best envisage these other lines as polar pairs, pulling men in opposite directions and therefore creating tensions. These tensions confronted sixteenth-century men with the multitude of particular decisions that they had to make.

Two of the polar pairs—Catholic–Protestant and Church–State—have long been in use by historians. Pollard deals with them. He more or less identifies Catholic with Church and Protestant with State. Then —in accord with his conception of the prime factors in modern history —he assimilates Catholic and Church to universal–feudal–medieval on the one hand, Protestant and State to national–middle-class–modern on the other. This propensity, strong in Pollard and his contemporaries and still strong today, seems to mark the triumph of a desire for simple order over a desire to face the facts. For in the sixteenth century Protestantism, especially in its Calvinist version, was *not* markedly middle-class. It attracted Norfolk and Gelderland squires and the Western Highlanders as powerfully as it did burghers in London, Amsterdam and Edinburgh. And it was the 'internationalism' of the Calvinists—their readiness to render material aid and undergo bodily danger to render assistance to the persecuted Saints in foreign lands—that prevented the Papal counter-offensive from destroying Protestantism. The conviction which Calvinism ultimately developed with respect to the relation of State to Church received its most eloquent expression when the Scottish minister, Andrew Melville, plucked that would-be divine-right monarch James VI of Scotland by the sleeve, called him 'God's silly vassal', and informed him that, although James was King of Scotland, Jesus Christ was King of the Kingdom of the Church, 'whose subject King James VI is, and of whose Kingdom not a King . . . nor a head but a member'. And Melville adds that the ministry 'whom Christ has called and commanded to watch over His church have sufficient power . . . of Him so to do . . . the which no Christian prince should control or discharge'. To the convinced Calvinist, the *Regnum Christi* was not a promise of pie in the sky but a call to present action. To many a European prince it was a clear and present danger. Until we grasp that the claims of Presbytery were *not* national or middle-class, that they were quite as universal, quite as catholic, and, in that dubious sense, quite as medieval, as the claims of the Papacy, we shall ill understand the events of the later sixteenth century. But then the taxonomy that completely subsumes Catholic under medieval and feudal is itself peculiar. It is a somewhat arbitrary way to classify a faith which flourished almost twenty centuries ago in the great cities of imperial Rome and which today enjoys firm support among the urban populace of the greatest cities of industrial America.

The study of sixteenth-century history during the past fifty years, then, has not sustained Pollard's decision to assimilate Protestantism and the defection from universalism to each other, and to reduce them to epiphenomena thrown up by the rise of the middle class and of nationalism. In Karl Marx's language, neither is mere superstructure. Moreover, during the past fifty years, historians of various aspects of the sixteenth century, as we have noted, have felt impelled to deal with other polarities besides Catholic–Protestant and Church–State. Among them are town–hinterland, lay–clerical, secular–religious, *Realpolitik*–legitimacy, realm–province, dynasty–region, *gubernaculum–jurisdictio*, court–country. No more than the Catholic–Protestant polarity will these others fit the patterning of history that makes the sixteenth century the great divide between feudal–universal–medieval on the one hand and middle-class–national–modern on the other. But although we recognize this one *negative* similarity, we must not conceive of these other polarities as complete historical analogues to the Catholic–Protestant polarity. For in the common opinion of the sixteenth century, the Catholic–Protestant polarity was absolute, unconditional. That is to say, both Catholic and Protestant claimed to possess the sole, saving, and God-given truth, necessary for the redemption of man. The logic of both the Catholic and the Protestant position, therefore, called for unremitting warfare on the opposite position. The principle was one of mutual exclusion, indeed of mutual extermination. If we adopt this point of view in examining the other polarities we have mentioned, however, we court confusion, for the Catholic–Protestant pair is eccentric, atypical in its absoluteness. Although between the opposed members of each of the other pairs there is tension, the issue is *never* either–or; it is *always* more-or-less. With respect to the interests of town and hinterland, of laity and clergy, of dynasty and region, of court and country, the question in the sixteenth century is never how one can annihilate the other; it is how to strike a viable balance between them, how under varying conditions to work out ever anew the terms of adjustment and reconciliation.

Failure to keep this point in mind can be fatal to our understanding of the sixteenth century, and nowhere more so than in grasping the relationship between *Realpolitik*, or political realism, and legitimacy. We are likely—as Pollard did—to note the discrepancy between the sixteenth-century statesman's profession of concern for the rightful public order of Christendom and his complete opportunism in practice, and to write off the profession as a cynical bit of fraudulence. By parity of reason we then ascribe the statesman's frequent advocacy of legality in the internal affairs of his master's realm to hypocrisy, too. Yet it is more likely that the major statesmen of the age—Gattinara and Perronet, Robertet and L'Hôpital, Cecil and Walsingham, even Wolsey and Thomas Cromwell—were *both* political realists *and* men concerned with legitimacy. The trouble was that, in the sphere of relations *among* rulers, the medieval structure of institutions was wholly shattered and afforded no foothold for aspirations toward a legitimate order. In this sphere men with power might talk, and even believe, the old pieties; but they acted, perforce, like a gang of disingenuous cannibals. Within the realm, however, where much of the framework of institutions remained relatively intact, the gap between profession and practice, between what men of power felt it right to do and what they felt it necessary and desirable to do, was a good bit smaller. In this sphere a concern for legitimacy had something substantial to hang on to. If this is so, then between the professions and the intentions of people like Henry VIII and Elizabeth I there may be a closer correspondence than most historians have been willing to grant.

Among the polarities mentioned earlier there are two that may be worth a little further discussion, because it seems likely that in the near future a good deal of the historical writing on the sixteenth century will focus on them, or at least it seems desirable that such writing should. They are dynasty–region and court–country. We have already watched Garrett Mattingly make short work of the illusion that national interest was the guiding star on which sixteenth-century monarchs set the course of their policy. But if not on national interest, on what did they set their course? Professor Mattingly says,

> The sixteenth-century struggle for power had a *dynastic*, not a national, orientation. The Kingdom of Naples and the Duchy of Milan were wealthy and famous provinces. The conquest of either would increase the apparent strength of the prince who could effect it, and indubitably increase, for a time, the benefits he would be able to bestow on his captains and councilors. Whether such conquests would be worth to his people the blood and treasure they cost was an irrelevant, absurd question. Nobody expected that they would (*Renaissance Diplomacy*, pp. 152-3).

What counted most in high politics in Europe from 1450 to 1550 was not the French or English nation, much less the German or Italian nation. It was the Houses of Tudor, and Valois, and Burgundy, and Trastamara, and Hapsburg; and when dynasticism attained its fullest development and its greatest eccentricity, it was the monster House of Trastamara-Burgundy-Hapsburg, embodied in the person of Charles V.

At the pole opposite to the dynasty was not the nation; that much is certain. But to give a name to what was at the opposite pole is not easy. The word 'region' may be the best word available; but it is most unsatisfactory. It is as near as one can come in English to the more satisfactory but not perfect French word, *pays*. In the sense intended here France, England, and possibly Spain were *pays*, but hardly Germany or Italy. And, although they were parts of the *pays de France*, Brittany, Languedoc, and Burgundy were also *pays*. Aragon was a *pays*, and so were the parts of Aragon called Catalonia and Valencia. In the first half of the sixteenth century the Netherlands were one *pays* comprised of about a dozen *pays*. Ireland was a *pays*, and so was Wales, and so, possibly, was the region that Englishmen simply called the North; but Sussex and Wiltshire were not. What then, constituted a *pays*, or, understood simply as a translation of that word, a region? Roughly, a *pays* or region was a territory whose inhabitants shared a sentiment of identification with that territory and with each other, sufficiently strong to make it regularly necessary for politicians to take that sentiment into account in their political decisions. The more resistant regions almost always had regional liberties, charters, *fueros*, well-preserved ancient customs. They often had special regional political organs, too, which enabled them to do some highly effective foot-dragging when dynastic policy ran overmuch against the regional interest. It was not the nation that set limits to the pursuit of dynastic policy in the sixteenth century; it was the *pays* or region. What the results might be, if the tension between dynasty and region ran too high, Philip II learned at great expense in his dealings with the Netherlands.

The court–country polarity is more difficult to define than the dynasty-region polarity, because in historical fact the boundary between court and country is far less distinct than the one between dynasty and region. Indeed, the effective monarch in the sixteenth century was precisely the one who prevented a sharp delimitation of those boundaries from taking place, who avoided the dangers inherent in the isolation of court from country. In England, for example, the grooms of the chamber and gentlemen-in-waiting were wholly court, the great officers of state only slightly less so. Lord-Lieutenants, on the other hand, were betwixt and between, half-court half-country; and the justices of the peace were almost wholly country. Roughly speaking, the court was at once a source of patronage, a focus of power, a way of life, and a repository of administrative authority at the center of which stood, not the abstract crown, but the living, breathing prince. Country was the miscellaneous lot of interests, concerns, and habits of thought and action that were essentially *local* in character, although certain local interests and concerns might be common to almost all the localities in a realm. Research into the internal development of European states that, explicitly or otherwise, takes fully into account the court–country polarity has not been under way for more than a decade or so. Implicitly it is taken into account in Sir John Neale's great work on the Elizabethan Parliaments and in the later sections of William Dunham's recent study of the fee'd retainer, explicitly in Trevor-Roper's *The Gentry*. A further orientation of research to the court–country polarity might at once add flesh to the lean history of sixteenth-century governance and provide some bones for the invertebrate mass called local history.

So far in this rather long-winded examination of an old book, we have dealt with matters of substance or body and matters of form or mind. In the Christian tradition, we ought to end up by dealing with the spirit; but pronouncements about the spirit of one's own day, or even of an earlier day, with respect to almost anything are tricky affairs. In this area, above all, each man is likely to confuse the voice of the age with the echo of his own prejudices and prepossessions. Nevertheless, the voice of the age—of any age—does speak from many mouths. The voice of Pollard's age certainly spoke from his. Notions, so much in the air at a particular time that the people of that time scarcely are aware of them, yet leave subtle but indelible marks on the things those people write. The assumptions historians make permeate their work by conditioning the way they order their data and the importance they ascribe to the various arrays of events that come under their consideration. At the moment we are not concerned with 'inexplicit assumptions', dear to the hearts of practitioners of the sociology of knowledge. For Pollard makes at least one assumption with all the explicitness the heart could desire. He does so in such statements as: 'There have been changes sudden in their outward manifestations. The French Revolution is a more striking example of them than the transition from medieval to modern history. But even the French Revolution was a summation of causes which had been working for ages. Even here it is true to say that *Natura nihil facit per saltum'* (*Factors in Modern History*, p. 33). Nature does nothing by leaps. Or again:

> Whatever factors we take in the making of that change from medieval to modern history . . . they have their roots stretching far back into the past and buried far out of sight. The growth and decay are silent, gradual, almost imperceptible. The dramatic events which catch the eye and ear, and by which we date the progress or backslidings of mankind, are, like the catastrophes which convulse the sphere of nature, but the outward and visible manifestations of causes, working without rest, without haste, without conscious human direction, in the making of the history of the world (*ibid.* p. 51).

Pollard's Latin tag—*natura nihil facit per saltum*—is a dead giveaway. It dates *Factors in Modern History* very tidily as the intellectual emanation of a period when the idea of progress and, indeed, the whole domain of social thought in general had taken on the color and tone of Darwinism. It comes earlier than the emergence of those doubts about the gradualness of transformations in the sphere of organic nature, which were engendered by the study of genetics. If I have not got mutation theory all mixed up—and I probably have—biologists today would be likely to suggest that organic nature does nothing important in the way of change *except* by jumps. But for historians of an era precommitted to find in human history an analogue to the process of gradual, even glacial, change that they believed characteristic of natural history, the particular sort of factor analysis which Pollard adopted was something of a godsend. Consider Pollard's own procedure. As we have seen, he selects as the crucial factors in modern history the advent of the middle class and nationalism. Now the middle class and nationalism did not exist in Europe in the tenth century. They may perhaps be dimly discernible in the twelfth century; they attain undeniable ascendancy only in the nineteenth century. Since we start with the middle class and nationalism at low ebb, and, about six hundred years later, end up with them at high flood, what more natural for a historian committed to evolutionary gradualism than to connect the starting point and the end point on his time scale in the simplest way possible—by an ascending straight line. Pollard and his contemporaries did the natural thing: they drew that straight line. And ever since in the pages of our history textbooks, 'emerging nationalism' and the 'rising middle class' century after century have toiled steadily upward along it.

In fact, there is no reason to assume that the slopes of the curves of ascent of the middle class and of nationalism during more than half a millennium were straight lines, or even that they trended continuously upward over their whole course. To work out empirical methods just for roughly gauging the slope of such a curve over its whole course would tax the ingenuity of the shrewdest analytical historian. Naturally Pollard was not aware that his views involved any empirical problem of measurement. That straight line of his is wholly *a priori*, a purely imaginary construction that does not set historical facts in order, but altogether escapes and soars above their dreary restrictions. It is the product not of historical investigations but of the spirit of Pollard's age, the age of historical Darwinism.

If we give serious consideration to those varied polarities mentioned above, our very image of the historical process will differ drastically from Pollard's. The sense of inevitable, straight-line trends, so strong in him, diminishes. The sense of the catastrophic, which Pollard minimizes, increases. For a while at the turn of the fifteenth century, the tensions among various poles stand in rough and complex balance, and the adjustments necessary to maintain a workable equilibrium are relatively small. Then a couple of wholly unpredictable things happen. Luther successfully defies the Pope; the conquistadors discover the precious metal hoards and mines of America. Within a few decades these events drastically augment the tensions in the system. The areas in which men can get along on the more-or-less type of decision shrink. The areas in which they have to face either–or decisions expand. As such decisions increase in number, they also increase in importance; both what decisions will have to be made next, and what their proximate consequences will be, become increasingly hard for contemporaries to predict, and the stream of happenings flows not with glacial majesty but with devastating violence.

The catastrophic character of history at times of crises is reflected in the kind of history writing that can deal with such times. Analytical history, the sort of history that Pollard wrote in *Factors*, and the sort that has become increasingly popular in academic circles since, runs into trouble amid the convulsions of a world in upheaval. It often pretends that they really weren't convulsions, or that they really didn't matter. But, of course, they really were convulsions, and they really did matter. At this point, the narrative historian must take over from the analytical historian; for it is his art not to demonstrate that the course of events was inevitable, but, in the midst of mounting uncertainties, to render the decisions men made intelligible.

And here, in the past fifty years, our movement has not been progressively forward, or even, crablike, sideways; but simply backward. Living in the tradition of both Macaulay and Ranke, A. F. Pollard did not need to be told that history is an intricate sequence of the acts of men in time; and that ultimately, to do justice to that sequence, one needs to tell a story. That his own volume in the Political History of England series, written in 1910, remains even now the best single treatment of the era it covers sufficiently testifies to Pollard's mastery of narrative. Today, however, orthodox academic historians tend to put story-telling under a ban. To tell a story well is to commit the scandalous sin of being popular if one is not an academic, or of being a romantic historian if one is an academic. Putting story-telling under a ban does not, of course, make it possible to traverse the period between say, Luther's breach with Rome and the Edict of Nantes without telling a story. It does, however, make it possible for some academic historian to tell such stories incompetently while smugly regarding their ineptitude as an infallible mark of redemptive merit, of their superiority to those damned historians who tell their stories well.

Having dealt with an explicit assumption that colored Pollard's view of what happened in modern history, we may conclude this essay with a brief examination of one of his tacit or inexplicit assumptions. This assumption is still current among many historians, and in all likelihood it remains tacit, I suspect, because historians are not aware that they are making it. Since the assumption is not directly expressed, it is rather difficult to find the right words to describe it. The assumption of the conservation of historical energy is reasonably satisfactory, although the wages-fund theory of the historical process, or the teeter-totter or seesaw theory, might do just as well. The model in this instance, one may guess, was taken from Newtonian physics rather than from Darwinian natural history. Stated rather abstractly, the idea is that in a given society the energy expended on a single pair of polar elements is fixed, so that any flow of social energy in the direction of one such pole can only take place by way of subtraction from the flow of energy to the opposite pole. So abstractly stated, the idea, I fear, may seem trivial, or unintelligible, or both. Let us try to make it a little more concrete. Earlier we mentioned secular and religious as polar phenomena. In so doing, we aimed to point up the contrast between aspirations and actions directed toward this-worldly and those directed toward other-worldly goals. Granted that in particular cases it is not always possible to make a clear-cut distinction, still, to suggest an extreme instance, it is not too hard to decide toward which pole the lustful glutton tends, and toward which the martyr, toward which Alexander VI and toward which Savonarola. Now, on the assumption of the conservation of historical energy, if in a society there is an increase of activity in the direction of the secular pole, there *must* be a corresponding decrease of energy in the direction of the religious pole. Moreover and therefore, for the historian who makes the assumption, *the increase in the secular direction is itself sufficient evidence of the decrease in the religious direction.* Although this corollary to the assumption of the conservation of historical energy is an intellectual trap of the most lethal sort, I fear that the abstractness of my exposition still conceals the clear, present, and practical danger which I have been trying to reveal. Perhaps the surest, if not the kindest, way to reveal the danger of this trap is to show what happens when someone falls into it.

In *Factors in Modern History*, A. F. Pollard falls into it. Throughout his book, but especially in the chapter on 'Henry the Eighth and the Reformation', Pollard makes a very good case for the intensification of this-worldliness in the sixteenth century. And he does not nearly exhaust the evidence supporting his case. Consider the boast of Elizabethan statesmen—a strangely secular boast in view of the Christian tradition in such matters—that they intended to punish no one for his religious beliefs. Consider the French *politiques*—French Catholics, who yet preferred the hope of this-worldly peace, held out by the Edict of Nantes, to their Christian duty to extirpate heresy. Consider even Philip of Spain, who, long after the Pope had excommunicated the English Jezebel, was still ready to negotiate for a peaceful settlement of his differences with her.

The evidence, then, strongly indicates that many sixteenth-century men aimed at, and even openly avowed, secular goals which almost all men of the thirteenth century would have rejected with an outward show of horror and, quite possibly, with real inward loathing. These being the facts about this-worldliness, the secular, in the sixteenth century, what inferences about other-worldliness, about the religious, can we properly draw from them? The answer, of course, is that we can properly draw no inferences whatever about other-worldliness in the sixteenth century from these facts. Any commitment with respect to other-worldliness in the sixteenth century, that is, with respect to any historical phenomenon in any century, should follow and never precede the historical investigation of that phenomenon at that time. It must not be derived from the investigation of the opposite or polar phenomenon alone. Yet without a moment of hesitation Pollard, and a great many historians since Pollard, have habitually, perhaps even unconsciously, inferred from the facts about this-worldliness in the sixteenth century the decline of other-worldliness in that age. Why did Pollard do it? He did it because he had fallen into the lethal trap I have been trying not very successfully to describe, the trap created by the corollary about evidence which follows from his assumption about the conservation of historical energy. He took the demonstrable increase in the flow of energy and activity to the secular pole to be adequate evidence of the flow of activity and energy away from the religious pole. And here in a quite concrete instance the assumption about the conservation of historical energy has exercised a practical and very malign influence on historical imagination. Since they have already *taken it as given* that other-worldliness declined in the sixteenth century, Pollard and many other historians have had either to disregard facts which suggest that things were otherwise or they have had to explain such facts away. Neither alternative is a very happy one, since both, instead of helping us to make sense of one of the most conspicuous sequences of facts in the sixteenth century, force us to make nonsense of it. That conspicuous sequence of facts is the one which runs from the religious revival, exemplified but not exhausted by Christian humanism, through the Reformation and the Counter-Reformation, to the Wars of Religion. That this series of events indicates that the sixteenth century underwent an intensity and extension of religious concern beyond anything which had been experienced or imagined in the fifteenth century is a historical inference practically beyond doubt.

Only something *extra-historical* could blind able historians to a fact so obvious. We have identified that extra-historical entity—the assumption of the conservation of historical energy. If we get rid of the assumption, we get rid of our difficulty and can look squarely at the historical facts. Once we realize that the religious and the secular, although polar to one another, *can*, both at once, rise to higher levels of intensity, we will recognize that they both *did* so rise in the sixteenth century. From 1517 on, the religious revival which had begun earlier got caught up in the one historical polarity of the sixteenth century which was unconditional and absolute—the polarity between Catholic and Protestant. Under such circumstances its very intensity threatened the civil order and the security of every land in Western Christendom.

But men—almost all men—are concerned not only with matters of creed and ideology; they are also concerned with civil order, which is the framework of their living from day to day. And for secular rulers the maintenance of civil order is at once a necessity and, according to the views current in the sixteenth century, a part of their duty to God. When the intensified pull toward the religious pole found expression in mortal strife between Catholic and Protestant, is it really any wonder that men of theory, like Bodin, felt impelled to think through afresh the problem of political obligation, that men of judgment, like Montaigne, felt the need to dampen the fires of sectarian ardor, and that statesmen, regardless of their religious preference, felt driven to play the European power game with a cold and careful calculation of the consequences of each move? Whether in the particular situation domestic order, or place in the European state system, or both, were involved, the conflict over religion had set a painfully high price on errors or weakness in the game of power in the sixteenth century. So Mary Stuart learned to her cost in Scotland, and Philip II to his cost in the Netherlands. So the French learned through a generation of devastating and bloody religious civil war. If, in the sixteenth century, many men displayed an intense preoccupation with chilly computations of this-worldly advantage, it was in part at least because they felt at their backs the burning heat of religious conflagration.

It was my intention to bring this essay to a close with an apology for its scantiness in the *matter* of history, the massing of fact, and for its preoccupation with the *forms* of historical explanation. Yet after all, had the deployment of a mass of fact seemed more desirable to me on this occasion than a contemplation of problems of historical form, there was nothing to prevent such a deployment. But history writing is more than a piling up of facts; it is an arraying, an ordering of facts. Its goal is not only to state what happened, but to render what happened increasingly intelligible; and we must concern ourselves not only with ways of getting data, but with ways of putting data together. Our refined methods of assessing evidence and establishing facts, of which we are justly proud, should not be the only tools of our craft. Historians need to be a most eclectic band of workers, jacks-of-many-trades, if not of all. We should be ready to bring to bear on the problems of ordering intelligibly those facts at our disposal, the whole range of our remembered experiences—what we know about other disciplines, the insights we have gained from literature, and, perhaps most important, though surely least cultivated, a certain good sense and solidity of judgment which we may acquire if we go reflectively about the business of living our own lives. In the indispensable fervor of collecting vast stacks of 4 in. by 6 in. cards, covered with priceless, although somewhat incoherent bits of information, let us not forget what Pollard knew so well and exemplified so clearly in *Factors in Modern History*: 'He also serves', who sometimes sits and thinks.

4

The Education of the Aristocracy in the Renaissance [*]

IN AN INQUIRY concerning education the historian may take one of several starting places, launch his investigation with one of several major questions. He may ask what people thought education should be at a particular time. Or he may ask what education at that time was like in fact; and as every teacher knows to his sorrow, there is usually a world of difference between the answers to those two questions. He may also ask who got the education that was offered, and this third question is surely no less significant than the other two. If one believes that knowledge in some measure is power, particularly if one is an educational anarchist and believes that in society at large a man who has received almost any kind of rigorous intellectual discipline stands in a position of competitive advantage, other things being equal, over a man who has received none, then the question of who got an education becomes acute for the writing of social history. Now about what certain men during the period of the Renaissance thought education should be like we know a great deal, and about what education in fact was like we know somewhat less, but still a considerable amount. About who got the education—about the social appropriation and distribution of these very valuable scarce goods—we know almost nothing.

That this was the case was sharply brought home to me in the course of an investigation of the aristocracy of the new monarchies in the age of the Renaissance. Not being able to find any study of the matter in print, I decided to try myself to reach at least a tentative answer to the above questions about the education of the aristocracy. The rather fragmentary sketch that follows is the result of this inquiry. A casual investigation of the situation in Spain did not produce any result worth recording, so any generalizations that appear hereafter apply only to England, France, and the Netherlands. What, then, was the education

[*] An earlier version of this essay appeared in the *Journal of Modern History* in March 1950.

of the aristocrats during the Renaissance, how many of them received it, when historically did they begin to receive it, and what did they want with it?

The most superficial examination of the most conspicuous data tells us with certainty at least this: that in the sixteenth century there was a great deal of complaint about the education of the aristocracy, and that with a few exceptions the Jeremiahs of the time were all saying pretty much the same thing. The well-born were ignorant, they were indifferent to learning, and they preferred to stay that way. John Skelton compressed the essence of a century of criticism into a capsule of doggerel:

> Noblemen born
> to learn they have scorn,
> but hunt and blow a horn,
> leap over lakes and dikes,
> set nothing by politics.

It was in almost identical terms but more emphatically that an unnamed gentleman stated his attitude on learning to the humanist diplomat Richard Pace. 'It becomes the sons of gentlemen', he said, 'to blow the horn nicely, to hunt skillfully, and elegantly to carry and train a hawk'. He added that 'the study of letters was for rustics', that it was stupid, and that all learned men were beggars. 'Rather my son should hang', than be learned, he concluded. Another Englishman later in the century added dress, dining, drinking, and gadding about to hunting and hawking in the list of current aristocratic attainments. Noble folk charge anyone who talks wisely with preaching, he said, and contemptuously call all men more learned than themselves penmen.[1] Across the Channel the story is the same. La Noue speaks of the present sunken generation of noblemen, great hunters and brawlers, who take little care to educate their young to *choses honnestes*. They let themselves be ruled by custom and think it enough if their children can read and write. Noël du Fail's country gentleman in the *Contes d'Eutrapel* reads a translation of the Bible, a dismal series of medieval romances and

---

[1] John Skelton, *Poetical Works*, ed. A. Dyce (London, 1843), i. 334; Richard Pace, *De fructu* (Basel, 1517), preface cited in *Early English Meals and Manners*, ed. F. J. Furnivall (Early English Text Society, original series, no. 32) (London, 1868), pp. xii–xiii (hereafter cited as '*English Meals*'); Sir Thomas Elyot, *The Boke Named the Gouernour*, ed. H. S. Croft (London, 1883), i. 99: 'Some . . . without shame dare affirm that to a gentleman it is a notable reproach to be well learned and to be called a great clerk'; and Hugh Latimer, *Sermons and Remains* (London, 1844), i. 68–9.

saints' lives, and nothing else. Another Frenchman deplores 'the nobles' Gothic fashion of hating learning and learned men as if books and arms were things incompatible.' And yet another in an untranslatable pun says that the only use most nobles had for a *plume* was to put it in their hats.[1]

So ran the refrain—a chorus of condemnation against the unlearnedness and hostility to learning of the noble and the gentle. What is the meaning of this denunciation? It fits well into a time-honored pattern of historical explanation. It may be but one more note in that running-down-the-scale of feudalism which, played contrapuntally with the ascent of the middle class, is taken to be the all-sufficient explanation of practically everything that happened in Europe for seven hundred years. Before adopting this explanation out of hand we had better examine somewhat more closely the circumstances surrounding the complaints. We have the criticism of the aristocracy, and we have the situation criticized—the ignorance of the wellborn. Was the complaint new or of long standing? The situation—was it old or new? And, finally, was the situation real or unreal; to what extent was the sixteenth-century aristocrat actually an ignorant man?

For purposes of comparison we may begin our investigation with Geoffrey Chaucer's pilgrims on the Canterbury road at about the end of the fourteenth century. In that motley band there were only three men who were certainly aristocrats or near-aristocrats—the knight; his son, the squire; and the franklin. The knight and the squire received identical training; and to it we must give our earnest attention. The franklin tells us why: he has a son, he says, and he

> . . . levere than twenty pound worth lond,
> Though it right now were fallen in myn hond,
> He were a man of such discrecion

as the squire. Then, instead of dicing and spending wildly, he would commune with gentlemen and rightly learn what belongs to gentility.[2] The Yorkshire landlord feels that the training of the squire is just what

---

[1] [François] de la Noue, *Discours politiques et militaires* (Basel, 1587), pp. 129–30 and 137–9; Noël du Fail, *Œuvres facétieuses*, ed. J. Assézat (Paris, 1874), ii. 166; Droit de Gaillard, cited in Paul Porteau, *Montaigne et la vie pédagogique de son temps* (Paris, 1935), p. 312; and Henri de Mesmes, *Mémoires inédites*, ed. Édouard Frémy (Paris, 1886), p. 125. See also the story of the situation of the French nobles unable to communicate with the Latin-speaking nobles of Poland (Porteau, p. 313, n. 1) and Michel de Montaigne's observation on the aversion to letters of the French nobles (*Les Essais*, ed. P. Villey [Paris, 1930], i. 337–8).

[2] Geoffrey Chaucer, *Canterbury Tales*, ed. J. Manly (New York, 1928), pp. 378–9.

that of a gentleman should be. His own education is somewhat deficient;[1] the squire's is at once the average and the ideal, the pedagogic goal toward which gentlemen and would-be gentlemen direct their children. It is *the* education of the aristocrat.

The squire's formal education had two branches. He learned music —to sing it, to play it, to compose both tune and lyric. He learned to dance, to draw and write; he learned to speak and move gracefully. This was courteous aesthetic training, the learning of love, dedicated to the lady fair. He exercised his body. He rode, shot, handled lance and sword; he ran, vaulted, and leaped. He carved before his father at table. This was practical knightly training, preparation for warfare and for the honorable service a gentleman owed his lord. The squire's education began when he became a page in about his seventh year, it continued for fourteen years, and its goal was knighthood. In the course of these fourteen years the noble youth was supposed to acquire not only a set of accomplishments but a code of morals, as well. He was to come out of the educational mill lowly and serviceable, gentle and worthy, loving chivalry, truth, and honor, freedom and courtesy.[2]

In Chaucer's time this pattern of gentle education was about two hundred and fifty years old, and almost a century later it was still the only kind of aristocratic education the court of France knew. In this long time much had changed but not the training of a gentleman. William the Marshall, who served Henry II well in the twelfth century, would have found nothing in the education of Chaucer's squire in fourteenth-century England or of La Tremouille in the fifteenth-century court of Louis XI that he would not have prescribed for his own sons.[3] But it was not the kind of education that the lament-makers of the sixteenth century were prescribing for gentlemen in their time. Indeed, some of the squire's very attainments were a target for their

[1] The franklin disavows any knowledge of Cicero (ibid. p. 380), so he could not have spent many years in grammar school where Cicero was a pedagogic staple, being introduced probably around the fourth or fifth form. See A. F. Leach, *The Schools of Medieval England* (New York, 1915), pp. 300–4.

[2] Chaucer, p. 151. The catalogue of moral qualities supposed to result from this education is drawn from the virtues ascribed to the knight and the squire in the prologue, ibid. pp. 150–1. The pattern of knightly learning appears over and over fragmentarily or in full in medieval vernacular literature, for example, in *King Horn*, ed. J. R. Lumby and G. H. Knight ('Early English Text Society, original series', no. 14) (London, 1866), p. 7.

[3] Sidney Painter, *William Marshall, Knight-Errant, Baron, and Regent of England* (Baltimore, 1935); and Jean Bouchet, Le Panégyric du Chevalier sans Reproche (*Collection complète des mémoires rélatifs à l'histoire de France*, ed. C. B Petitot, 1st ser., vol. xiv) (Paris, 1822), pp. 363–4.

criticisms. In his old age the squire himself, like his sixteenth-century successors, probably retired to his estate, sloughed off his no longer useful graces, and spent his time in the hunting, hawking, and reading of old romances that so disgusted our band of Renaissance critics. Many of these critics were coolly indifferent even to those aspects of knightly training which they did not overtly sneer at. In their eyes the squire's education suffered from a fatal flaw. Partly practical, partly moral, partly aesthetic, it was quite unlearned. Bookish learning could rarely be expected among men in whom the ability to read and write was a good but supererogatory work.

Such learning, the squire's sixteenth-century congener said to his critics, was clerkly, for the men of the church and the men of the schools, not for men of the world. So would the squire have said, and so said his ancestor in William the Marshall's time. But—and here lies the core of the difference—they did not say it in answer to criticism, because in those days there was no criticism to answer. Before the Renaissance few people demanded or expected that a gentleman should be a clerk, and if aristocrats drew a sharp line between clerkly education and their own, they had the support of the clergy in so doing.[1] Yet in the sixteenth century we have a spate of words dedicated to the proposition that all gentlemen worthy of the name must be clerks, deep in learning and the intellectual virtues; and the words come, mind you, not merely or mainly from clerks but from the gentlemen themselves—from men like Sir Thomas Elyot and Sir Humphrey Gilbert, Jean de Saulx Tavannes and François de la Noue.[2] Ignorance and indifference to letters in the aristocracy was not new in the sixteenth century; what was new and radical was the suggestion that things should be otherwise.

What educational reality underlay the mass of exhortation and criticism directed at the aristocracy in the sixteenth century? Were the English gentlemen, say, of that age as innocent of and indifferent to school learning as Chaucer's squire was, and as the squire's contemporaries felt that he had a perfect right to be? Some of their doings suggest that the answer is, 'No'.

---

[1] C. R. Potter, 'Education in the Fourteenth and Fifteenth Centuries', *Cambridge Medieval History* (Cambridge, 1913–36), viii. 700; and Rudolf Limmer, *Bildungszustände und Bildungsideen des 13. Jahrhunderts* (Munich, 1928), p. 23, n. 85.

[2] Elyot, *passim*; Humphrey Gilbert, *Queene Elizabethes Academy* (Early English Text Society, extra series, no. 8) (London, 1869), p. 2 and *passim;* La Noue, pp. 129–59; Jean de Saulx Tavannes, Mémoires de Gaspard de Saulx Tavannes (*Collection complète des mémoires rélatifs à l'histoire de France*, ed. C. B. Petitot, 1st ser., vols. xxiii–xxv) (Paris, 1822), i. 152–6.

Beginning some time in the reign of Henry VIII, the scions of the titled nobility of England swarm into those citadels of clerkly training, the English universities.[1] Greys, Brandons, Manners's, Cecils, and Devereux all appear on the college registers. Between 1525 and the end of the century six peers of the Howard family alone matriculate at Oxford or Cambridge. In his years at Cambridge as tutor and master of Trinity, Archbishop Whitgift supervised the education of Herberts, Norths, Cliffords, Cavendishes, and Zouches.[2] Among the great crown servants who surround Elizabeth—the Cecils, the Bacons, Walsingham, Smith, Coke, Hatton, Sydney—there is scarcely one without a university education. Never before had the lay councillors and titled nobility of an English ruler been so learned. But these are the men at the top, the very apex of the pyramid of gentility.[3] What happens if we descend a little? Around 1550 the fiery preacher Hugh Latimer, who had once complained that the nobility was so ill-trained that churchmen had to be employed in the royal service, thunders angrily and not altogether consistently, 'There be none now but great men's sons in the colleges, and their fathers look not to have them preachers'. In the third quarter of the century William Harrison accuses the sons of the rich of filling up not only Oxford and Cambridge but the great grammar schools, too, and pushing the poor out of the scholarships.[4] Such charges suggest that we take a look at what was happening during the Renaissance in those institutions originally founded for the instruction of poor clerks.

[1] I have not intended to imply that aristocrats who did not enter the church never went to universities in the Middle Ages. The death of an elder son sometimes turned out into secular life a younger son, in school preparing for an ecclesiastical career. There always seems to have been a scattering of noblemen who went to school through some temperamental quirk or whim, but this was the result of individual idiosyncrasy, not a response to a social pattern.

[2] This list is by no means exhaustive. Information concerning most of the men mentioned can be found in the *Dictionary of National Biography*.

[3] The writer realizes that he is running counter to a fashion, current but by no means universal, of assimilating all men less than titled peers to a Hydra-headed monster known as the middle class. For an example of this procedure see R. H. Tawney, 'The Rise of the Gentry 1558–1640', *Economic History Review*, xi (1941), 1–38. However respectable its sponsors, a view that separates the gentry from the titled nobility and binds them to merchants and tradesmen finds little justification in Tudor habits of thought. See 'The Myth of the Middle Class in Tudor England', in this volume.

[4] William Harrison, *Description of England*, ed. F. J. Furnivall ('New Shakespeare Society publications', 6th ser., nos. 1, 5, and 8) (London, 1877–81), i. 77–8; and Latimer, i. 179. Latimer's statement seems to conflict with his criticism of the ignorance of the nobility (see n. 1, p. 46). Which judgment is the more correct will become evident as we progress.

A complete register of the boys enrolled was not kept at Eton until late in the seventeenth century. The biographical register of Eton College is a modern compilation put together from such bits of information as happen to have survived at Eton or are deducible from other school lists. Because of the bond between Eton and King's College, Cambridge, a disproportionate number of King's Scholars, usually headed for the church, appear in the register, while the commensals, sons of great and powerful gentlemen, are under-represented, and the oppidans, who lived in town, are scarcely to be found. Keeping all this in mind, we may profitably open the register not quite at random. We come to a page full of Clarks, and especially of William Clarks, no less than seven Williams between 1444, when the college opened, and 1567. Almost to the end the list runs as it should in a school the prime intent of which is to raise up clerics. The first six William Clarks are all King's Scholars both at Eton and later at its twin foundation, King's College Cambridge. Several become fellows of King's, one makes his career in the university, the others become vicars, rectors, or chaplains. But the last William Clark, William of 1567, turns from the well-worn path of ecclesiastical preferment; he goes from Eton to the Middle Temple and knighthood. Is this a symptom of change? What does a further glance through the C's in the register tell us?

There are about a hundred C's from 1444 to 1600 concerning whose later careers the register carries information. Almost three-fourths of these men end up in suitably clerical positions—as university fellows and schoolmasters or in benefices. If the period is divided through the middle around 1520, just about half our clerical Etonians fall on each side of the line. The case of those who do not follow clerical careers is different. Of twenty-eight such men in the register twenty-six fall into the second half of our period. The secular careers followed by the twenty-six are in the main those in which gentlemen predominated. A dozen go on to the Inns of Court, five are Members of Parliament, two are soldiers, three become knights, and one a peer. The social complexion of Eton has begun to change.

The presence of five members of the House of Commons in our group suggests another approach to the register. How many future members of the Commons went to Eton between its founding and the death of Elizabeth, and how are they distributed chronologically? A search of the register unearths about fifty of them. Only one Etonian of the half-century and more between the founding and 1500 appears on the register as a member of the Lower House; fewer than ten enter in the first full century of the school's history. But among the Etonians of the forty-odd years of Elizabeth's reign one finds no less than forty future Parliament men. Now this appearance of Parliament men among the Etonians coincides neatly with a significant change in society and politics—the rush of the gentry to get themselves elected to the House of Commons for borough seats. Who are these forty Etonians who later turn up in Parliament? Eighteen are sons of knights or of peers, six sons of knights' or peers' daughters. Twenty become knights themselves, six become peers, and a considerable number marry daughters of knights or peers. In the case of only six of the forty is no connection with folk bearing titles of honor indicated in the slight biographical sketches of the register, and, when we note a Temple, a Hampden, and a son of the Archbishop of York among the six, we need not take the exceptions over-seriously. When we further note that several of our future Parliament men were King's Scholars, Harrison's complaint about the sons of the great bumping the poor off the foundations takes on an appearance of accuracy. The impression that men of gentle birth in England were beginning to take bookish learning with unprecedented seriousness in the sixteenth century is strongly reinforced when we observe that every single one of the forty Etonian Members of Parliament went from Eton to the universities and that more than two thirds of them proceeded thence to the Inns of Court.[1]

Two rather scandalous episodes in the history of other English schools indicate that the development at Eton was not unique. Late in the fourteenth century William of Wykeham founded Eton's elder sister, Winchester, to restock with learned men a clerical body depleted by the Black Death. As an afterthought he provided that his own kin

[1] Wasey Sterry, *Eton College Register 1441–1698* (Eton, 1943), *passim*. The synthetic character of the register and the difficulties encountered in compiling it are described in the introduction. A number of extraneous situations conspire to make the register distort the image of the careers of Etonians in the period with which we are concerned. The most important is the lack of an Oxford matriculation register before the 1550s. The considerable amount of information made available about later Etonians through that register suggests the extent of the lacuna resulting from its absence in the earlier period. The effect is to increase the apparent weight of the scholarship students whose names have largely been preserved in the register of King's College, Cambridge. The same effect results from the difficulty of pinning down any name in the late fifteenth century, far greater for that era than for the Elizabethan age, thus again unduly accentuating the role of the King's Scholars for the earlier period. With all reasonable allowance for these distortions, however, I think that the strong impression conveyed by the register of the increasingly predominant role in the college played by sons of the gentry aiming at secular careers is a true one.

should be admitted as scholars on the foundation. During a century and a half Winchester fulfilled Wykeham's intention by becoming a forcing house for the higher clergy. The founder's kin availed themselves of their privilege but little at first, and then, for a hundred years, almost not at all. Then in 1569 the son and heir of Lord Saye and Sele requested and received admission. The grounds were kinship to the founder. Unwittingly Winchester had opened the floodgates. Wykeham's aunt, it seems, had thirteen extremely philoprogenitive daughters whose sequelae two centuries later knew a good thing when they saw it. For several years scions of gentle houses—Sacheverells, Barkers, Blounts—poured into Winchester, all claiming descent from Wykeham's family. Only the judgment of a commission headed by the Lord Chancellor, recommending that but ten of the founder's kin at one time be allowed on the foundation, prevented Wykeham's gentle-born descendants from taking over the school altogether.[1]

Twenty years before the Winchester affair there was a dispute in the commission to refound the Canterbury Cathedral school. Some of the commissioners argued that only the sons of gentlemen should be admitted. When Archbishop Cranmer pointed out that the children of the poor were often more gifted than gentlemen born, he was flatly told that plowmen's sons should plow, artificers' sons follow the paternal trade, while 'gentlemen's children are meet to have the knowledge of government and rule in the commonwealth'.[2]

In the Canterbury and Winchester episodes the sixteenth-century English gentlemen do not appear in an altogether flattering light. They are edging the clergy out of one school and trying to bar all but their own sons from another. The stories, however, hardly point to an aversion to learning on the part of the wellborn. Rather they seem to show the aristocracy in a stampede toward bookish education, in which the poor and weak are likely to be crushed by the great and strong.

We have already noted that the Etonians of Elizabeth's day, who later sat in Parliament, all went on from school to the universities. This appears to be a further symptom of the English aristocracy's new attitude toward education. True, entries with respect to 'literate laymen' begin to appear in the registers of the church as early as the end of the fourteenth century, and in the reigns of Henry VI and Edward IV the parvenu Pastons for a couple of generations sent most of their young

---

[1] A. F. Leach, *History of Winchester College* (New York, 1899), pp. 307–8.
[2] *Narratives of the Days of the Reformation*, ed. J. G. Nichols, 'Camden Society Publications', 1st ser., lxvii (London, 1859), 271–3.

men to the universities. Still it is my impression that, except for such as were planning careers in or through the church, English gentlemen did not ordinarily go to Oxford or Cambridge in the later Middle Ages. In this connection the case of the Stonors is significant. An Oxfordshire county family since the late thirteenth century, they lived within convenient distance of the university. They served on commissions to settle university disputes; they befriended impoverished gentlewomen on the request of the chancellor of the university; generation after generation of Stonors as sheriffs of the county collected for the king what was due him from the colleges. They were even benefactors of the university. Yet in two volumes of correspondence there is no evidence that they ever sent their children to school at Oxford.

By the third quarter of the sixteenth century the squirearchy has elbowed its way into Oxford in force. For every five men matriculating there as *filii plebei*, three describe themselves as gentlemen's sons. At the beginning of the seventeenth century the proportion is six gentlemen to five plebeians. Such a record is reasonably imposing, yet it is by no means the whole record. English university registers of the sixteenth century are not altogether reliable and are less likely to mark the presence of the wellborn than of the baseborn.[1] Moreover, no English school record will tell us of the education in letters of men like Sir Thomas Elyot, who acquired his learning from private tutors, or like Lord Mountjoy, who got his while traveling abroad.[2]

We have caught our gentlemen acquiring clerkly learning in the schools. Let us see what they are doing after school days are over. The lord-lieutenants of the shires and their deputy-lieutenants were responsible for taking the musters and exercising the county militia—the feeble

[1] M. Deanesley, *The Lollard Bible and Other Medieval Biblical Versions* (Cambridge, 1920), p. 209; *The Paston Letters* ed. J. Gairdner (Edinburgh 1910), i. 42, 82 and 434, ii. 143 and 312, and iii. 77 and 485; *Stonor Letters and Papers*, ed. C. L. Kingsford (Camden Society Publications, 3rd ser., vols. xxix–xxx) (London, 1919), i. 12, 67–8, 88, 90–2, and 115, and ii. 137–8; and C. E. Mallet, *A History of the University of Oxford* (London, 1924–7), ii. 141–2 and 142, n. 1. An undeterminable number of gentle-born did not bother to matriculate in Oxford at all, although they had lodgings in a college (e.g. Oliver Cromwell, *Writings and Speeches*, ed. W. C. Abbott [Cambridge, Mass., 1937–47], i. 27–8).

[2] Elyot, i. pp. xxxvii–xl; and *Dictionary of National Biography*, *s.v.*, 'Blount, William'. A considerable amount of education at a high level by tutors in aristocratic households went on throughout the sixteenth century as a preparation or a substitute for school and university training, in England (*English Meals*, pp. ii, viii–xi, xv, and xx–xxi, *Original Letters Illustrative of English History*, ed. H. Ellis, 1st ser., [London, 1825], i. 341–3; Roger Ascham, *The Whole Works of Roger Ascham*, ed. J. A. Giles [London 1864–5], i. pp. i and x–xvii) as well as in France (La Noue, pp. 140–2 and 147–8).

and somewhat perfunctory English alternative to the standing armies of the continental powers. They were also in part in charge of that *bonne police* of their neighborhood with which contemporary French writers were so much concerned. The line between their part and that of the justices of the peace in the maintenance of order in the country was not sharply defined, but it did not greatly matter since they themselves were all on the commission of the peace. Deputy-lieutenants were also likely to crop up in the House of Commons as representatives of neighboring boroughs or of their county and to do a turn or two as sheriff. Of the men who served in the lieutenancy commission between 1607 and 1619 in Northamptonshire most had come of age in the reign of Elizabeth. There were nineteen of them in all, including the lord-lieutenant himself. What kind of education had they received, or, to put it more pertinently, to what extent had their Elizabethan fathers been satisfied to allow them to grow up as great hunters and hawkers untouched by formal education? Two of the nineteen left no discoverable trace on the educational record of the age, and concerning two others the evidence is ambiguous. Of the remaining fifteen at least eleven matriculated at Oxford or Cambridge, and of the eleven, seven were admitted to the Inns of Court. Four others, who do not appear on the university registers, also went to the great English schools of law, and one of the four traveled on the Continent under the supervision of a tutor, making occasional though educationally unprofitable stops in university centers. In other words, of our group of nineteen men almost four-fifths were exposed to some kind of higher learning, almost three-fifths spent time at the former centers of clerical training, the universities, and well over a third topped their university experience with a dab, and sometimes much more than a dab, of education in the laws of England. And these figures, note, are an absolute minimum, representing only those men who left indubitable traces on the various school registers. Given the fairly casual way in which the registers were sometimes kept and our uncertainty about two names actually on them, we must recognize that there well may have been more schooling scattered among our deputy-lieutenants than the numbers we have given indicate. Yet the very minimum involves a goodly number of gentlemen of a single county in a kind of education that Chaucer's squire knew not. Moreover, among these gentlemen were very few younger sons, put to school because—perennial Saturday's children of the English system of primogeniture—they would have to work or beg for a living. In their school days most of our deputy-lieutenants had been heirs-apparent to substantial fortunes, under no immediate economic pressure to seek place by the route of learning.[1] And there is no reason to believe that the situation with respect to the schooling of the deputy-lieutenants in the other counties was markedly different from what it was in Northamptonshire. Even in remote and backward Cornwall, at least four of the eight gentlemen in the commission during Sir Walter Raleigh's lieutenancy were university educated.[2] Nor does it seem likely that there would be an abrupt change if we descended slightly in the social scale and gave our attention to the education of the justices of the peace. Whatever the validity of the indictment at the beginning of the sixteenth century, it was certainly not true at its end that English gentlemen as a group were indifferent to formal schooling. By that time men who received what once was called clerkly training no longer remained concentrated in the schools, nor did they make a beeline for the church or the offices of the central administration of the realm. Bookish learning had gone with them out into the shires and was widely scattered among the men who ruled the countryside.[3]

In the last quarter of the fifteenth century Philippe de Commines, a shrewd and observant Fleming, looked at the French aristocracy and its education and found neither good. 'They are raised', he said of the nobles, 'only to be fools in dress and words; they know nothing of reading French and they do not have a single wise man around them.' Even the poor ones were both too ignorant and too stupid to take care of their own affairs, so they were robbed by their servants and only woke up to the consequences of their loutishness when it was too late.[4] Such was the opinion of a shrewd observer of the French noblesse in the

---

[1] For the names and the education of the Northamptonshire deputy-lieutenants, 1607–19, see the Rev. H. Isham Longdon in *The Montagu Musters Book*, ed. J. Wake, Northamptonshire Records Society Publications, vii (Peterborough, 1935), 245–8. A survey of other available sources of information has enabled me, however, to place two more and possibly four more deputies in school.

[2] Richard Carew, *Survey of Cornwall* (London, 1602), fol. 83v.

[3] While this essay was first in the press, its central thesis was confirmed by J. E. Neale, *The Elizabethan House of Commons* (New Haven, 1950), pp. 302–8. In his excellent study, *Oxford and Cambridge in Transition 1558–1642* (Oxford, 1959), Mark Curtis has recently demonstrated how the flood of laymen into what were, up to the sixteenth century, seminaries for clerics, drastically modified the effective organization and the method and substance of instruction in the two English universities. The role of the Inns of Court in spreading their kind of learning both in the sixteenth century and earlier should not be underestimated (John Fortescue, *De laudibus legum Angliae*, ed. and trans. S. B. Chrimes [Cambridge, 1942], pp. 114–21). That the gentle-born came to the Inns in considerable number even before the sixteenth century seems beyond doubt.

[4] Philippe de Commines, *Mémoires*, ed. J. Calmette (Paris, 1924–5), i. 69–70.

1480s. There are signs of a change as the fifteenth century draws to a close. The Cairons of Bretteville, who for one hundred and fifty years had been satisfied with adding bit by bit to their holdings on a slow climb from burgherdom to gentility, began to send their children to the university at Caen.[1] Antoine de Montchrétien was educated in the same school in the suite of two lords.[2] Noël du Fail, a man proud of his noble lineage, went to Paris for the arts, elsewhere for law training, and returned to his province to a judgeship and a literary career.[3] While at Toulouse, Henri de Mesmes met in the university not only the *gens de robe* but also scions of the great families of Joyeuse and Foix.[4] Training in the classics acquired somewhere, somehow, left its marks where we would least expect them—on gentlemen soldiers such as François de la Noue and that old war horse Blaise de Monluc.[5] The Du Bellays, faithful and active servants of Francis I in war and council, were owners of a considerable library.[6] Another soldier, the Comte de Brissac, had his eldest son educated according to a scheme that out-romanized the humanists since the young count was allowed to speak and hear no language but Latin until he was seven years old.[7]

Indeed, it is worth noting that most of the standard citations in criticism of the education of French gentlemen in the sixteenth century are drawn from the writings of sixteenth-century French gentlemen who had received good clerkly educations—Noël du Fail, Jean de Saulx Tavannes, François de la Noue, Michel de Montaigne. La Noue, moreover, admits that three or four hundred sons of 'good houses' travelled abroad each year to learn languages. He adds that, 'believing not without reason that the sciences are a great ornament to nobles and make them worthy to administer all public charges', some French lords sent their sons to universities.[8] When Montaigne speaks of the 'hatred of books' of 'almost our whole nobility', he is not being just another censor of aristocratic dunderheadedness; for this contempt of learning,

---

[1] Abbé Aubert, 'Notes extraites de trois livres de raison de 1473–1550', *Bulletin historique et philologique du Comité des Travaux historiques et scientifiques*, 1898, pp. 445–99; and Marc Bloch, *Caractères originaux de l'histoire rurale française*, Instituttet for Sammenlignend Kulturforskning Skriften, ser. B, no. 19 (Oslo, 1931), 143.

[2] Henri Baudrillart, *Gentilshommes ruraux de la France* (Paris, n.d.), 149.

[3] Emmanuel Philipot, *La vie et l'œuvre littéraire de Noël du Fail* (Paris, 1914), pp. 32–70. [4] Mesmes, p. 144.

[5] La Noue, pp. 129–59; and Blaise de Monluc, *Commentaires*, ed. A. de Rublé (Paris, 1864–7), *passim*.

[6] Martin and Guillaume du Bellay, *Mémoires*, ed. V.-L. Bourilly and F. Vindrey (Paris, 1908–19), i. 3–6.

[7] Montaigne, i. 334. [8] La Noue, pp. 142–6.

he tells us, is bred not of ignorance but of familiarity under depressing circumstances. It results not from lack of education but from too much bad education. His attack was on the unsuitable philological pedantry which the humanists themselves had set up as a pattern of education for the aristocracy. According to Montaigne, the sixteenth-century French nobleman acquired his contempt for learning not outside school but in it.[1]

In the passage previously quoted from Commines a contrast is clearly implied between the French nobles proud of their ignorance, poor in their worldly and intellectual endowments, and another nobility that was not as they. Where had Commines come into contact with such a nobility? His impression of the French lords was formed

[1] Montaigne, i. 312–15 and 337–8. Since the historical destiny of the English gentry and the French *noblesse* was perhaps in some way linked with the extent to which each appropriated the available means of learning, a few general observations may be apropos. While late in the sixteenth and early in the seventeenth centuries the concern of Frenchmen with the inadequate training of nobles does not abate (Montaigne, i. 251–341 and Saulx Tavannes, i. 155–76), at least one Englishman admits that the gentry is showing an ample zeal for the acquisition of learning. Speaking of English women, he says, 'This nevertheless I utterly mislike in the poorer sort of them, *for the wealthier do seldom offend herein*, that being themselves without competent wit, they are careless in the education of their children' (Harrison, iii. 155–6, italics mine). Note also his observation on the high level of training at court (ibid. i. 271–4). A comparison of the data cited in this essay on the English situation with those cited on the French may enhance the impression that activity was greater among the former. In part the disparity in the volume of evidence is due to my concentration of the larger part of this study on the English materials and to the greater abundance of printed material from England available. Yet, granted these reservations I feel that the general impression left by the data in the essay of a greater zeal for education among the English than among the French aristocrats corresponds to the actual situation. In this connection the remarks of Saulx Tavannes are especially significant. After saying that the children of French nobles should be put into the universities and kept there until they are twenty-three, he adds: 'The ignoble did not take the judicial offices (*estats*) from us; ignorance deprived us of them. The door is open to all who make their children study, who then cannot be barred from office. . . . Stupid is the opinion of oafs that presidents and councillors are not gentlemen' (i. 155–6). La Noue has a more charitable and very interesting explanation of this situation. He says that the nobles withdraw their sons from the universities just at the point when they would begin to profit, because, of the two learned careers, church preferment goes by favor rather than by learning, and judicial office goes to the highest bidder. Besides, 'the most splendid honors are won by the sword', and fathers are anxious to start their sons early in this most lucrative career (pp. 145–6). That the nobility of the sword was in fact failing to make a place for itself in the great law courts and the legal profession generally is indicated by the small number of nobles with places in the great sovereign courts (Louis Wolff, *La vie des parlementaires provençaux aux XVI⁰ siècle* [Marseilles, 1924], pp. 6–7). In this matter the contrast between France and England seems to be beyond dispute, and it may be one of the keys to the later history of the noble order in the two countries.

before he knew Italy at all. At that time he knew only one nobility, the one among which he, Philip van den Clite, was born and raised, the Netherlands-Burgundian lords who had grown to manhood in the reign of Philip the Good. Could it be those lords whom he is contrasting with the French nobles?

Embedded in our ordinary conceptions or preconceptions about the forms of initiative, new life, new vigor, in the fifteenth century lies the historical trinity of 'humanism', 'Renaissance', 'Italy', almost sacred and untouchable. Historians with a taste for antithesis sometimes set up Italy and the Burgundian lands as polar phenomena, the new and the old, the future and the past, the on-driving and the quaintly archaic; Italy the land of the classical revival, of free and easy manners and morals, of religious indifference veering toward skepticism; Burgundy the land of medievalism on its last legs, of formalism and rigid etiquette, of orthodoxy. The big thing in Italy was the rediscovery of classical antiquity; in Burgundy under Philip the Good the big thing was the revival of chivalry, that bête noire of so many humanists. While Italians were going into a philological frenzy over each newly discovered manuscript of classical Greece and Rome, countless medieval romances in insipid verse were being turned into even duller prose by Burgundians. The height of society in Italy was the informal court circle of intellectuals and dilettantes gathered around the Gonzagas, the Montefeltros, the Medicis. In Burgundy the height of society was the pompous chivalric order of the Golden Fleece, the creation of the chivalry-bewitched prince, Philip the Good himself. So on first thought it does not seem very profitable to look for an early drive toward learning among the knightly followers of the Grand Duke of the Occident, whom we have been taught to think of as the resplendent but overripe fruit of the autumn of the Middle Ages.

Yet the Fleming Commines himself complained of never having learned Latin in his youth although other young men of his rank and age 'went to study the tongue of Cicero and Vergil at the schools of Louvain, Cologne, and Paris'.[1] A glance at the Louvain matriculation register during its first thirty years in a measure confirms what Commines suggests. It contains a reasonable sprinkling of men designated as *nobilis*, nothing like Oxford had to show a century and a half later, but still a significant number. Some of the names registered as noble are Glymes, Lalaing, and Brederode, representatives of the proudest

---

[1] Kervyn de Lettenhove (ed.), *Lettres et négotiations de Philippe de Commines* (Brussels, 1867–74), i. 49.

families of the most vainglorious nobility in Europe. Also on the register is Edmond de Dynter, a Brabant knight, author of a Latin chronicle of his native land, himself one of the chief instigators of the establishment of the university, and, as his matriculation records, 'secretary to our illustrious master the duke'. There were other names as eminent as any we have mentioned— Croys, Lannoys, Borsellens— but they do not bear the designation *nobilis*. Nevertheless, they may have been scions of the great families, since also among those with no *nobilis* following his name we find one Gregorius Casteleyn, who became Georgius Casteleyn when he received his Bachelor's degree in 1432. This Gregorius or Georgius Casteleyn was no bourgeois's son aspiring to preferment in the church or to a place in the ducal bureaucracy. He was Georges Chastellain, faithful servant and historiographer to the House of Burgundy and, despite what the register fails to say, a man of immaculate if minor noble lineage. Among Chastellain's contemporaries at Louvain was no less august a personage than Cornelius, the Great Bastard of Burgundy, eldest son of Philip the Good, whose name does not appear in the register at all. How many other names in the Louvain register list belong to men with a lineage at least as distinguished as Chastellain's we do not know. Nor do we know how many nobles followed Cornelius's lead and went to school there without matriculating, nor how many went to Cologne or Paris.[1]

We do know, however, that Philip the Good established another university at Dôle in Franche-Comté. Dôle, too, attracted a share of the Burgundian aristocrats, Vergys, Grammonts, La Tours, Colignys. Chastellain's friend and disciple, Oliver de la Marche, a minor Comtois noble, who carried on the Burgundian historiographic tradition, was a student at Dôle. While there he received a gift of twenty francs from Philip the Good's sister Catherine to pay for his fees and clothes. The interest of the ruling house in encouraging the lay nobility to acquire learning did not stop at the emission of occasional *douceurs*. The *studium generale* at Dôle came into being on the initiative not of a town, a cathedral chapter, or a community of scholars, but on the initiative of

---

[1] *Matricule de l'Université de Louvain*, vol. i, *1426 (origine)–30 août 1453*, ed. E. Reussens ('Commission royale d'histoire') (Brussels, 1903), *passim* (for Chastellain's matriculation and degree see p. 45, entry 4). Cf. Georges Chastellain, *Œuvres*, ed. Kervyn de Lettenhove (Brussels, 1863–6), ii. 76. Matriculation registers for Cologne for the period with which we are concerned are available: *Der Matrikel der Universität Köln*, ed. H. Keussen, Publikationen der Gesellschaft für rheinische Geschichtskunde, vols. vii and viii (Bonn, 1892–1919); but the register does not help much in identifying noble students.

Philip himself. He helped it with a public subsidy; and he provided it with a set of statutes offering the nobles, as such, greater privileges and a more elevated position than did any other university in Europe. He seems to have been doing his best to give his nobility a strong incentive to go to school at Dôle.[1]

That we should find the earliest impetus toward education—clerkly, bookish education—for the aristocracy among the nobles of Burgundy, that Philip the Good should gently shove the sons of his great lords into the universities, may come to us as a surprise. Historians have tended to see only archaism in the Burgundian revival. Yet the court of Burgundy in Philip's time was after all the most hospitable place in Europe, hospitable to men, hospitable to ideas and arts and ways, to anything new or old that showed signs of vigor and life. It found a place for Jan van Eyck's painting, for courtly pageantry, for Ghillebert de Lannoy's schemes of political reform, for the romances which celebrated chivalry, the satires which laughed at it, and the *Cent nouvelles nouvelles*, which disregarded it altogether. In that court it was not considered a mark of distinction for the nobility to be ignorant of letters, to scoff at letters, or to regard them as the peculiar and dull domain of clerks. The tradition of the Valois Maecenate, fallen on evil days in the land of its birth, reached its apogee in the Netherlands under the good duke. Philip even had an informal literary council that examined books before recommending them for illumination and incorporation into the duke's library. Among his literary advisers were Jean de Créqui and Jean, comte d'Étampes, two of his best generals; Philippe Pot, the richest lord in the duchy of Burgundy; Anthony, another of Philip's bastard sons; Anthony's son Philip, and scions of the illustrious houses of Cleves, Luxembourg, Brimeu, Croy, and Lannoy. There was scarcely a churchman among them. To judge by the content of the duke's library the taste of these men was remarkably catholic. There were numerous books of piety; there were chronicles, romances, and medieval custumals; but there were also the *Digest* and works of Christian and pagan antiquity—among the latter, writings by Aristotle, Josephus, Vegetius, Livy, Sallust, Ovid, Juvenal, Cicero and Seneca.[2]

Among the lordly amateurs of learning at Philip's court was Jean de Lannoy, member of an ancient family of Walloon Flanders. It was

[1] H. Beaune and J. d'Arbaumont, *Les Universités de Franche-Comté* (Dijon, 1870), esp. introd., pp. xxxvi–xxxviii and lxxxiv–xciv.

[2] Georges Doutrepont, *La Littérature française à la cour des ducs de Bourgogne*, Bibliothèque du XVe siècle, viii (Paris, 1909), 498; and J. Barroit, *Bibliothèque protoypographique* (Paris, 1830), nos. 705–1612.

a family that attained great distinction and high honor in the service of the House of Burgundy, providing it with captains, *baillis, gouverneurs,* councilors, ambassadors, generals, and viceroys. In three generations the Lannoys gave eight members to the Order of the Golden Fleece. They were *grands seigneurs;* it was their French counterparts whose smug loutishness evoked the contempt of Commines. Jean de Lannoy, as we shall see, was neither smug nor a lout. Born in 1410, he was nephew to Antoine and Jean de Croy, for four decades principal advisers of Philip the Good. For many years Jean fought in the ducal armies and for fourteen years he was *gouverneur* or stadholder of Holland, the office borne by William of Orange a century later. He led a contingent of six thousand Dutch volunteers to aid the duke against the rebels of Ghent. He served on special missions to France and England. In 1451 he became the fourth of his family to enter the Order of the Golden Fleece. At the age of fifty-two he was transferred from the governorship of Holland to that of Walloon Flanders, his ancestral home. Two years later his wife gave birth to a son, his prospective heir, who furnished the occasion for a remarkable undertaking on the part of his father.

Shortly after Louis de Lannoy was born, a night passed when Jean slept little because of the thought that he could 'never hope to see' his boy 'at the age when he will have much understanding'. 'I realize that my son and I can never be of the same time, for he comes and I go. . . . Therefore I decided to write this letter to my son so that if I do not live to the day when he can understand me, at least he will know by letter what my lips could not say to him, as often it is with lovers, who when they are together for love they cannot speak.' The letter Jean wrote in his own hand is dated at its end May 3, 1465. Its purpose is to advise Louis on his education. Jean disclaims any design to write for the general enlightenment. Such work he leaves to 'wise men, clerics, historians, and rhetoricians'. He is moved only by the 'natural love I bear my son'. After instruction in the house of some honorable man up to the age of twelve, he tells Louis, 'you can go to the Latin schools at Louvain, Cologne, or Paris with a priest who speaks German, that you may know how to talk that language'. Besides applying himself diligently to acquiring Latin, young Lannoy must take part in the school disputations. When his formal schooling is over, he will get much good from the books his father will leave and from those that he will find means to acquire himself. He should give attention to the Bible, to the books on ethics and economics, and especially to those on politics.

In many respects, Jean de Lannoy's tract is the most significant of all the documents bearing on the education of the aristocracy during the Renaissance. It is early. It is eminently practical in tone. It is the work of one who was himself a great noble. But most important of all, Jean de Lannoy tells us in the most forthright and personal fashion exactly why he wants his son, sole heir to a great seigneurial fortune, to receive a kind of education hitherto deemed peculiarly appropriate to preachers and teachers:[1]

> Those who have learned and retained much, and who have the greatest desire to learn and know, attain great good, honor, and riches. . . . This has often caused me deep displeasure not for envy of them, but, because of my simplicity and slight knowledge and because I was never put to school. I therefore know and can know nothing. I realize that this chance is for me lost and gone, never to be recovered, for I do not see or expect any remedy as to Latin or other studies. No day passes that I do not regret this, and especially when I find myself in the council of the king or of the Duke of Burgundy, and I know not nor dare not to speak my opinion after the learned, eloquent legists and *ystoryens* who have spoken before me. For I do not know the order or manner of speaking and can say nothing, but 'Master John or Master Peter has spoken well, and I am of his opinion'. Whence I have often felt deep shame and humiliation in my heart.

Sixty years earlier in date, his theme is identical with Elyot's in *The Boke Named the Gouernour*. The aristocracy must become learned that they may perform well their duty of service to their prince in council, in embassies, and in the governance of the commonwealth. Here we reach the heart of the matter.

We have looked at the schools, the sanctuaries of clerkly learning, and we have tried to determine the composition of the student body. We have observed in the period of the Renaissance a marked influx into these schools of sons of noble houses, coming to acquire a kind of education hitherto deemed suitable to clerics. These aristocrats are at school not in order to pursue an ecclesiastical career but for some other reason. Our ways of taking count are not entirely precise; they are rather impressionistic, but the impression itself is strong. While the movement of the gentle-born into the schools seems greatest in England

---

[1] Baudouin de Lannoy, *Jean de Lannoy le Bâtisseur, 1410–1492* (Paris, 1937), pp. 13–112; and 'Coppie des lettres envoyées par Jehan Seigneur de Lannoy à Loys son filz', ibid. pp. 119–210, esp. pp. 119–21, 138–40, and 147–8.

during the Renaissance, still, in other lands too it has a force well beyond what it had in the age immediately preceding. And we have seen reason to believe that our work as school inspectors has given us but a fragmentary notion of the full strength of the quest for learning by the nobility. The high standard of home education that we glimpse in a few aristocratic houses suggests a general leveling-up of that type of training, full evidence concerning which is irretrievably lost.

And now at the very place where the movement started, at the very time it was getting under way, a *grand seigneur*, Jean de Lannoy, by telling his son why he should acquire learning, has given us the reason for the drive of the aristocracy toward education. It is the same in the end, on the threshold of the seventeenth century, as it was in the beginning in the midst of the fifteenth; it is the same in the other realms as in the Low Countries: the noble and gentle must become learned in order to play their part in the government of the commonwealth—as soldiers, ambassadors, councilors, governors, judges, administrators, in whatever office they are called to. Indeed, we may say that even before new methods of education were proposed, education itself was held forth as the means whereby men nobly born should win a place in the service of the princely commonwealth. Ghillebert de Lannoy was Jean de Lannoy's cousin, his granduncle's son; but he was of an older generation than Jean, of the generation that grew up with Philip the Good rather than during his reign. He, too, wrote an essay of advice to his son on education, and the difference in generations is clearly reflected in the books of Ghillebert and Jean. Both spend what may seem to us an inordinate quantity of ink on mere moral exhortation, but in Jean the exhortation is interspersed with, and even incidental to, a fairly specific educational program. Ghillebert, on the other hand, is almost purely hortatory; yet his purpose is quite practical and is the same as Jean's. If his son follows his advice, the prince having heard of his virtues 'and perceived them in action will commit to you so exalted an office whence so much good and profit will accrue to you that you will become rich and powerful without doing anyone wrong'. Such service is honorable. Read 'Valerius Maximus, Tully, Lucan, Orosius, Sallust, Justin, and other historians', Ghillebert tells his son, 'and you will wonder at the many virtuous examples of how our predecessors loved honor and the public weal and faced death for the good of the land'.[1]

We have heard much of the aspiration of the Renaissance Italian to be an *uomo universale*, to devote himself to the development within

[1] Ghillebert de Lannoy, *Œuvres*, ed. C. Potvin (Louvain, 1878), pp. 443–72.

himself of a rounded personality, a complete individuality. In the north, among the aristocracy, there is little of this. When a gentleman considers the education of gentlemen, it is with one end in view. We have already heard the Burgundians directing their children into the government of the commonwealth; Sir Thomas Elyot sets the pattern in England. He heads one of his chapters of *The Boke Named the Gouernour*, 'The education or form of bringing up of the child of a gentleman, which is to have authority in a public weal'. Thomas Starkey and Roger Ascham echo the same idea. Sir Humphrey Gilbert has a scheme whereby gentlemen's sons will be crammed like Strasbourg geese with knowledge and skills, the better to serve 'in Parliament, in council, in commission and other offices of the Commonwealth'. And just in case his nephew may be under the illusion that his impending tour of the Continent is solely for his own edification or amusement Francis Walsingham reminds him no less than six times in a scant two-page letter of his obligation to make the trip fruitful for the public service and the commonwealth. In France, La Noue emphasized the importance of providing adequate training for an aristocracy destined to serve as 'great generals, commanders, governors and high officials, ambassadors and captains', and Montaigne's indictment of the French grammar-school pattern of education in his treatise for Diane de Foix on the rearing of her son is grounded on the thesis that the schools are useless for nobles whose life will be spent in high office—military, diplomatic, and civil.[1]

If during the period there is any development of ideas on the proper training for aristocrats—and our habit of thinking in terms of evolutionary growth often leads us to read development into texts where it is not—it is a development in precision and clarity. The end—education for service in the princely commonwealth—remains unchanged; the means and methods needed to attain this end become better understood. The first impulse, as we find it expressed in Jean de Lannoy and Commines, is to say, 'Get ye to school!' and to refrain from overmuch curiosity about the suitability to the end they had in view of the education the schools were offering. When the tide of humanism begins to move north, any questioning of the educational program of the apostles of antiquity and light is drowned in a deluge of expletives and ink,

[1] Elyot, i. 28; Thomas Starkey, *A Dialogue between Reginald Pole and Thomas Lupset*, ed. K. M. Burton (London, 1948), pp. 21–39; Ascham, iii. 138; Gilbert, pp. 2–12; Conyers Read, *Mr. Secretary Walsingham and the Policy of Queen Elizabeth* (Cambridge, Mass., 1925), i. 18–20; La Noue, pp. 148–9; and Montaigne, i. 275–341.

accompanied by shrill cries of 'Barbarian!' 'Ignoramus!' 'Hunter and hawker!' Only later in the sixteenth century did men who doubted whether either scholastic logic or classical philology were the best possible foundations for the new role of the nobility formulate their ideas precisely enough to deserve a full hearing. Then, however, in all three lands, men of gentle birth—Humphrey Gilbert in England, Montaigne and La Noue in France, Philippe de Marnix in the Netherlands—proposed schemes of education specifically framed to meet the needs of an aristocrat whose career was to be public service.[1]

The assertion in the sixteenth century that the aristocrat has a special claim on office is, of course, nothing new. On the contrary, what is new is an overt recognition on the part of some nobles that the claim is not indefeasible and absolute. The day is past when there was almost a one-to-one coincidence between the number of a lord's 'tall men' or the extent of his acres and the role he could arrogate to himself in that management of common concerns which is government. Instead of simply assuming that political authority belongs of right to them, the aristocrats profess that, other things being equal, preference in office should be theirs; and the very claim to preference is made on the grounds of its utility to the commonweal. It is no longer always presupposed as it formerly had been, that a prince who chose parvenus to serve him did so out of mere whim or to spite those born to rule. Not only bitter preachers like Latimer but the more perceptive members of the upper class recognized that a prince who would be well served had no alternative but to take help where he could find it. The recognition by a gentleman of the paramount claim of prince and commonwealth to good service is almost always coupled with an exhortation or a plan addressed to the members of the aristocracy to educate themselves to the point where they can render such service.[2] Jean de Lannoy, after

---

[1] Gilbert, pp. 1–12; La Noue, pp. 148–54; Montaigne, i. 275–341; Philippe de Marnix, 'Ratio instituendae juventutis', Œuvres, ed. E. Quinet and A. la Crois (Brussels, 1857–60), viii. 17–107.

[2] Two main reasons are alleged for preferring the noble- over the baseborn: (1) that the subjects will render a better and more willing obedience to men born to authority than to nobodies and (2) that when men bound only by a cash nexus and careerism are given offices instead of those bound by duty and honor, other things being equal, the lack of a bond of obligation increases the ultimate cost to the commonwealth of their service (Claude Seyssel, Grand monarchie de France [Paris, 1558], fol. 37a–b [1st ed., 1519]; Jerónimo Castillo de Bobadilla, Política para corregidores [Madrid, 1597], i. 72–88; Gilbert, pp. 10–12; Montaigne, i. 296; and Great Britain, Historical Manuscripts Commission, Calendar of the Manuscripts of the Most Hon. the Marquis of Salisbury . . . preserved at Hatfield House [London, 1883–99] [hereafter cited as 'Hatfield MSS'], i. 163). These arguments,

paying respects to the ability of the legists and *ystoryens*, urges his son to be as learned as they. Ascham inserts his criticism of the incompetence of aristocrats to fill the great offices of the land into an elaborate pedagogic manual designed to overcome that incompetence. And William Cecil plans obliquely to undermine the place of the baseborn in the service of the realm by forcing education on the nobility by Act of Parliament.[1]

One of the most impressive and universal traits in the complex of writings about the education of the aristocracy for service to the commonwealth is the subordination of questions of right and privilege to questions of responsibility. Something is made of the rights of the aristocrats to office, more of their responsibility through education to prepare themselves for office, and most of their responsibility to turn the education they get to the service of the public weal. In Starkey's dialogue Lupset brusquely overrides Pole's suggestion that the contemplative life may be a legitimate end of a nobleman's education. A man of Pole's position, he answers, is duty bound 'to handle matters of the commonweal here in his own nation'. Men such as he are born 'to common such gifts as to them be given . . . and not to live to their own pleasure and profit'. Osorius in his book of *Civil nobility* speaks slightingly of those who take their learning with them into seclusion and do not 'employ the benefits of their arts and sciences to the avail and commodity of the commonwealth'. Even Montaigne, himself so little given to conventional judgments, feels bound to make a rather elaborate apologia for his conduct and career in view of 'the complaints daily buzzed in mine ears . . . that touching public office I am over singular and disdainful'.[2]

From the assertion of the duty of gentlemen to acquire an education and turn it to the service of the princely commonwealth, it was not far to the assertion that the head of the commonwealth was obligated to provide the necessary education for his noble servants. Erasmus gave early expression to such an idea, but without limiting it to the nobles.

not always free from suspicion of personal interest, seem yet to have contained a germ of truth. Cf. *Letters and Papers of Henry VIII*, ed. J. S. Brewer, J. Gairdner, and J. H. Brodie (London, 1862–1910), xi. 319–20; and Jehan Masselin, *Journal des États Généraux de France . . . en 1484*, ed. A. Bernier, Collection des documents inédits sur l'histoire de France (Paris, 1835), pp. 354–61.

[1] Baudoin de Lannoy, pp. 119–210; Ascham, iii. 123 and *passim;* and *Hatfield MSS*, i. 163.

[2] Starkey, pp. 21–6; Osorius, cited by Ruth Kelso, *The Doctrine of the English Gentleman in the Sixteenth Century*, University of Illinois Studies in Language and Literature, xiv, nos. 1 and 2 (Urbana, Ill., 1929), 125; and Montaigne, i. 338–9.

In his tract, *De pueris instituendis,* he declares that the provision of an adequate supply of teachers 'is a public obligation in no way inferior to the ordering of an army'. The idea that there exists a public duty to provide learned training specifically for the aristocracy comes later in the century. In preparation for Elizabeth's first parliament Cecil drew up the scheme before mentioned, which, besides binding the nobility by law to bring up their children in learning at some university from the age of twelve to eighteen, would have set aside one-third of all university scholarships for gentlemen. Toward the end of the century La Noue in France and Sir Humphrey Gilbert in England came up with far more elaborate and carefully wrought plans. Gilbert suggested one academy in England, La Noue several in France, in which the curriculum, fully set out in their respective schemes, was entirely focused on training noble youth for public service. The full cost of maintaining these schools was to be a public charge on the royal revenues.[1] As we run across one after another of these plans in which the education of the aristocracy was to be subsidized out of the common purse as a matter of public responsibility, the startling demand of the gentlemen of the Canterbury school commission that all but men of good birth be excluded from the benefits of the foundation comes into a more intelligible perspective. In a rough and highhanded way they were reflecting the demand of the aristocrats for a sufficient share of the available education to prepare them for public careers in a commonwealth that required to be served not only faithfully but intelligently.

At the outset of this essay we entered into a small empirical study of the extent to which the nobility acquired education during the Renaissance. As we proceeded with our search, we came perhaps to recognize that this question had implications with respect to the entire social history of the age, that it cast a shadow of doubt on some of our most cherished prepossessions about the direction and character of social change during the Renaissance. Two clichés concerning this era are deeply embedded in our historical tradition. One of those clichés concerns the rising middle class climbing to power over the prostrate body of the degenerate aristocracy. The other tells us how royal absolutism transformed some feudal lords into feeble court butterflies and left the rest to grumble and rot in the country, secluded from any role in government. These two clichés are by no means irreconcilable with one another; on the contrary, they are usually served up well-blended in the same dish.

[1] La Noue, pp. 148–54; and Gilbert, *passim.*

Yet how prostrate is a social group that, facing the challenge of new times, rises to meet it by engaging in an altogether new kind of activity —that of acquiring a kind of learning hitherto almost monopolized by clerics? The aristocrats who went chasing education with the ardor we have noted, can they be the same men as the aristocrats who, we are told, lolled about in a somnolent stupor while brisk businessmen were snatching the seat of power out from under them? On the contrary is not their quest for learning a mark of the flexibility of Renaissance aristocrats, who, having lost the influence over the course of affairs that their bands of stout fellows had afforded them, were seeking, in a measure successfully, to exercise power in a changed world through new channels?

A description of the relationship between the aristocracy and the new monarchs that seeks to do justice to the actual complexity of the situation is a delicate and difficult business, but even this little study should have sufficed to show how inadequate to cope with it are banalities about Renaissance despots and a monstrous nobility, half court insect, half bucolic vegetable. Doubtless the nobility had its full share of such insecta and flora, as what grouping of the sons of men does not; but the kind of education that Renaissance aristocrats were seeking and to some extent getting did not have as its object the multiplication of rural *fainéants* or courtly sycophants. There is a difference between serving honorably in a princely commonwealth and decorating a court —all the difference, let us say, between Louis XII and Louis XIV or Philip the Good of Burgundy and Philip III of Spain.

The sixteenth-century aristocrat, when he assumes governmental tasks, is not rendering the service that a man owed his personal lord in the days of high feudalism. Nor is he performing that unlimited earthly worship which subjects were presumed to owe to God's vice-regents by some writers of the seventeenth century. He is serving a commonwealth prince, who in the words of one of the ablest of those princes stands highest 'in his estate royal' when he is 'conjoined and knit together' with his people 'in one body politic'.[1]

The conception of service to the commonwealth cannot be written off as mere verbiage in all the outpourings on the education of the aristocracy that we have examined. If that conception gave a certain moral legitimacy to obedient service rendered by the aristocracy to the prince, it also established psychological limitations on such service and

[1] Henry VIII's statement cited in Raphael Holinshed, *Chronicles* (London, 1587), iii. 955–6.

set some bounds on the duty of obedience. Montaigne makes quite explicit a fundamental distinction implied in the thought of his time. The tutor of the nobleman 'shall frame his charge's will to be a most loyal servitor of his prince, very well affected and courageous, but he will dampen in him any desire to attach himself to the court except out of a sense of public obligation'. The educated nobleman will thus retain that liberty impossible in 'a man waged and bought . . . a courtier who can have neither the right nor the will to speak or think otherwise than favorably of a master who has chosen to foster and raise him up from among so many other subjects. Such favor and usage dazzle a man's eyes and corrupt his freedom'.[1] It is not without significance that Francis Walsingham, the great councilor of Queen Elizabeth, in his letter of advice on education through travel speaks of public service, speaks of serving the country, speaks no less than three times of duty to the commonwealth, but does not even once mention the obligation to serve the prince.[2] Education to serve the commonwealth is not training in servility to its ruler; quite the contrary.

It is the express distinction of Montaigne and the patent habit of thought of Walsingham that become action on the part of many of the aristocrats in the revolt of the Netherlands, in the civil wars in France, and in the Puritan Revolution in England. They owe obedience to the prince as head of the commonwealth, but when the prince divorces himself from the commonwealth the whole question of obedience must be examined anew. Here we enter paths which we cannot at this time follow. What we have already said may be enough to show that a revaluation of our whole conception of social ideas, social structure, and social function in Europe in the age of the Renaissance is long overdue. It may also suggest that we start our revision by thinking in terms not of the decline of the aristocracy but of its reconstruction.

[1] Montaigne, i. 296.   [2] Read, i. 18–20.

5

The Myth of the Middle Class in Tudor England *

I

THE TUDORS 'courted the middle classes'; they were especially favorable 'to commerce and the middle classes on which the new monarchy rested'.[1] 'The growth of the middle class' was favored by 'the rise of the Tudors . . . a bourgeois dynasty'.[2] This is the myth of the middle class in Tudor England. Although the general myth of the ever-rising middle class is considerably older, that particular part of it dealing with the Tudor period became orthodox dogma only fifty-odd years ago, when Professor A. F. Pollard pronounced its authenticity in *Factors in Modern History*. His essay on 'The Advent of the Middle Class' attributed to this ostensibly omnipotent group every significant phenomenon in European, and especially in English, history for three centuries—the Renaissance, the Reformation, the colonial expansion of Europe, the New Monarchy, nationalism, the rise of the House of Commons, the Puritan Revolution.[3] His conclusions have won almost universal acceptance; the roster of those following Pollard's lead includes nearly every distinguished historian who has discussed Tudor history in the past forty years.

* This essay is a complete rewriting with very considerable additions and revisions of a paper read before a session of the American Historical Association in December 1948. That paper appeared without scholarly apparatus in *Explorations in Entrepreneurial History*, **2** (1950), 128–40.

[1] R. H. Tawney, *Harrington's Interpretation of His Age*, British Academy, Raleigh Lecture on History, 1941 (London, 1942), p. 15. Ibid. *The Agrarian Problem in the 16th Century* (London 1912), p. 197.

[2] Louis B. Wright, *Middle-Class Culture in Elizabethan England* (Chapel Hill, 1935), p. 5.

[3] A. F. Pollard, *Factors in Modern History* (London, 1907), esp. chap. 11, 'The Advent of the Middle Class'.

So we have on our hands a full-blown myth, which by explaining everything has come to emanate an aura of sacredness, of mystical untouchability. To doubt it smacks of heresy, blasphemy, and sacrilege.

Now to make an end of a myth is not always necessarily desirable, for myths may serve as a vigorous stimulus to intellectual as well as to social effort. There is, however, a point hard to define when the myth, instead of evoking thought, acts as a substitute for it, or when, in the face of patent disintegration of the myth men spend vast amounts of time and effort in shoring it up, instead of setting out to build newer and more solid intellectual structures. The myth of the middle class has become both of these kinds of barrier to understanding. A large group of historians uncritically ascribes every major historical change in the Tudor period—and a long time before and after—to the desires, aspirations, ideas, and intentions of the rising middle class; a second group turns great scholarly resources to preventing the very concept of a Tudor middle class from vaporizing before our eyes and turning into such stuff as dreams are made of.

Yet at the outset it seems more than ordinarily easy to subject the myth of the Tudors and the middle class to an empirical test. We know who the Tudors were and what the middle class was, and we can proceed from there. Never was there a fonder illusion. The Tudors are reasonably stable, but the middle class is as fluid as water. A concept that at a distance seems solid gold turns out on closer inspection to be mere melted butter.

Only gradually does the high priesthood of the Myth of the Middle Class impart to that class an infinite capacity for ramification. At first the middle class appears quite innocently in association with commerce. It is comprised of 'rich burghers'. It is 'of the counting house . . . a commercial middle class'. Or as Professor Louis Wright puts it with commendable precision, it is a group 'whose pre-occupation was trade'.[1] Clearly we have here a bounded sector of society, sharply distinguished from the rest, a satisfactory object for discourse or investigation. We have indeed the *bourgeoisie*, precisely the group that an able sixteenth-century Frenchman, Claude Seyssel, described as the *estat moyen*.[2] But, alas, as soon as we start our survey of the middle class we discover that the very sponsors of the idea we wish to investigate have already obliterated most of the boundary marks, and that the

[1] Wright, *Middle-Class Culture*, p. vii.
[2] Claude Seyssel, *Grand Monarchie de France* (Paris, 1519), fol. 13–13v.

middle class has begun to spread all over the social map. The two processes by which the limits of the class are extended are a fascinating study in historical casuistry.

The first method is that of procreation—the theory of the continuity of mercantile germ plasm. According to this theory Sir Francis Walsingham, for example, was middle class because one of his great-grandfathers was a merchant, four generations on the land apparently being insufficient to attenuate the effect of merchant blood.[1] The possibilities latent in this method of extending the middle class are enormous, and will serve to explain away dozens of otherwise anomalous facts. Does a nobleman display an aptitude for making money? We trace his pedigree through all its branches until we come on a City man, and there is our explanation. The beauty of this method is that it can be turned on and off at will. If the particular aristocrat we are investigating is a blockhead bankrupt, we can stop genealogizing short of the merchant ancestor and point to the bankruptcy as a symptom of the inevitable collapse of the old nobility before the rising middle class. The procreative theory attains its ultimate triumph perhaps when through her maternal great-grandfather Geoffrey Boleyn, Lord Mayor of London, it links Queen Elizabeth herself to the middle class.[2]

An even more useful procedure is the extension of the middle class by assimilation, since it spares us an arduous and uncertain job of genealogical research. The argument, implicit rather than expressed, seems to run this way: the middle class were business men; business men get rich; whoever gets rich is middle class. The reasoning here might find critics among finicking logicians, but for historians on the hook between a very simple theory and some very complicated data it cannot be beat. By this reasoning the job of extending the middle class to the countryside is accomplished. Since they seem to have prospered, the

[1] According to Pollard, *Factors*, p. 40, Walsingham was 'upstart gentry'. Walsingham's mother was the daughter of a knight. His paternal uncle was a knight and Lieutenant of the Tower. In the paternal line his father, his grandfather, his great-grandfather and his great-great-grandfather owned land in Kent. His grandfather was once sheriff of that county, and his great-grandfather was buried at the family estate over a half century before the birth of the 'parvenu' Francis. Francis's lawyer father—a younger son—was a justice of the peace in Kent. He was also Under-Sheriff of London, a position ordinarily held by men of considerable professional eminence, Sir Thomas More, for example. On page 2 of his *Middle-Class Culture*, Dr. Wright groups the more important members of the learned professions with the nobility and gentry as the upper class. Conyers Read, *Mr. Secretary, Walsingham and the Policy of Queen Elizabeth*, 3 vols. (Cambridge, Mass., 1925), i. 2–12.

[2] Pollard, *Factors*, p. 40.

copyholder of the fourteenth and fifteenth centuries, the large lease-hold farmer and the yeoman of a somewhat later era are drawn into the middle class. And above all the gentry, all of the gentry, even those who received titles of nobility from the Tudors. Meantime there is the small industrial master. Neither spiritually nor economically is he very distant from the lesser merchant clothier. It would be invidious, impolite, to exclude him from a party to which we have invited so many. He is *bourgeois*, too. The limits of the middle class thus become most elastic, and that fine scholar, Professor Tawney, who has perhaps done as much as anyone to stretch them, takes full advantage of his handiwork. According to the exigencies of his argument, the middle class is composed of men of the town and commerce, or of men of town and country alike; it includes small masters or it excludes them, includes the well-to-do copyholder or excludes him, includes the yeoman or excludes him, includes the gentry or excludes them. The conception of the middle class thus attains all the rigor of a rubber band. Like Humpty Dumpty Professor Tawney is a master of words; middle class means what he wants it to mean when he wants it to mean it.[1]

[1] In *Religion and the Rise of Capitalism* (Pelican ed., 1947) Professor Tawney rather closely hews to a line that identifies the middle class with the *estat moyen* of Seyssel, the *bourgeoisie*. The identification is indeed so close that where the index (not made by the author, but, I assume, approved by him), has 'middle class' the page referred to mentions only '*bourgeoisie*' (e.g., pp. 15, 77, 78, 98). Even in *Religion and the Rise of Capitalism*, however, the concept is expanded sufficiently to include yeomen (pp. 168–9) and small masters (pp. 172–3) on the grounds of their affinity, partly economic, partly spiritual, with the trading and commercial classes. (For further references see index, ibid. p. 276.) In the same work, however, a rather sharp line is drawn between the 'business classes' and the gentry (pp. 173–5). In *The Agrarian Problem* Professor Tawney speaks of a 'rural middle class' of large copyholders in the fourteenth and fifteenth centuries (p. 82). In his 'Rise of the Gentry, 1558–1640', *Economic History Review*, xi (1941), 1–38, class lines are rather differently drawn. The commercial and trading group remains, but we hear no more of the yeoman and the small master as members of the middle class. So much of the landlord group is incorporated, however, as to leave scarcely anyone in the class above the middle. The rural 'middle class' is composed of the owners of 'small and medium sized estates . . . the gentleman farmer', not only the 'man who works his land as a commercial undertaking', but landlords living 'mainly on rents', who engage in some sideline enterprise (pp. 16–17). 'The landowner living on the profits and rents of commercial farming and the merchant or banker, who was also a landowner . . . judged by the source of their incomes . . . were equally *bourgeois*' (p. 18). A substantial part of the peerage becomes *bourgeois* in this generous conception. Despite the disappearance of the middle-class yeomen from 'the Rise of the Gentry' and from Professor Tawney's Raleigh lecture, in the opinion of the learned historian of the yeoman they 'were a substantial rural middle class': Mildred Campbell, *The English Yeoman under Elizabeth*

The ultimate triumph in extending the boundaries of the middle class, however, rests with Dr. Louis Wright. The Tudors, he has told us, were a 'bourgeois dynasty'. Since he originally described the middle class as men of trade and the town and since the first four Tudors, uncontaminated by Boleyn blood, did not have middle-class chromosomes, we note the proof of this point with interest. Henry VII, he suggests, was bourgeois because he had 'the habits of a usurious merchant', while his son was bourgeois, too, because he 'enjoyed his wealth with the abandon of any *nouveau riche*'.[1] We have here two infallible marks of the middle class—thrift and extravagance. And since in the words of Private Willis, but in a somewhat different sense, all men are born 'either a little liberal or else a little conservative', we have arrived at the *ne plus ultra*, a conception of the middle class that includes the whole human race from time immemorial.

Thus has the conception of the middle class been expanded. At the risk of seeming ungrateful to my predecessors who have displayed so much ingenuity in the work, for the purpose of this paper I will try to dispense with the mighty gothic structure they have reared and rely instead on a puritan simplicity. In this paper the middle class is Seyssel's *estat moyen*—merchants, financiers, industrialists, the town rich, the *bourgeoisie*.[2] I am impelled to this Draconian measure by the conviction that otherwise the middle class becomes so fluid, indeed so ethereal, as to defy attempts to say anything about it.

---

and the Early Stuarts, Yale Historical Publications, no. 14 (New Haven, 1942), p. 61. Professor Tawney has recently pointed out the intellectual pitfalls created by casual and contradictory use of the terms employed in class specification. R. H. Tawney, 'Rise of the Gentry: A Postscript', *Economic History Review*, 2nd ser., vii (1954), 97. We may expect that in the future Professor Tawney's multitude of disciples and admirers will follow the precept of the master rather than his example.

[1] Wright, *Middle-Class Culture*, p. 5.

[2] One group that Seyssel includes in his *estat moyen* does not belong in the English middle class. In France in the sixteenth century the principal offices of justice and the upper ranks of the legal profession were filled by *bourgeois*. The investigations of my classes in English History at Queens College (New York) for 1955 and 1956 seem to show that the men who attained eminence in the legal profession in England under the Tudors were usually the offspring of landed families. This result is in accord with the observation of Sir John Fortescue in the fifteenth century. Sir John Fortescue, *De laudibus legum Anglie*, ed. and trans. S. B. Chrimes (Cambridge, Eng., 1942), pp. 118–19. In neither England nor France were there any explicit status bars to training in and the practice of law. As in France a few sons of landed folk so in England a few men of humble origin attained legal eminence. But in Tudor England townsmen were but a scattering among the mass of the sons of the gentry at the Inns of Court and later at the bar.

II

Devotees of the myth of the middle class adduce several sorts of evidence to demonstrate the rise of that class in the Tudor period. One of the favorites is the addiction of the landed aristocracy to marriage with merchant fortunes and incidentally with any persons that might be appendant thereto. Certainly when they married, impoverished Tudor gentlemen of some acres and more debts went where money could be found, and this often meant going to the towns. In the days of the later Stuarts there were probably not many fine old Tory families that could climb their genealogical trees to the height of four or five generations without finding a city father or a country clothier or some other equally bourgeois progenitor ensconced in one of the branches. An unusually efficient Eros made this sort of provision for three noble families at one swoop, when through marriage three great-grand-daughters of William Stump became the Countesses of Rutland, Suffolk, and Lincoln; for Stump, the great Western clothier, was the very model of a Tudor middle-class man.[1]

There may, indeed, have been some propensity among the upper aristocracy to regard marriage to City money as a sort of indefeasible privilege of their class. From the hard-pressed Lord Stafford, lineal descendant of the fifteenth century Dukes of Buckingham, Lord Burleigh once received an inadvertently comic letter with a rather pathetic undertone. The poor peer complains out of bitterness and frustration. A rich merchant father with whom he is dealing is about to break off negotiations. He is going to withhold from the anxiously waiting arms of Stafford's son the prized daughter so essential to the restoration of a decayed noble lineage.[2] Stafford patently felt himself the victim of a peculiarly urban bit of double-dealing.

The evidence of the rise of the middle class most dearly beloved by the devotees of the myth, however, is the record of its land purchases under the Tudors. The facts alleged in support of the thesis do not admit of doubt. Tudor moralists were condemning, Tudor statesmen worrying about the extensive acquisitions of land by the merchants of their day, the extensive sales of land by its former owners.[3] Merchants

[1] G. D. Ramsay, *The Wiltshire Woollen Industry in the Sixteenth and Seventeenth Centuries*, Oxford Historical Series (Oxford, 1943), pp. 36–7 and p. 37, n. 1.

[2] *Original Letters Illustrative of English History*, ed. H. Ellis, 3rd ser., 4 vols. (London, 1846), iv. 90.

[3] In his heyday Thomas Cromwell considered limiting the amount of land a merchant might buy. G. S. Thomson, *Two Centuries of Family History* (London,

were indeed buying estates of the titled nobility and the gentry in the sixteenth century. On this the record clearly supports the present-day historians and the contemporary moralists and statesmen. Wherever men were making considerable fortunes in trade and industry, they were putting at least part of their profit into land.[1] In the West the country clothiers, made newly rich by the booming sales of unfinished English white cloths in Antwerp, were all landbuyers from the great William Stump with his vast estates to more modest but yet substantial folk like the Hedges with their pair of manors.[2] In the East we have Thomas Cony of Bassingthorpe, Merchant of the Staple, husband of a London alderman's daughter, who at the start of his career had a wool business and land bringing him £200. At his death sixty years later he is no longer in the foreign trade in wool, dormant since the middle of the century. But he now holds land worth about £450 at the old rent, perhaps more than twice as much at the improved. This quadrupling of his income from land was quite an achievement for Cony since in the interim he had launched nineteen children into the world.[3] A member of the London Mercers Company, Richard Manningham, whose obscure origin is imprinted on his memorial brass, *honesta natus familia*, buys an estate at Bradbourne in the parish of East Malling and retires to it. He thus joins the exodus that makes the Londonward part of Kent a place of choice for the newest gentry of England, a sort of Britannic Westchester. Finally his money sets his cousin John, the diarist, on a safe way to the gentry, mounted on that reliable nag, the profession of law.[4] From the relatively modest acquisitions of Maningham one may ascend to the dizzy pinnacle attained by another City family, the Greshams, great purchasers in the lively market created by the sale of monastic lands.[5] Along the path of land purchase stretching from the Manninghams to the Greshams stood or climbed many a

1930), p. 17. William Cecil had the same idea. Tudor Economic Documents, ed. R. H. Tawney and E. Power, *Tudor Economic Documents*, 3 vols. (London, 1924), i. 326.

[1] Tawney, 'Rise of the Gentry', pp. 17–18. 'By the middle years of James . . . it is difficult to find a prominent London capitalist who is not also a substantial landowner'. p. 18.

[2] Ramsay, *Wiltshire Woollen Industry*, pp. 31–49.

[3] ' Extracts from the Household-Book of Thomas Cony. . . .', ed. Edmund Turner, *Archeologia*, xi (1794), 22–33.

[4] John Manningham, *Diary of John Manningham*, ed. J. Bruce, Camden Society Publications, 1st ser., xcix (London, 1868), introd., pp. i–x.

[5] J. W. Burgon, *Life and Times of Sir Thomas Gresham*, 2 vols. (London, 1839), i. 37–9 and App. 3 (p. 460); *Original Letters*, 3rd ser., iii. 270–1.

London merchant. As one writer melodramatically puts it, it was a period 'when an Ingram . . . could afford to buy, and a Verney was forced to sell'.[1] It is only when we consider the revolutionary implications imputed to the undeniable facts of the case that we feel some sense of doubt. The allegations as to the facts are true; is the situation itself of earth-shaking import? Is it new?

As we approach the entrance to the Tudor era we come on our first hint that we may have misunderstood the significance of merchant land buying. William Caxton, the printer, lived most of his adult life in Flanders, where great town families spent centuries in trade. In London, he complained, there were no such mercantile dynasties.[2] Here on the very verge of the Tudor period we find a suggestion that the exodus of business men from trade was not a peculiarity of that era. Miss Thrupp's fine study of the medieval London merchant has shown what became of the commercial families that disappeared in one, two, or three generations. Some merely died out in the male line. Some receded into obscurity, rural or urban. But a considerable number of the most considerable merchants purchased estates and set themselves up as gentlemen. Such men and their families were likely soon to be absorbed (in some instances merely reabsorbed) into the country gentry.[3] The many fifteenth-century London business men who died without male heirs often left behind a well-dowered widow or a few nicely fixed daughters. The fifteenth-century Pastons, with their perpetual negotiations for London heiresses,[4] Sir William Stonor with his successful marriage to a

---

[1] L. C. Knights, *Drama and Society in the Age of Jonson* (London, 1937), p. 107.

[2] *Prologues and Epilogues of William Caxton*, introd. and ed. W. J. B. Crotch, Early English Text Society, original ser., clxxvi (London, 1928), 77–8. 'One name and lineage . . . in this noble city of London . . . rarely continue unto the third heir or scarcely to the second.'

[3] Sylvia Thrupp, *The Merchant Class of Medieval London* (Chicago, 1948), pp. 118–30.

[4] *The Paston Letters*, A.D. 1422–1509, ed. J. Gairdner, 4 vols. (London, 1910). The Pastons worked hard to get rich city marriages all around. John P. to Sir John P., 'I am proferred a marriage in London worth 600 M' (iii, 109, no. 739). Sir John to John P., 'The matter of Mistress Barly' is 'but a bare thing. . . . It passeth not [blank] marks' (iii, 177, no. 789). John P. to Margaret P., 'Mother, I heard while I was in London where was a goodly young woman to marry, which was daughter of one Seff a mercer, and she shall have £200 in money to her marriage and 20 M a year of land after the decease of a stepmother of hers which is about 50 years of age. . . . I spoke with some of the maid's friends and have gotten their good wills to have her married to my brother Edmund' (iii, 219, no. 812). Edmund P. to William P., 'Here is lately fallen a widow . . . which was wife to one Bolt, a worsted merchant and worth £1500 and gave his wife 100 M in money . . . and £10 a year in land. . . . I will for your sake see her' (iii, 278, no. 858).

rich City widow,[1] are but instances of the general truth that before the Tudor period country families had discovered the tonic effect on their more or less blue blood of a transfusion of *aurum potabile* from the City.

A century before Caxton the history of a yet more famous man of letters follows the very course which Caxton was complaining about —from town to country. Father a vintner; son a vintner, public official, landlord in Kent, and a poet; grandson a man of vast estates. Such seems to have been the story of Geoffrey Chaucer's family.[2] From the fourteenth century comes that classical example of the rise of the middle class, the de la Poles who went from trade at Hull to the Earldom of Suffolk in two generations.[3] William de la Pole was but the brightest star in a galaxy. Lesser English financiers of Edward III's dubious ventures in conquest cap the genealogical tree of many a later aristocratic family.[4] A refugee from the seventeenth century, I lose my bearings in the strange terrain at the turn of the twelfth. Yet even in that unfamiliar region, I seem to discern familiar lineaments in the misty figure of Henry Fitzailwin, the first Lord Mayor of London. Before his Mayoralty he was a tenant in sergeantry. At his death after a long period in office, he held two knights' fees and land in four or five counties.[5]

And so back through the centuries, as far as the record will take us, we find the rising middle class making its way out to the land, buying estates from aristocrats too unlucky or thriftless to hold them. The feckless young Lord whom Chaucer's Reeve was fleecing was as utterly foredoomed to lose his land as any of his spiritual successors under Elizabeth.[6] The gentleman waster of the fourteenth-century poem who frittered away in an orgy of boozing and whoring estates accumulated by more prudent ancestors could have found companions in every century from the twelfth to the nineteenth.[7] And, in the late twelfth

---

[1] *The Stonor Letters and Papers*, ed. C. L. Kingsford, 2 vols., Camden Society Publications, 3rd ser., 29, 30 (London, 1919), I, xxvi–xxvii.

[2] R. D. French, *A Chaucer Handbook* (New York, 1939), pp. 40–74, esp. p. 74 and n. 20; Martin B. Ruud, *Thomas Chaucer*, University of Minnesota Studies in Language and Literature, ix (Minneapolis, 1926).

[3] *Dictionary of National Biography*, s.v. Pole, Michael de la (1330?–89), and Pole, Sir William de la (d. 1366).

[4] Alice Law, 'English *Nouveaux Riches* of the 14th Century', *Transactions of the Royal Historical Society*, new ser., ix (1895), 49–73.

[5] *Dictionary of National Biography*, s.v. Fitzailwin, Henry (d. 1212).

[6] Geoffrey Chaucer, *Canterbury Tales*, Prologue, lines 593–612.

[7] *A Short Debate Between Winner and Waster*, Select Early English Poems, ed. Sir I. Gollancz, iii (London, 1920), lines 263–85.

century northern knights, including, as one would expect, a Percy, having their lands in hock to the Jews, found a new way to pay old debts by destroying pledge and pledgee in a common holocaust at York.[1]

The process then on which historians have laid such emphasis in their account of the rise of the middle class in the Tudor period—the movement of rich merchants and industrialists out to the land, the decay of landed families, and the linking of gentility with city riches by marriage—in all this there is nothing novel. Merchant Ingrams indeed were buying and landed Verneys were selling at the turn of the sixteenth century; but our impulse to drop a tear for the passing of the old order or to sing hosannah at the advent of the new is somewhat damped by the knowledge that only a century earlier landed Zouches and Stonors were selling, while in the person of Sir Ralph, Lord Mayor of London, merchant Verneys were buying.[2] Indeed we may suspect that a considerable number of those ancient families declining under the Tudors were rising under Lancaster and York, the *parvenus* of a hundred years before, and so on, back through the centuries.

For getting and spending, gaining and losing, winning and wasting —these are not traits of one order of men or one or two special eras of human history; they are a trait of every era when some men have what other men want, of every age when some men have the strength, the cunning, the tenacity, and the fortune to take what they want, while others lack the strength, the cunning, the tenacity, and the fortune to keep what they have.

It remains to ask why, under the circumstances, historians of the Tudor era have concluded that merchant land-buying in the sixteenth century marks an especially significant phase in the rise of the middle class. To understand this peculiar conclusion, we do well to recognize it not as a unique idiosyncracy but as one species of a considerable genus. One of the odder performances in contemporary historiography takes place when the social historians of *each* European century from the twelfth to the eighteenth with an air of mystery seize the curtain

[1] *The Jews of Angevin England, Documents and Records*, ed. J. Jacobs (New York, 1893), pp. 117–30, 385–92.
[2] *Stonor Letters and Papers*, i. p. xiii. *Letters and Papers of the Verney Family*, ed. John Bruce, Camden Society Publications, 1st ser., lvi (London, 1853), 22–3. For the rise in one century of a late medieval manorless family to be holders of 200 manors, see J. L. Kirby, 'The Hungerford Family in the Later Middle Ages' (Summary of Thesis), *Bulletin of the Institute of Historical Research*, xviii (1940), 83–4.

cord and unveil the great secret. 'Behold', they say, 'in *my* century the middle-class nobodies rising into the aristocracy'. After an indefinite series of repetitions of this performance one is impelled to murmur 'But this is where I came in', or even, 'What of it?' And then one begins to wonder why each highly competent specialist thinks that his particular sector of the apparently oft-repeated process is so remarkable as to be worthy of the name of social revolution. Perhaps an answer is to be found in the didactic writing of contemporary moralists.[1] Not only do Tudor writers contemn the new-made gentleman, and lament the decay of old aristocratic families; with scarcely an exception they say, or imply, that things were never thus before, that in the good old days nobles were liberal and hospitable but never prodigal; they did not sell their land. And merchants, industrious and honest, never greedy or grasping, did not seek to buy it, but were satisfied in the place to which God had called them. To historians committed to raising the middle class, willy-nilly, in the Tudor period, these denunciations of the movement as an outrageous novelty are as manna; but how much significance can we attach to them? On the face of the medieval history of land transactions, of which we have just had a glimpse, not much; on the face of the writings of earlier moralists, even less.

When

> Boys of no blood, with boast and pride,
> Shall wed landed ladies, and lead them at will

Domesday is nigh, and nowadays it is clear to see, 'It will soon come, or perhaps is here'.[2] So sang a fourteenth-century poet, lamenting the 'novelty' of the rise of the middle class in his own age. And in his bitter indictment of the sinful and degenerate world he lived in, Piers Plowman included as one count the successful social ascent of the base. 'Soap sellers and their sons for silver knights are made.' [3] Thus medieval didactic literature of each era denounces climbing merchants, land-getting nobodies, and aristocrats who waste their substance or marry business fortunes, as new things of evil. And thus from age to age the process so denounced went on and on.

Why the moralists themselves for centuries blandly ignored the

[1] For a fine survey of part of this literature, see Helen C. White, *Social Criticism in Popular Religious Literature of the Sixteenth Century* (New York, 1944). The texts of a number of these writings will be found among the publications of the Early English Text Society. Select passages are printed in *Tudor Economic Documents*, esp. vol. iii.

[2] *Winner and Waster*, lines 15–17.

[3] Qtd. G. G. Coulton, *Medieval Panorama* (New York, 1955), p. 245.

facts of the past in favor of elegant fictions we can only conjecture. Perhaps they did not ignore the facts of the past as they understood them. Their social ideal was the hierarchical society of fixed social orders, and such a society they found in the 'histories' which were their regular diet—the romances of chivalry.[1] Here indeed was the society of the moralist's dream, where knights were liberal and generous, town folk industrious, humble, or preferably non-existent, peasants docile and dutiful, a society above all without an economy, where there were no scarce goods, spending but no getting, always enough for everybody in his appointed place.[2] This cloud-cuckoo land may be a world of dreams to us; to many men up through the sixteenth century it was no dream at all but a fact as living, more living, than anything that had actually happened in the days long before their birth. When Henry VII named his first son Arthur he was not making a casual curtsey to a lightly held fairy story;[3] he was attaching his new dynasty to that segment of the past which contemporary Englishmen most vividly knew. Like Mark Twain, medieval men remembered best the things that had not happened.[4]

[1] G. R. Owst, *Literature and Pulpit in Medieval England* (Cambridge, Eng., 1933), p. 332. 'All (the preachers) with one accord look back from their own day and generation to some golden age of chivalry . . . "when there were many chivalrous knights in this land, alike of the Round Table as of the *gartir*." ' See also pp. 311, 314, 337.

[2] The new printing press devoted itself to a remarkable extent to the publication of medieval vernacular literature. An especially popular variety was the *mise en prose* of the metrical romance of chivalry. This bastard form, which enjoyed great popularity in the court of the Duke of Burgundy, was brought back to England by William Caxton and provided grist for the first English printing press. For the *mise en prose*, see Georges Doutrepont, *Les Mises en Prose des Épopées et des Romans Chevalresques du XIVᵉ au XVIᵉ Siècle*, Academie Royale de Belgique, Classe des Lettres, Memoires en 8ᵉ, 2 serie, 40 (Brussels, 1939). For Caxton's connection with Burgundian society and culture and the predominance of medieval chivalric and didactic works in the output of his press, see *The Prologues and Epilogues of William Caxton*, biographical introduction by Crotch, and *passim*.

[3] The commissioners whom Thomas Cromwell chose in 1535 to assess the taxable value of the monasteries were probably not selected for their addiction to chivalric myths. Yet they exempted a considerable sum of the income of Glastonbury from the tenth on the grounds that by the terms of the will of King Arthur the monks were bound to use it for alms. A. Savine, *English Monasteries on the Eve of the Dissolution*, Oxford Studies in Social and Legal History, i (Oxford, 1909), 230 and 230, n. 1.

[4] In this respect the difference between medieval and modern man may be less than modern historians like to believe. Contemporary American legends also look back to a golden age of innocence peopled in our case by Founding Fathers, pioneers, and so forth, all conspicuously endowed with virtues which we, their degenerate descendants, conspicuously lack.

III

When we have proceeded so far in our analysis of the myth of the middle class, we run head on into the indisputable fact of drastic agrarian change in the sixteenth century—the so-called agrarian revolution. The commercialization and rationalization of agriculture;[1] the decline of subsistence farming;[2] the new literature of farm improvement and scientific surveying;[3] crop specialization; enclosure, rackrenting, and sheep-farming;[4] the decay of hospitality[5] and the replacement of the intimate, the personal, the customary, the medieval relationship between lord and man by the cold cash nexus of employer and laborer or hireling farmer (the typical economic form of middle-class capitalism)[6]—these are the symptoms of change. The whole process is shot through with the appetite for gain and the cold, rational pursuit of profit, alien to the custom-bound countryside, native to the business habits of the city. The agricultural revolution is simply what happens when the rising middle class of the town turns its attention to the

[1] Tawney, 'Rise of the Gentry', pp. 12–18.

[2] Tawney, *Agrarian Problem*, pp. 200–13, 254–65.

[3] Two examples of the new literature on husbandry and surveying, Thomas Tusser, *Five Hundred Pointes of Good Husbandrie*, ed. W. Payne and S. J. Herrtage, English Dialect Society Publications, xxi (London, 1878), and William Norden, *Surveyors Dialogues* (London, 1607). E. G. R. Taylor, 'The Surveyor', *Economic History Review*, xvii (1947), 121–33 presents an interesting discussion of the new art. The mere replacement of the book survey by the accurate estate plan hanging on the landlord's chamber wall created a standing invitation to economic rationality.

[4] On the land hunger of the Tudor era and its social and economic impact see Tawney, *Agrarian Problem*, and Campbell, *English Yeoman*. From Thomas More on, almost every social critic of the century used sheep-running, rackrenting, or enclosure as the fulcrum of his attacks on the landlords. The 'economic' character of the grievance contrasts interestingly with complaints registered in later medieval sermons which tended to charge the landlords with *force majeure*.

[5] The cry about the decline of hospitality can hardly be taken at face value unless we can get some idea of what that hospitality was. The old aristocrat, the third Duke of Buckingham, on a Christmas Day fed almost two hundred at dinner, of whom twenty-two 'from the town', thirty-two 'from the country' and eleven others *might* be poor. The rest were largely hangers-on or hangers-on of hangers-on, and if any others benefited it does not appear in the household accounts. *Extracts from the Household Book of Edward Stafford, Duke of Buckingham*, ed. J. Gage (London, 1834), pp. 8–11. The performance, if it was one, does not compare favorably with that of the parvenu Sir Edward Montague of Boughton, said to have fed 1,200 at his gate one Christmas. *The Montagu Muster Book*, ed. Joan Wake, Northamptonshire Record Society Publications, vii, p. xxii.

[6] For the transition from a medieval to a modern capitalist economy and the contrast between the two see Tawney, *Agrarian Problem*, pp. 98–135, 213–80.

exploitation of land for profit. And thus to the support of the legend of the rocketing middle class and the plummeting aristocracy comes the fable of the city slicker and the rube, the clever, ruthless Londoner and the pudding-headed countryman. The combination is a most happy bit of economy in scholarship, since precisely the same evidence used in defense of the legend—the financial embarrassments of aristocrats, the land purchases of merchants—can be trotted out and used again to defend the fable.

Of course if one looks for indebted peers and bankrupt knights in the Tudor period one finds them;[1] but then in the records of the debtors' court all classes are always equally bankrupt. If, instead of looking for the economic lame ducks of the landed aristocracy in the places where we are sure to find them, we move in a less constricted circle our incompetents are offset by men of a different stamp, men who export cloth,[2] invest in the metallurgical industry and coal mining,[3] improve the tin-smelting process,[4] work at marsh draining,[5] and save 10,000 acres of bottom land by a new cut in the Bridgwater River.[6] On the shady fringes of legality, no doubt, but in the bright sunlight of profit we find aristocratic corn broggers, enclosers, and rackrenters.[7]

[1] Lawrence Stone, 'The Anatomy of the Elizabethan Aristocracy', *Economic History Review*, xviii (1948), 1–53.

[2] Gentry and peers interested in wool and cloth trade: for Sir Wistan Brown and William Sydney, see *Letters and Papers of Henry VIII*, revised, i, pt. 1, no. 1172 (2); for Lord Cobham, see *Hatfield MSS.* (Historical Manuscripts Commission), ii. 103.

[3] For the interest of Burleigh, Leicester, and Pembroke in the metallurgical industry, see William R. Scott, *The Constitution and Finance of English, Scottish and Irish Joint-Stock Companies to 1720*, 3 vols. (Cambridge, 1910–12), i. 46; ii. 415. For the interest of the aristocracy in coal mining, J. U. Nef, *Rise of the British Coal Industry*, 2 vols. (London, 1932), ii. 9–17, 52–4.

[4] Richard Carew, *Survey of Cornwall* (London, 1602), fol. 13. The alert genteel tinner was Sir Francis Godolphin who 'entertained a Dutch mineral man, and taking light from his experience [built] thereon far more profitable conclusions of his own invention'.

[5] For the activities of Lincolnshire Wellbies, Ogles, and Harringtons in fen draining, see *Hatfield MSS.* (Historical Manuscripts Commission), i. 119.

[6] Robert Ricart, *The Maire of Bristow is Kalendar* (London, 1872), Camden Society Publications, new ser., v. 57–8. The danger of flooding was 'prevented and foreseen' by the 'Commissioners of sewers, namely Sir Hugh Paulet, Sir George Speke, Sir Maurice Berkeley, Mr. Humphrey Coles, esq., Mr. Henry Portnam, esq., and many other of the said commission with the advice of the best heads of good yeomen of the said country'.

[7] Corn brogging appears to be imputed to Sir William Paston and the Lord Admiral in the reign of Elizabeth, *Hatfield MSS.* (Historical Manuscripts Commission), xiii. 168–9. For aristocratic enclosers see n. 1, p. 91 below. In the North, a region hardly notorious for economic precocity, one of the economic grievances

So active was the landed aristocracy between 1540 and 1640 in enterprises other than agriculture that Lawrence Stone requires 7500 words more to present a summary of the wide-ranging business undertakings of a small fraction of that aristocracy, the lay peers. Mr. Stone even feels the need to distinguish between the more sober and conservative business interest of most of the gentry and the bolder, more speculative activities of the peers, who with equal insouciance were willing to take a flyer on a race horse, a piratical expedition, a coal mine, or anything else going. Of the families in the peerage between 1560 and 1640 fully two thirds were engaged in colonial, trading, or industrial enterprise. Nor did intensity of activity clearly correlate with recentness of title.

> In the Elizabethan period the most active entrepreneur in the country was not some busy merchant or thrusting member of the new gentry, but a peer of ancient stock, George Talbot, ninth earl of Shrewsbury. He was the largest desmesne farmer of whom we have record, he owned a ship which he employed in seeking out new trades and in exploration, he was one of the largest iron-makers in the country, with three separate works under his control, he operated steel works, he sponsored technical innovation in refining his lead, he owned coal mines and glass works. In addition to all this he was an active investor in trading and exploring ventures. . . . It is a remarkable record. . . . [1]

So among these enterprising rubes there were but few parvenus in the ordinary sense and many old families. But historians of the rise of the middle class use the terms 'parvenu' and 'old aristocracy' in a sense different from that of ordinary discourse—in a Pickwickian sense indeed. In common speech a parvenu is a man of recent riches or gentility; and the title of old aristocrat is reserved for men with longish pedigrees. But for those who write of the rise of the middle class a gentleman who is not a blithering incompetent about his own affairs becomes thereby a parvenu though his acres were in his family since the Conquest. Conversely, he who is enough a fool to lose the lands his father won becomes an old aristocrat by his virtuosity in stupidity, though the paint is barely dry on his blazon.

of the peasantry involved in the Pilgrimage of Grace was the taking of gressums, a regional variety of rackrenting. M. H. R. Dodds, *The Pilgrimage of Grace, 1536–1537*, 2 vols. (Cambridge, Eng., 1915) i. 369–73.

[1] Lawrence Stone, 'The Nobility in Business, 1540–1640', in *The Entrepreneur, Papers Presented at the Annual Conference of the Economic History Society* at Cambridge, England, April 1957, pp. 14–21.

An early sixteenth-century memorandum from a landlord to his steward typifies that commercial spirit which city men are supposed to have brought with them to the land. Amid a mass of other minutiae the steward is instructed to try to arrange with Lord Brooke an exchange of one of his employer's estates for the lordship of Wardere. The steward is also to attach Sir John Pickering's goods and arrest him for debt. He is also to bargain with Lord Ferrers for some furs, and to 'drive the lowest price thereof'. And he is to sell off £100 of timber out of a wood in Amersham, reserving the best to his master, and getting 'Thomas Bynks, the carpenter of London', to go to Amersham with him, 'to help drive the most to our profit'. Thus does our landlord intone the ancient litany of commerce, 'Buy low, sell high'.[1] His painstaking attention to detail, his thorough knowledge of the state of his own affairs, his appetite for the last possible farthing of profit, his ruthless treatment of an unfortunate debt-ridden gentleman, do they not all bespeak the merchant, stirring the stagnant, medieval countryside with the spirit of capitalist exploitation? In theory, perhaps, but in fact the man who wrote the letter was Edward Stafford, third Duke of Buckingham, premier Duke and one of the most active enclosers and depopulators in all England.[2]

A look back into the Middle Ages previously turned up for us medieval land-buying merchants and medieval lamenters of the good old days. The discovery of a bourgeois kind of blue-blood duke straddling the conventional boundary between medieval and modern times suggests another look back. Of course we have no right to expect to turn up another memorandum from another calculating duke. There were very few dukes at all in England, and the preservation of a calculating memorandum from a calculating one is a bit of luck we could hardly hope for more than once every few centuries. Yet more than a century before Buckingham's day an even richer duke, John of Gaunt, wrote one of his stewards about the management of a great estate. He told him to lease all the lands of the new assarts under his administration, to throw out any tenants who refused the new terms, and to let the land to others willing to give more. And as to other lands that could be let more to his profit, the Duke of Lancaster wanted them leased at their true annual value 'without sparing anyone in this

---

[1] *Original Letters*, 3rd ser., i. 220–6.
[2] *Dictionary of National Biography*, s.v. Stafford, Edward, third Duke of Buckingham (1478–1521).

matter'.[1] Nor does the unsparing Duke stand alone. In the three decades after the Black Death the population of England fell about thirty per cent; but from this decreased population flinty-hearted landlords managed to exact an income only ten per cent less than what they received before the plague ravaged the land. In 1381, when the peasants rose in their wrath, it was against such as these, not against the mild, indulgent, paternal lords who exist only in the imagination of writers whose knowledge of the Middle Ages dates from the beginning of this century.[2] We do not have to recede as far into the Middle Ages as John of Gaunt before we come to noblemen whose aristocratic appetites for self-enrichment aroused their interest in enterprises usually associated with the coarser tastes and more rational economic proclivities of the middle class. In the fifteenth century a baron, an earl and a duke concerned themselves with mining matters.[3] In Edward IV's reign another earl got himself a concession for running a vacation cruise in his own ship to carry pilgrims from England to St. James of Compostella.[4] The provision of venture capital for the shipping business seems especially to have accorded with the entrepreneurial tastes of that Edwardian peerage. The Lords Howard, Herbert, and Fauconberg all owned a vessel or so. The Earl of Warwick, the Kingmaker, owned a whole fleet of them. He appears to have made use of his position of favor and power to plan a splendid commercial coup. When after a period of embargo the trade to Bordeaux was reopened in 1464, the Earl quickly got a license to carry a cargo there in his fleet and to return laden with much-prized barrels of claret. A fellow-Earl, Essex, engaged in a miscellaneous export of wool, cloth, tin, lead, hides, and coal.[5] And fairly beating the Tudors to the honor, King Edward IV won from modern historians the accolade of 'bourgeois' by his extensive shipments of wool for sale on the Calais market.[6]

The best-documented business career of the fifteenth century in

[1] *John of Gaunt's Register, 1372–1376*, ed. S. Armitage-Smith, 2 vols., Camden Society Publications, 3rd ser., xx, xxi (1911), ii. 2923, also 181.

[2] On the successful hardhandedness of the landed aristocracy after the Black Death see G. A. Holmes, *The Estates of the Higher Nobility in Fourteenth Century England* (Cambridge, Eng., 1957), pp. 114–15.

[3] Fitzwalter, Northumberland, Gloucester: Scott, *Joint-Stock Companies*, ii. 385, n. 2.

[4] *Original Letters*, ed. H. Ellis, 2nd ser., 4 vols. (London, 1827), i. 110–11.

[5] Cora Scofield, *The Life and Reign of Edward IV*, 2 vols. (London, 1923), ii. 417–19.

[6] Ibid. ii. 404–15.

England is that of another wool merchant. That merchant, who had a vivid flair for entrepreneurship, was also a country gentleman of ancient lineage and, eventually, the son-in-law of a Marquess. His name was Sir William Stonor, and he was heir to several generations of Cotswold graziers, long substantial men in their neighborhood. By a judicious marriage and careful commercial arrangements he set himself at the head of a vertically organized wool business. The clip of Sir William Stonor's Cotswold flocks and the wool he bought from his rustic neighbors was marketed at Calais by Sir William Stonor and associates, Merchants of the Staple. But before he became a merchant and after he ceased to be one, Stonor was an improving landowner, primarily concerned with estate management. His goal was to become 'the worshipfullest of the Stonors' that ever was. A City marriage and a plunge into the wool trade were no bar to his ambitions. His second marital venture brought him the widowed heiress of an Exeter fortune; and he crowned his career and achieved his goal by taking as his third wife Anne Neville, daughter of the Marquess of Montague, niece of the Earl of Warwick, the Kingmaker.[1]

Let us now move back a century and a half in time, down a step or two in the social scale, and look at the estate book of Henry de Bray compiled a little after 1300. There we can watch in action the preservation and improvement of an estate that, passing to the Dives family through Henry's daughter, was to remain there to the Civil War. Henry was a 500-acre man. His rent roll did not raise him to the level of a knight. Two or three centuries later he might have called himself esquire. He was proto-gentry. And he showed that proclivity for accumulation and for driving hard bargains that was to cause harassed peasants centuries later to feel there would never be good times while gentlemen were up. He went into the land-market in his neighborhood when he was a young man, and stayed in it for thirty years. He sold, exchanged, and bought, but in about thirty transactions his purchases were four times the number of his sales. By successive payments in three years he cut the rents on one of his large holdings by eleven-twelfths. For a period of twenty years Henry put an average of one-third of his rental income into building. Scarcely more than a fifth of his outlay for construction went to making himself a house. Most of the rest went into farm building—granges, pigsties, walls, watercourses, bridges, granaries, tenants' cottages. His mill brought him ten per cent a year on his investment, and he noted the gain in his estate

[1] *The Stonor Letters and Papers, passim.*

book. Henry, moreover, picked up enough law to serve as steward for a Northampton priory.[1]

Having guessed wrong on the War of the Roses, the Stonors suffered heavy land losses in litigation after the accession of Henry VII. The Staffords were almost ruined when Wolsey brought the Duke of Buckingham to the block partly, it seems, for the unpardonable crime of being almost as rich, eminent, and vainglorious as the Cardinal Archbishop himself. Thus Stonors and Staffords can serve as handsomely ruinous set pieces in that *mise en scène* of decaying aristocracy which the schematic exigencies of twentieth-century historiography demand to provide a background for the rise of the middle class. The considerable number of families who, like the descendants of Henry de Bray, held on to their land through Plantagenets, Lancastrians, Yorkists, Tudors, and early Stuarts remain recalcitrant to tidy classification, historical anomalies, neither decaying aristocratic fish nor rising middle class fowl.

Regardless of the divers destinies of their families a sixteenth-century Stafford, a fifteenth-century Stonor, and a fourteenth-century Bray—country men all—show a methodical interest in gain, in 'driving the most to their profit', that has come to be regarded as a kind of middle-class monopoly. Their very existence shows that tight-fisted, hard-headed landlordism was not an innovation of the Tudor merchants or of the Tudor age. Nor need we believe that Bray, Stonor, and Buckingham were exceptional or unusual. They were only so in the sense that enterprising men are always exceptional and unusual, a minority in all classes at all times. What is unusual is that the revealing documents about them have by accident survived. These documents lay bare the acquisitive spirit that moved to action the landed men who wrote them. For the most part the spirit that moved medieval landlords to action must be inferred from the actions themselves, but in the actions of some of those landlords a spirit of vigorous economic initiative and adaptability is unmistakably marked.[2] Too easily we

[1] *The Estate Book of Henry de Bray*, ed. D. Wellis, Camden Society Publications, 3rd ser., xxvii (London, 1916), *passim*.

[2] The stereotype of rural stagnation in the Middle Ages, long untenable, has received what one might hope (but not expect) to be its *coup de grâce* in the past twenty-five years. It has been replaced by a picture which displays a great deal of activity on the part of landlords, aimed, as the sixteenth-century Duke of Buckingham's activity was aimed, at driving bargains that would be most to their profit. See especially M. M. Postan, 'Chronology of Labor Services', *Transactions of the Royal Historical Society*, 4th ser., xx (1937), 169–93; ibid. 'Revisions in Economic History: The Fifteenth Century', *Economic History Review*, ix (1939),

conceive of the changes in medieval rural life as large impersonal secular movements. We forget that underlying those changes were a multitude of individual decisions on the wisdom of which depended, in some measure, the future course of events and, entirely, the success or failure of the men who did the deciding. Did a small twelfth-century landlord try to stand on his rights to labor service in the face of a tight labor market? He lost his labor force. If he was unduly obstinate he lost his land soon, too, since idle acres then as now made bankrupt landlords. The loss of incompetents is the gain of the economic opportunists among the landed, whose enterprises for clearing, ditching, and draining their estates helped to make twelfth- and thirteenth-century agrarian history the tale of a vast land-reclamation project. By the same token the lord who failed to take advantage of the labor glut of the thirteenth century to shift his relations with the peasantry in the light of the altered situation lost ground before others more acute or more ruthless than he. The hundred-year-long depression that lasted past the middle of the fifteenth century, with its shrinking markets and depopulation, meant dark days for landlords who did not trim their sails to the economic hurricane. And the times of the Tudors, turbulent but replete with opportunities, demanded a new economic strategy of the landowner, if he was to survive—a loosening of the rigid economic structure that as a matter of self-preservation his predecessors had imposed on the estates he inherited. The very phrase 'agricultural revolution', while it casts doubt on the scrupulosity of the landlords abundantly testifies to their vigor and adaptability. To all the vicissitudes of four eventful centuries, then, the landlords had to accommodate themselves or, as many did with each secular economic swing, lose their lands to men with a better head for managing their affairs.

160–7; ibid. 'Some Social Consequences of the Hundred Years' War', ibid. xii (1942), 1–12; ibid. 'The Rise of a Money Economy', ibid. xiv (1944), 123–34; ibid. 'Some Economic Evidence of Declining Population in the Later Middle Ages', ibid. 2nd ser., ii (1950), 221–46; E. A. Kosminsky, 'Services and Money Rents in the Thirteenth Century', ibid. v. (1935), 24–45; N. Denholm Young, *Seignorial Administration in England*, Oxford Historical Series (Oxford, 1937). Thomas Wilson, *State of England Anno Dom. 1600*, Camden Society Publications, 3rd ser., lii (London, 1936), Camden Miscellany, xvi. 18, astutely noted that 'gentlemen who were wont to addict themselves to wars are now for the most part grown to become good husbands, and well know how to improve their land to the uttermost'. For further details see Campbell, *The English Yeoman*, pp. 64–104. In view of the decline of estate revenues the resort to war by the aristocracy of the fifteenth century was not so irrational economically as it may seem at first sight. Postan, 'Some Social Consequences of the Hundred Years' War', pp. 7–8, 10–12.

Need we then believe that the sixteenth-century landowners waited for the example and inspiration of town merchants before they embarked on the course that was to create such an upheaval in the English countryside? Certainly some of the older aristocracy did not stay for such nudging from the townsmen. English peers and gentlemen of high lineage were quick to take advantage of the opportunity that the expansion of the woollen industry offered them. In the Government's earliest investigation of depopulation it found Brooke, Lord Cobham, Grey, Marquess of Dorset, and Sacheverells, Belknaps, and Hampdens among the active enclosers.[1] And in truth some of the basic procedures that wrought the agricultural revolution of the sixteenth century were not veiled mysteries of commerce accessible only to merchants. To throw up a hedge and throw out a tenant; to run sheep into a field; to hoist rents and raise entry fines: these were not strokes requiring economic genius or merchant lore or even moderate intelligence. In a period of rising prices the stupidest and most extravagant lout of a landlord could do these things—as the stupidest and most extravagant often did.

'I showed myself to my friends in court and after went down to my tenants and surveyed my lands, let new leases, took their money, spent it' in London 'upon ladies, and now I can take up at my pleasure.' So speaks the character in *Epicœne*, whom Ben Jonson called Sir Amorous la Foole.[2]

Moreover, the purchases of estates by city men do not always have the social implications usually ascribed to them. They are not always milestones marking the march of a conquering middle class into the enemy territory of the aristocracy. For when we see landowners losing land and city men acquiring land we cannot be quite sure that we are witnessing the collapse of ancient families and the rise of new ones. To classify every landlord who inherited his estate as an aristocrat and every man with a city father as middle class may not quite do justice to a complex social order that awarded status according to customs, rules, and habitudes the nuances of which are not easily discernible at a remove of three or four centuries. In this connection consider the case of James Whitelocke. James was the fourth son of a successful London merchant. Born, bred, and educated in the City, he himself became a successful lawyer. But James Whitelocke's father was the son of a

---

[1] *The Domesday of Enclosures, 1517–1518*, ed. I. S. Leadam, 1 vol. in 2, Royal Historical Society (London, 1897), pp. 188–9, 234, 350, 424–5.

[2] Ben Jonson, *Epicœne, or the Silent Woman*, act I, scene iv.

country gentleman, and James never forgot who his grandfather was. Although he was separated from the countryside by a generation of trade, few men can have been more conscious of land than he. Without showing any sign that he felt he was poaching or breaking the social game laws, he relentlessly chased after stewardships of foundations, the favorite small game of aristocrats on the hunt for auxiliary income. When money came to James Whitelocke, as money must come to all good lawyers who marry rich widows, he immediately bought out on to the land.

James Whitelocke did not enter on his estates, however, as a parvenu merchant's son crashing his middle-class way into the aristocracy; he entered as the grandson of a country gentleman to the place where he belonged, and to which he had always aspired. One of the Whitelockes had come home after the profitable interlude of a generation in the City.[1] The first Sir Ralph Verney, Lord Mayor of London, did not put himself on paper as James Whitelocke did. But one of his earliest purchases when he had made his fortune in town was the estate his family had lost some generations before. The fifteenth-century Lord Mayor, like the sixteenth-century lawyer, was arranging for a family homecoming.[2] The early Calvinist, they say, lived as if he were in the world but not of it; yet while waiting translation to his heavenly home, economically he often made a very good thing of his exile. How many sons and even grandsons of landed families lived in the town but were not of it, and yet won there that beatitude of riches which enabled them to go back where they came from? The question perhaps is not amenable to a precise answer, but it is one we must keep in mind when we find ourselves thinking of all merchant land buyers as middle-class parvenus thrusting their way by mere money power into the landed aristocracy.[3]

---

[1] James Whitelocke, *Liber Familicus*, ed. J. Bruce, Camden Society Publications, 1st ser., lxx (London, 1858), *passim*.   [2] *Verney Papers*, p. 22.

[3] In two interesting and suggestive studies Peter Laslett has shown that family connections with a country father, a country elder brother or even country cousins might have had a more decisive effect on the social orientation of a city merchant than his more obvious and conspicuous connections with his business associates and competitors. He regards this as particularly the case with seventeenth-century merchants of gentry origin, who were deeply imbued with the patriarchal tradition in their family circles. Peter Laslett, 'The Gentry of Kent in 1640', *Cambridge Historical Journal*, ix (1943), 148–64; and ibid. 'Sir Robert Filmer: The Man Versus the Whig Myth', *William and Mary Quarterly*, 3rd ser., v (1948), 523–52. The phenomenon in question was not uniquely Kentish or even uniquely Home County. Another instance of it is probably provided by the Barnardistons of Suffolk.

We might do well to be equally cautious about landlords who consumed their estates in an orgy of luxurious living. Blue blood is not indispensably prerequisite to the expeditious dissipation of a large estate. To blow a large rent roll, as to blow a large bankroll, all that is needed is the roll in the first place and the will to blow it. Consider the sad case of Toby Palavicino. He inherited one of the most magnificent landed fortunes in Cambridgeshire. His rake's progress from the time he came into his own to the time he lay 'in the Fleet for debts' took sixteen years; but then Toby was handicapped. His prudent father had laid an entail on the estate, and Toby was put to all the bother of getting an Act of Parliament passed to break it. Had it not been for this tiresome hindrance, he might have made it to jail several years sooner.[1] But those were not ancient, long-held acres that Toby went through at what—all things considered—was such a commendable clip. His father, Sir Horatio, had inherited not a foot of English land. Sir Horatio was a Genoese of a family that had been in large-scale trade longer than most of the families of the Tudor gentry had held manors. He had built his fortune on an alum monopoly and on the gains that came to him as Elizabeth's fiscal agent in the continental money market.[2] Of his large takings £20,000 went to purchase that splendid landed estate which in the end proved so inefficacious a barrier to son Toby's propensity toward bankruptcy.[3] The rapid dispersal of the Palavicino landholdings suggests that frugal fathers, whether of city or country, sometimes have frivolous sons, and that a not unusual correlative of the 'easy come' which sent one city generation out on to the land may have been an 'easy go' which took the next generation off it.

IV

The considerations and reservations just detailed have their bearing on the purchases of land by men of the town; but they must not be allowed to obscure the process which, at most, they qualify and moderate. In England men of the town and trade *did* purchase land; merchants, financiers and middle-class industrialists *did* acquire estates. As we have seen, however, this movement went on through many centuries of English history; and that sector of the movement which falls within the Tudor period seems not to manifest such peculiarities

[1] Lawrence Stone, *An Elizabethan, Sir Horatio Palavicino* (Oxford, 1956), pp. 310–14.

[2] Ibid. pp. 41–97.   [3] Ibid. p. 275.

as to warrant setting it off from the general process. But the process over its whole course is one of the most important phenomena of English social history, and we ought not to shirk the task of assessing its significance.

The movement out onto the land of men who made their fortunes in the towns and in trade is obviously a two-sided affair: it brought such men into the country; it took them away from the city. It is the former aspect of the process that has engaged the attention, or rather the imagination, of historians; for out of it and a bit of whole cloth they have woven the legend that the arrival of the townsmen in the country broke the old patriarchal rural economy and replaced it with a hard ruthless bourgeois commercialism.[1] We have already seen grounds for doubting whether this version of the matter, dramatically so pleasing, is quite in accord with the evidence which shows that merchant transplantation to the land was a very ancient habit, and that many country folk needed no nudging from transplanted merchants to persuade them 'to drive the most for their profit'. Do we have any evidence as to what the impact on the countryside of middle-class land buying actually was, as to what happened when men who had made their fortunes in trade acquired estates? We know something of what happened in the case of one group of such men. In the boom decades of the Western woollen industry all the successful clothiers bought land. Yet of the whole lot of them only one, William Stump, became a real country magnate, whose name was noteworthy beyond his little neighbourhood. For the rest—men like the Hedges with one or two manors—the established aristocracy buffeted them about at the portals of county society long enough to give them a clear idea who the lords of the land really were and then gradually admitted them, to become in a little while indistinguishable, undistinguished, amid the ruck of the lesser gentry.[2] Thus it was when the Wiltshire clothiers bought out onto the land. It is doubtful that things were very different when the same process took place elsewhere in England.

The intensity of the movement of the urban well-to-do from town to country probably varied from time to time, synchronously with the general tides of economic change. Any effort to measure the shifting force of the movement over a considerable span of time is fraught with difficulties. I am not acquainted with any attempt to make such a measurement. Yet without the need to resort to measurement one

[1] Tawney, *Agrarian Problem*, pp. 177–200; ibid. 'Rise of the Gentry', *passim*.
[2] Ramsay, *Wiltshire Woollen Industry*, pp. 46–7.

thing is quite clear. The Tudor merchant landbuyer, like his predecessor in the fifteenth century and his successor in Stuart times, came to the country as an individual seeking admission to the cadres of a flexible, vigorous, self-confident landed aristocracy, a society which a man might enter quietly but which he could scarcely take by assault. Many parvenus did make their way in. They were absorbed by that society without visibly altering it; and the grandsons of these parvenus —now indistinguishable from their country neighbors—assisted in the absorption of the parvenus of a later day. Through the centuries, then, the impact of the merchant landbuyers on rural society was probably slight. At any given time their numbers were too small in proportion to the established families, and their yearning to be accepted was too strong. The so-called middle-class economic traits that merchants are supposed to have brought with them to the land were unmistakably present among many of the men who were already on the land; but while the public exhibition of such traits could do little harm to the social position of families fully established, they might prove hurtful indeed to the social aspirations of a man still smelling of the warehouse and the counting house. Such is the disciplinary power of social snobbery on the climber. What little we know of the history of the parvenu suggests that he was the captive, not the conqueror, of the countryside.

The other side of merchant landbuying—the withdrawal of the buyers from the middle class—has not attracted much attention; yet it is probable that the flight of merchants to the land had a more forceful impact on the class that merchant landbuyers so willingly deserted than it did on the class they tried so hard to enter. For centuries it adversely affected the middle class in the three main ways a group can be affected —in personnel, material and morale. As to personnel some of the most competent members of the middle class were constantly being skimmed off and thereby the complex web of established commercial connections was being snapped. On the level of material—the economic level —we have the story, centuries long, of the drain of capital from commerce and industry to land. Extensive capital accumulations won in the town were spilled out on to the countryside instead of going to finance commercial and industrial expansion. What may be involved is not merely a run of cash from city to country, but a continuous constriction of credit as men whose success had raised their credit high moved slowly but steadily out of trade. There was, of course, some movement in the opposite direction. Some large landowners directly supplied capital for commercial ventures.[1] Merchant landowners with a foot still in the city used their estates for commercial credit.[2] And out of agricultural profits landlords provided younger sons with the where-withal to set up in trade.[3] But however much these processes aug-mented the available commercial credit, when a merchant took him-self and his capital out of town, he decreased it.

The effect of access to gentility through land acquisition on middle-class morale was ambivalent. In one direction it ran a floor under that morale. The preachers in the pulpit might thunder against mercantile greed,[4] the Church look with a somewhat jaundiced eye on many of the processes by which a business man got rich,[5] yet to men not blind to the glories of this world, the transactions that opened the way to those glories could scarcely appear contemptible, let beggarly friars say what they would. And it was quite clear that aristocratic glory was available to city families which invested appropriate quantities of the profits of trade in ways befitting a gentleman.

But as a concomitant to the floor under middle-class morale went a ceiling over it. By moving out to the land the merchant might soon become a gentleman; by the same token, however, he soon ceased to be one of the middle class. Now historians ordinarily assign to the early modern merchant a special point of view that dominates, almost controls, his economic transactions. That point of view leads him to make the prospect of profit, rationally assessed, the primary motive of his business decisions.[6] In sixteenth-century London a man with capital could lend it on good security for ten per cent per annum even when he took no more than the legal rate.[7] The return ordinarily anticipated from the purchase of land was about five per cent.[8] There cannot have been many estates on the land market that offered the merchant a return as good as and much more secure than he could get from doing

[1] The Earl of Leicester: Scott, *Joint-Stock Companies*, i. 79; Sir Edward Sandys and the Earl of Warwick: ibid. i and ii, *passim*.

[2] Thrupp, *Merchant Class*, p. 122.

[3] Ibid., pp. 214, 218, 227.

[4] One preacher attributed the creation of the traditional three orders to God, that of burghers and usurers to the Devil. Owst, *Literature and Pulpit*, p. 554.

[5] Benjamin Nelson, *The Idea of Usury*, History of Ideas, ser. iii (Princeton, 1949), deals most learnedly with one aspect of the Church's complex attitude toward the economic activities of urban enterprisers.

[6] See, for example, Joseph Schumpeter, *Capitalism, Socialism, and Democracy* (New York, 1942), pp. 121–30.

[7] 15 Elizabeth I, c. viii, 2; Thomas Wilson, *A Discourse on Usury*, introd. R. H. Tawney (New York, n.d.), pp. 155–69.

[8] Stone, *An Elizabethan*, p. 275.

business in town.[1] When such a merchant bought land, he was not ordinarily following the lead of rational profit calculation to the place where money grew thickest. By investing money where a greater effort brought a smaller return than it did in town, the rich London landbuyer was sacrificing profit to purchase prestige. When a merchant bought a large estate, he was—and he knew it—buying his way out of his class at a premium price. Such a course of action is destructive of a sense of class solidarity. It is hard to feel unlimited pride in a group whose leading members are fleeing it so persistently. The direction of the flight of the successful men—to the land directly or indirectly—left those who stayed behind no possible doubt as to where they stood. It was a social signpost unmistakably pointing toward the land: This Way Up. Far, then, from testifying to the growth in power of the middle class the process we have examined weakened its head, bled it of wealth, and prevented the stiffening of its backbone. Or, to vary the metaphor, the open door to gentility was an escape hatch whereby the middle class was kept to size. The steady traffic on the social ladder was not a sign that the ladder was shaky or that the rungs had come unstuck; it was on the contrary one of the surest signs that the ladder was stable and the rungs tight.

The place where the actual relations between social groups most effectively display themselves is perhaps at the point of tension or friction between them. Then attitudes buried under layers of amenities in times of harmony are uncovered and displayed. Consequently the letter of an aggrieved knight to the middle-class rulers of a borough throws more light than volumes of routine correspondence on the attitude of the rural aristocracy to the urban middle class. Such a letter Sir George Grey wrote in the 1590s to the rulers of Leicester about a felon they had taken into custody contrary to what Sir George regarded as his right. 'Have him I will', he wrote the mayor,

> ... therefore send him me, for as I live I will try all the friends I have in England, but I will be righted of this your fond and unjust dealing with me. . . . You and your brethren have already annoyed me and all the rest of Her Majesty's Justices in the shire in taking out of my hands what neither belonged to you nor your shallow

---

[1] The degree of security achieved by investment in land in the Tudor period is easy to exaggerate. Legal uncertainties with respect to overall title and with respect to the precise extent of the landlord's rights in a particular estate were concealed liabilities in many a land purchase. In Tudor England good lawyers might cost a new landlord quite as much as bad debts cost an old City hand.

capacities could understand. . . . You and your town have no reason to offer me this wrong . . . for if you be able to cross me in one thing I can requite your town with twenty, and therefore I wish you not to begin with me, for as I am a gentleman I will be revenged one way or another to my contentment and to your dislikes.

To the consternation of the merchant oligarchy, Sir George was as good as his word. He got himself appointed to the commission for assessing the town's subsidy, and all their efforts to dislodge him from the post were in vain. His riposte to the town of Leicester was more than brutal rhetoric. When he said, 'If you be able to cross me in one thing, I can requite you in twenty', he was performing a rough but accurate piece of social analysis.[1]

The elder Cecil once received a nervous and apologetic letter from the Lord Mayor of London that reveals the obverse of the Leicester affair. The Lord Mayor understands that Her Majesty and the nobles have taken offense at the 'excessive spending of venison and other victuals' in the Halls of the Livery Companies. Therefore Common Council has now forbidden excessive feasts and the consumption of venison in the Halls. The major leak of venison, however, is into the taverns, 'resorts of the meaner sort'. The Lord Mayor has drawn up an act to cover the taverns too, 'if your lordship have liking thereof'.[2] The psychology of the Tudor middle class could scarcely be more sharply revealed. No law or command from above is involved here, only an expression of annoyance at the presumption of the Livery Companies in showing a taste for display that is the prerogative of the aristocracy. On the other side there is no protest, no claim of right and no complaint of its infringement. Only the immediate, docile compliance of the subordinate who accepts his position, and the subordinate's trick of laying the blame on *his* inferiors—'the meaner sort'. These pliable men, who are they? The members of the Livery Companies, the Common Council, the very Lord Mayor of London—the *crème de la crème* of the Tudor *bourgeoisie*. It is not thus that the leaders of a ruling class speak and act, nor the leaders of a class that is on its way to rule or that aspires to rule. In the nineteenth century, hungry for game, the middle class with its 'silver bullets' made a shambles of the two-hundred-year-old game laws despite the anguished protest of the upper

[1] *Records of the Borough of Leicester*, ed. M. Bateson, 4 vols. (Cambridge, Eng., 1899–1923), iii. 385–6, 412–14.

[2] *Original Letters*, 2nd ser., iii. 37–8.

class.[1] In Elizabeth's day those 'silver bullets' had barely enough powder of middle-class morale behind them mildly to irritate the prince and the aristocracy.

V

There is little evidence, then, that the Tudor period saw any extraordinary development in the middle class of group consciousness, group pride, or will to power; but of princely concern for the welfare of the middle class and favor to its members the evidence is abundant. Tudor sovereigns elevated merchants and sons of merchants to positions of high public trust; they took a myriad of measures to foster commerce and industry, they granted extensive privileges to certain merchant groups; and finally, they more than once asserted that the welfare of the commonwealth stood in trade.

By concentrating on this set of particulars a historian can make a strong case for the theory that the Tudors especially favored the middle class, that they 'attached themselves to the rising commercial classes', that it was on those classes that 'the new monarchy rested'.[2] But it is not a very fruitful deployment of the historian's art to construct out of one set of particulars a tidy pattern which on consideration of another equally available set of particulars will have to be obliterated or altered drastically. If we undertake a reasonably careful examination of the evidence that purports to demonstrate Tudor favor to the middle class, that evidence either dwindles to insignificance or loses its shape in a mist of ambiguity. If Tudor princes and politicians on certain occasions spoke of merchants and traders as if they were the pillars of the commonwealth, this is a manner of speaking rather widespread among politicians, and to be swallowed with the customary grain of salt. Our inclination to estimate highly the praise Tudor princes and politicians heaped on the merchants must accommodate itself to the fact that those same princes and politicians were lavish in their praise of all sorts of groups and callings—handicraftsmen, sailors, town folk in general, peasants, yeomen, gentry, and noblemen—as the momentary exigencies of politics or rhetoric required.[3] Another set of exigencies was

---

[1] Chester Kirby, 'English Game Law Reform', *Essays in Modern English History in Honor of Wilbur Cortez Abbott* (Cambridge, Mass., 1941), pp. 345–80.

[2] See above, p. 71.

[3] *The Journal of Sir Roger Wilbraham*, Camden Society Publications, 3rd ser., v (London, 1902), *Camden Miscellany*, x, 54. The Council, as Elizabeth neared death, declared the nobility should be ready to 'withstand all attempts against the

likely to call forth another sort of rhetoric, sometimes transforming the mercantile pillars of the commonwealth into 'covetous and insatiable persons, coveting their own lucre', men of 'uncharitable and inordinate covetis', guilty of 'greedy appetites', and 'crafty conspiracies'.[1] In their less public pronouncements the Tudors do not seem to have displayed any passionate addiction to the *bourgeoisie*. A Venetian ambassador noted that they 'rarely troubled themselves about men of business', and Henry VIII once told the Emperor that he was well aware of the 'inordinate desire of gain . . . naturally given to merchants', and stated his intention, 'to give no further credit to them in their suits, clamors, and complaints than is convenient'.[2]

If we can afford to write off the sporadic public assertions by the Tudors of their fondness for the merchants and traders, we cannot write off the reliance of the Tudors on statesmen drawn from the middle class or with very recent middle-class antecedents. From the middle class—or lower—the Tudor monarchy recruited some of its greatest servants—Wolsey, Cromwell, Cecil, Gresham—and many of its lesser ones. Of this fact, however, it is not a necessary consequence that the Tudors felt particularly beholden to the class from which these servants came. And especially it does not follow that the middle class or the common people profited from the elevation to eminence of a few of their members. In their choice of their servants the dominating principle of the great Tudors was an invincible determination to be

peace of *the kingdom whereof they were the principal pillars*'. For ascription of a sustaining role in the commonwealth to the peasantry, townsmen in general, handicraftsmen and sailors, *Statutes of the Realm*, 39 Elizabeth I, c. 2; 1 and 2 Philip and Mary, c. 7; 5 Elizabeth I, c. 7; 32 Henry VIII, c. 14.

[1] The above unflattering descriptions of the rising middle class, engaged in the pursuit of profit in ways to be considered quite legitimate at a later date, are all drawn from official documents: *Statutes of the Realm*, 1 and 2 Philip and Mary, c. 5; 12 Henry VII, c. 6; and a proclamation on the price of sugar, Georg Schanz, *Englische Handelspolitik gegen Ende des Mittelalters*, 2 vols. (Leipzig, 1881), ii. 654–5. See also below, p. 107, for speculators described as 'wolves and cormorants'. A random selection of business men denounced and vilified by the Tudors at one time or another includes speculators in sugar, grain, and dairy products, country clothiers, bankers, the mercantile community of London, and the Company of Merchant Adventurers. A more zealous examination of the statutes would no doubt turn up others. The scope and vehemence of the Tudor indictment of businessmen and business practices lends considerable support to Mr. Stone's reversal of the myth of the middle class in Tudor England: 'All Tudor governments were the most resolute theoretical opponents of . . . those new bourgeois classes from which they are supposed to have derived most support.' Lawrence Stone, 'State Control in 16th Century England', *Economic History Review*, xvii (1947), 115.

[2] The author regrets that he has lost the references for the above quotations.

served well. They chose many of their servants from the middle class because after all that class provided a sizeable pool of talent from which to draw able men, and also because for some purposes, but not for all, it suited their ends to have officials whose fortunes depended primarily on the ruler's favor and not on strong territorial links in the countryside. Precisely because the Tudors chose their servants so well, the advancement they gave to middle-class men conferred no benefit on that class. The men with former mercantile connections or recent mercantile antecedents that the Tudors raised to high position did not carry with them into office any particular sympathy for the middle class or any concern for its special aspirations, if it had such aspirations. On the contrary several of the favorite examples of Tudor reliance on the middle class for Crown servants point in precisely the opposite direction. The aristocracy did not hate Thomas Cardinal Wolsey, son of a butcher of Ipswich, because of any propensity on his part to offend their noble sensibilities by an unseemly display of middle-class traits. In a large measure they hated him—'the haughtiest man alive', 'the proudest prelate that ever breathed'—so passionately because he far surpassed them all in two particularly aristocratic virtues—magnificence and arrogance.[1] Far from seeking to counteract the hatred of the courtiers by wooing the middle class—small good a successful wooing would have done him anyway—Wolsey thoroughly alienated the merchants by imposing heavy burdens on them in order to support his megalomaniac foreign policy.[2] When Thomas Cromwell, a man of antecedents inordinately obscure and mean,[3] reached the pinnacle of his power, he displayed an arrogance and magnificence not far surpassed by his old master Wolsey. He indicated his feeling for the middle class whence he came, when he considered a measure to prohibit merchants from acquiring any considerable amount of land. The proposal, if put into law and enforced, would have interposed a permanent barrier between the middle class and the aristocracy in which Cromwell had gained a foothold for his family.[4] William Cecil's grandfather—a man of humble origins—had set his family on the way to greatness by acquiring office and acquiring land. Cecil's father took the further step of providing his son with a good education.[5] William Cecil himself,

[1] A. F. Pollard, *Wolsey* (London, 1929), *passim*, esp. pp. 318–19, 325–7.
[2] Edward Hall, *Chronicle*, ed. H. Ellis (London, 1809), pp. 645–6.
[3] R. B. Merriman, *Life and Letters of Thomas Cromwell*, 2 vols. (Oxford, 1902), i. 1–5.　　　　　　　　　　　[4] Thomson, *Two Centuries*, p. 17.
[5] Conyers Read, *Mr. Secretary Cecil and Queen Elizabeth* (New York, 1955), pp. 17–32.

however, gave consideration to a measure that would have prevented families of like origin from following a similar path to glory. Besides incorporating Cromwell's plan for keeping the middle class out of the land market, this scheme would have reserved public office for the aristocracy and barred middle-class families from the kind of education that would fit them for the public service.[1] At least Cecil tried to provide his grandfather, whose family policy he profited from and repudiated, with a fancier set of ancestors than that wise old man was ever likely to have claimed. In his ardent quest for release from his middle-class or lower-class antecedents he resorted to genealogical fakers with a patience and a persistence and at a cost that deserved a better reward than the flimsy fantasies which his hired ancestor-manufacturers turned out for him.[2] Sir Thomas Gresham was for many years the financial agent of the Tudors in Europe's money markets, England's nearest approach in his day to a great financier of the continental type. If any middle-class servant of the Tudors should have been dominated by the concerns of his class, it was Gresham. Yet he, too, proved a Judas. For he hatched the neat dishonest little scheme whereby Elizabeth held the English cloth fleet to ransom. She refused to let it clear port until the merchants had agreed to pay her debt in Antwerp in good Flemish money and, at a considerable loss, accept repayment in London in English pounds.[3] Thus the Tudor public service deprived the middle class of some of its ablest minds, and the risen men showed no inclination to favor the class whence they came in a way that might have compensated that class materially for its loss in personnel.

This statement may seem to run counter to the frequent allegation that the Tudors especially favored commerce. In fact the concern of the Tudors to foster trade was at once traditional and highly selective. It was part of a prince's duty to promote the prosperity of the commonwealth, and since the prosperity of many subjects depended on the advancement of commerce, the prince should support the effort of the merchants. This doctrine was at least a couple of hundred years old in the sixteenth century. Far from being a modern heresy of the middle-class Tudors, it was impeccably orthodox, accepted as axiomatic by every ruler in Europe. But the general axiom admitted of numerous

[1] *Tudor Economic Documents*, ii. 326.

[2] *Hatfield MSS.*, xiii. 103, 140, 198, 397.

[3] Burgon, *Gresham*, i. 257–62; also Raymond de Roover, *Gresham on Foreign Exchange* (Cambridge, Mass., 1949), p. 220.

exceptions. The domestic corn merchant and the cattle merchant, the exporter of the outports, the importer of luxury goods, the shippers of corn and timber, the entrepreneurs who organized the village cloth industry—at one time or another, all these learned by bitter experience that their particular business did not come within the bounds of the trade that the Tudors decided to foster.[1] The corn brogger, the wool bodger, the Bristol merchant, the country clothier, the independent exporter must have found in Tudor concern for trade a continuous frustration and impediment to their quest for profit, and in Tudor professions of love for the merchant in general a poor compensation for the constriction and prohibition of their particular business activities.

What remains then of the notion that the Tudors especially favored and relied on the middle class? Simply this: that an undeniably close relationship was maintained between the government of Elizabeth and a small inner coterie of Tudor merchant-bankers. To the best of my knowledge the members of this coterie have never been studied as a group, although they appear to have exercised a considerable influence on certain phases of Elizabethan policy. The line of policy, however, that they seem to have sponsored, while of uncertain impact on the other social orders, was clearly and immediately to the disadvantage of almost every member of the middle class except themselves. By means of charters granting trade monopolies in particular foreign lands to companies, admissions to which they largely controlled, they sought to squeeze out that bane of the cartel, the independent export merchant.[2] At the same time they made their monopolies a veritable

---

[1] See above, p. 100, n. 1, and below, p. 104, n. 1 and 2. See also 5 Elizabeth I, c. 12 (cattle merchants), 25 Henry VIII, c. 18 (country clothiers), 5 Elizabeth I, c. 7 (fine-ware imports).

[2] Scott, ii, *passim;* Ephraim Lipson, *Economic History of England*, 4th ed., 3 vols. (London, 1947), ii. 196–360; 364–7. *Select Charters of Trading Companies*, ed. C. T. Carr, Selden Society Publications, xxviii (London, 1913), introd. and pp. 1–43. The propensity of the adherents of the myth of the middle class in Tudor England to rely on metahistory and to avoid exact historical investigation is nowhere more evident than with respect to the Tudor mercantile community. The framework for a study of that community was provided forty-odd years ago by George Unwin's 'The Merchant Adventurers' Company in the Reign of Elizabeth', *Studies in Economic History* (London, 1913). It seems beyond doubt that the materials necessary for the reconstruction of the personnel and practices of this community are available, many of them in print. Such a reconstruction would do much to remove discussion of the Tudor middle class from the realm of banal generalizations rooted in ideological postulates rather than in historical data. But a comprehensive investigation of that community is yet to be made.

Barmecide's feast for the outport merchants, a groaning board at which such merchants could sit but not eat.[1] Their control of export channels placed them in a favorable position to put the squeeze on middle-class producers for the export trade and notably on the country clothiers.[2] Their exclusive chartered position in several of the great continental marts gave them an advantage over independent import merchants, and in the London market they aimed to prevent organizers of industrial production from winning a place for themselves in commerce.

If the privileges of the London clique hung like an anchor on other sectors of the middle class, yet they were not wrenched from the hands of reluctant princes. They were freely granted because Elizabethan statesmen firmly believed in what was called a well-ordered trade,[3] and the privileges were merely applications of that belief to a particular sector of commercial activity. But although the special position of the great London merchant was the result of the execution of pre-established Court policy, such favor was still to be had only at a price. For serving as financial agents of the Crown,[4] for holding their privileges as tenants-at-will of the Crown,[5] for splitting their take with insatiably greedy court caterpillars in order to hold on to their lucrative oligopolies,[6] for being squeezed out of some of their gains by needy rulers,[7]

---

[1] See, for example, the complaint of Southampton about the effect on its trade of the London-controlled Muscovy Company, and the Spanish Company, both having charters of exclusive privilege. Alwyn Ruddock, 'London Capitalists and the Decline of Southampton in the Early Tudor Period', *Economic History Review*, 2nd ser., ii (1949), 149–50; see also the complaint of the merchants of Hull, *Tudor Economic Documents*, ii. 49–50.

[2] *Acts of the Privy Council*, new ser., iii. 19–20.

[3] Dozens on dozens of Tudor measures of economic regulation make the due and proper ordering of one activity or another their theme and their pretext. As one example among many, see 5 Elizabeth I, c. 12.

[4] F. C. Dietz, *English Public Finance, 1558–1641* (New York, 1932), pp. 124, 194. For scattered but significant observations on the 'court' merchants, see H. R. Trevor-Roper's most interesting study, 'The Gentry, 1540–1640', *Economic Review*, Supplements, 1 (1953).

[5] The suspension of the Levant Company charter prior to its expiry in 1599 was a fitting prelude to the abolition of the privileges of the Merchant Adventurers in 1614 in favor of Alderman Cockayne's crackbrained scheme. For the former see Scott, *Joint-Stock Companies*, ii. 87; for the latter, Astrid Friis, *Alderman Cockayne's Project and the Cloth Trade* (Copenhagen, 1927).

[6] For a particularly scandalous combination of courtier chicanery and low commercial maneuvering, see the account of the Earl of Cumberland's monopoly in Friis, *Alderman Cockayne's Project*, pp. 72–3.

[7] In addition to the ransom job on the Merchant Adventurers, mentioned above, p. 102, see the description of the squeeze put on the Levant Company's currant monopoly in Scott, *Joint-Stock Companies*, ii. 87.

for acting as receivers in bankruptcy to the more wildly extravagant among the court aristocracy,[1] for all these services the great London merchants were compensated even to abundance by the steady streams of gold and silver that flowed into their coffers. But underlying every explicit and specific grant of favor was a general but unexpressed condition—that the richest and most powerful members of the middle class should have their interest detached from that of their own class and the country at large and bound with shackles of gold to the court complex. This process was not uniquely English. Already on the continent an early generation of merchant-bankers of the Valois and the Hapsburgs had learned to their cost what happens to business men who put their trust in princes.[2] Yet for a good while to come, the Court rode the wave of the future, and in France for two centuries the unification of the middle class was impeded and the expansion of commerce and industry itself constricted by the intra-class schism that drew the most successful merchants and financiers into the role of court bankers, battening off royal finances and court-controlled monopolies, learning sometimes too late that the Court always took a very large *quid pro quo*. In Elizabethan England we can discern the configuration of just such a group of Court-bound capitalists. Their later political history is yet to be written. But it is surely of some significance that at the verge of the Civil War the City of London was secured for Parliament by a virtual *coup d'état* of the Common Council against the Royalist aldermen, the very inner circle of the Court-bound merchant bankers.[3]

VI

Despite apparent antithesis in word and action, the Tudor attitude toward the middle class was neither self-contradictory nor ambiguous, but intelligible and consistent in the light of Tudor policy. Although occasionally distorted by the immediate imperatives of war, diplomacy

[1] Stone, 'Anatomy', *passim.*

[2] R. Ehrenberg, *Capital and Finance in the Age of the Renaissance*, trans. H. M. Lucas (London, 1928), pp. 149–50, 159–60, 161–336; *Histoire de France*, ed. E. Lavisse, v, pt. 1, H. Lemonnier, *Les Guerres d'Italie—La France sous Charles VIII, Louis XII, et François Ier* (Paris, 1911), pp. 228–35.

[3] 'A letter from Mercurius Civicus to Mercurius Rusticus; or London's Confession, but not Repentance', *Somers Tracts*, ed. Walter Scott, 13 vols. (London, 1809–15), iv, 587–98.

and defense,[1] perverted by fiscal stringencies,[2] and inhibited by a tough legal structure of which the Henrys and Elizabeth were remarkably respectful, Tudor policy was fundamentally coherent and solid. Well it might be, since it was erected on old and deep-set ideas. The hierarchical organic conception of society, once the scholastic idealization of thirteenth-century realities,[3] then in the waning Middle Ages the vehicle of a vigorous social criticism,[4] becomes with the Tudors the mold of policy, the guide to action. To implement a social ideal older than Thomas Aquinas those imperious dynasts brought a new faith, as naïve as our own, in the efficacy of government regulation to cure all ills. The world was out of joint and—men being sinful creatures—it would always tend to get out of joint, but the Tudors had no doubt that they were born to set it right.[5]

What was new about Tudor policy lay not in the social theory at its base, but in its magnification of the active regulatory role of the royal government as the means by which society might approximate its own ideal. The whole matter was once put in a nutshell by men who had the highest authority for putting it there. A food shortage had hit England, caused a sharp and sudden rise in the cost of living, and then quickly vanished. Nevertheless, wrote Elizabeth's Privy Council to the Justices of the Peace of Norfolk, 'a great number of wicked people

[1] Bacon's famous aphorism about Henry VII subordinating considerations of plenty to considerations of power is far too categorical to apply to all the Tudors; limited to suggest that they put considerations of policy ahead of the desire of English merchants to enrich themselves it comes fairly close to the truth. Stone, 'State Control', *passim*.   [2] Dietz, *English Public Finance*, *passim*.

[3] Among the many expositions of this theory in its thirteenth-century version, Gierke's remains one of the best: Otto Gierke, *Political Theories of the Middle Age*, trans. with introd. by F. W. Maitland (Cambridge, Eng., 1900). Ruth Mohl, *The Three Estates in Medieval and Renaissance Literature*, Columbia University studies in English and comparative literature (New York, 1933), gives a fine account of variations rung on the theme in medieval popular literature.

[4] The use of the theory as a framework for social criticism has its most eminent English exemplar in *Piers Plowman*. Alain Chartier, *Le Quadrilogue investif*, ed. E. Droz, Les Classiques français du moyen âge, xxxii (Paris, 1923), is a good example in French of a similar use of the hierarchical organic conception. See Owst, *Literature and Pulpit*, pp. 210–470, for the clergy's habitual use of hierarchical theory as the basis of social criticism.

[5] While those who have written of Tudor regulatory activity—Tawney, Unwin, Cunningham—may differ as to its motive and efficacy, there is no difference of opinion among them about the unlimited range of that policy. The most recent studies of Tudor policy are F. J. Fisher, 'Commercial Trends and Policies in 16th Century England', *Economic History Review*, x (1940), 95–117 and L. Stone, 'State Control', *Economic History Review*, xvii (1947), 103–20. An autarkic policy based on fear accounts for much that seems erratic in Tudor social politics, according to Mr. Stone.

. . . more like to wolves and cormorants than to natural men . . . most covetously . . .' try to 'hold up the late great price of corn and all other victuals by engrossing the same into their private hands'. They do this by buying up victuals while they are still in the farmers' fields, forestalling the food supply before it can be 'brought to the ordinary market for to be bought by the poorer number'. The Justices of the Peace, the communication continues, have ample authority under existing laws and orders, to deal with the situation. They are commanded 'to cause diligent inquisition to be made . . . as well in places of liberties and towns corporate as in all other places' in their county to 'apprehend such engrossers . . . take from them such as they shall unlawfully buy, . . . compel them to revoke their unlawful bargains, and . . . send up to us some of the most notable offenders to be ordered by us'. The Justices were also to work out other ways 'to restrain these lamentable abuses and . . . to bring all manner of victuals to a reasonable price . . . so that the poor may not be longer oppressed. . . . We have heard,' the letter goes on indignantly, 'that men . . . of good livelihood and in estimation of worship . . . enrich themselves by this kind of engrossing. We do warn you all to have a special care . . . to certify us of their names and thereby to avoid the just offense of the inferior sort which cannot be but grieved to see such corruption in the better sort suffered without restraint.' [1]

Than commodity speculation no economic activity could be more middle-class; but in Tudor eyes men who engaged in it were as wolves and cormorants. The hand of government lay heavily on these men, for by driving the poor to despair they endangered the order of the commonwealth. But that hand was not indifferent to class lines. It fell most heavily on offenders of the highest rank. Necessarily so, since like their predecessors in the Middle Ages the Tudors relied on example no less than on command and coercion in the work of governance, and the greater the offender the more disastrous and widespread the psychological effect of his offense on those beneath him in status. But if the wrath of the Tudors was especially vehement against offenders 'in estimation of worship', still it was precisely to men 'in estimation of worship' that they turned in order to repress offenders of whatever class. For centuries the rulers of the towns had striven to keep the rulers of the countryside and the officers of the prince from meddling in their affairs. That was the crux of the struggle for town charters; and

[1] *The Official Papers of Sir Nathaniel Bacon*, Camden Society Publications, 3rd ser., xxvi (London, 1915), 140-41.

the more successful boroughs had even managed to have their own officials empowered as justices to enforce royal orders. But in the letter we have just looked at it is not magistrates of the towns who are called on to suppress engrossing among their own subjects. In the face of the royal command charters were of no avail to preserve the middle class from its betters; town liberties were paper walls that crumbled before the Justices of Peace, rulers of the countryside who were also officers of the Crown. The letter to the Justices of Norfolk was thus a precise reflection of the theory and practice of Tudor policy; and to reflect that policy the men who issued it—the members of Queen Elizabeth's Privy Council in 1597—had credentials that can hardly be impugned. From such a source at such a date, it epitomizes a century of experience in Tudor governance, an experience which, whatever ethical judgment be passed on it, was a remarkable feat of the art of politics. The ideal of Tudor statesmen was organic: society was made up of members performing different functions for the common good. The ideal was also hierarchical: though all parts of the commonwealth were indispensable, they were not equal, but differed in degree and excellence as well as in kind. The role of policy was to maintain and support good order as good order had been understood for several centuries—social peace and harmony in a status-based society.

To this end, on the positive side, it was royal policy to advance the prosperity of all estates and to remedy their legitimate grievances. On the negative side it was relentlessly to repress violent breaches of order, riot, sedition, and rebellion, and to subject the unregulated desires and particular interests of individuals and groups to the good order and harmony of the commonwealth. Many apparent inconsistencies in Tudor policy are merely expressions of the positive and negative sides of that policy—positively to encourage and support men and groups that served well in their place, negatively sharply to rap the knuckles of men and groups that pushed out of their place and disrupted the social order. The Tudors did not believe that the governing power should align itself on the side of one class and against another. From the point of view of Tudor social theory such an alignment would be stupid and perverse. Theory here had roots in experience. In his essay, 'Of Seditions and Troubles', Francis Bacon, the most articulate though not the wisest Tudor statesman, epitomized both theory and experience.[1] Seditions and troubles, the bane of commonwealths, are not

[1] Francis Bacon, *The Essayes or Counsels Civill and Morall*, Essay XV, 'Of Seditions and Troubles'.

prevented but evoked by the fixed alliance of the prince with or against particular groups and interests. Such alliances drive the repressed to rebellion out of desperation and encourage the oppressor to sedition out of arrogance. The conspiracies of the overmighty and the wild violence of the downtrodden are but heads and tails of the same coin —a disordered commonwealth.

Tudor policy was usually quite tender of vested interests. It protected old ones and created new ones in the emergent forms of enterprise. It thus sought to establish itself in a regulatory position *vis à vis* the whole range of commercial and industrial life.[1] Vested interests should be protected and the more vested the more protected, since to such interests the hopes, aspirations, and security of so many men were bound. The idea that a whole local industry should be wiped out because the same goods could be produced cheaper elsewhere made no sense to the Tudors, and if their economics were rather crude, their knowledge of the cost of suppressing the riots and rebellions of men thrown out of work, being founded on experience, was most precise.[2] A well-regulated trade and a well-regulated industry were simply corollaries of a well-regulated commonwealth, just as a well-regulated agriculture was. It was not the policy of the Tudors either to stand mulishly athwart the path of change, or to allow it free rein, but to guide it, to bring it as they said to some good rule conformable with good order. The vast mass of Tudor legislation on economic activities rests solidly on three principles—privilege, regulation, supervision. The purpose was to prevent the unchecked greed and ambition of any group—middle-class or other—from dislocating the social order.

The men of the middle class had an important function in this organic hierarchical commonwealth, as the leading people of the towns, 'the better sort', the 'discreet, sad, and well-disposed persons', the 'abler people' at least in a fiscal sense. Such men could effectively be held responsible for the 'good rule, governance, and political demeaning'

---

[1] J. U. Nef, *Industry and Government in France and England, 1540–1640*, Memoirs of the American Philosophical Society, xv (Philadelphia, 1940), 25–57. Nef doubts the efficacy of the Crown's efforts, but his most telling evidence of failure is based mainly on judicial decisions after 1603.

[2] Many Tudor policies that stood athwart the path of economic 'progress', as we with the advantage of four hundred years of hindsight view it, even policies doomed to failure at the outset, served the purpose of saving their subjects from despair. If in effect the Tudors could do nothing for this or that depressed group, they at least made it clear that it would not be from want of trying. They knew well that 'the politic . . . nourishing and entertaining of hopes . . . is one of the best antidotes against the poison of discontentments', Bacon, *loc. cit.*

of their charges; they could also be held to make good out of their pockets any deficits in the taxes due from their boroughs. The Tudors, interfering as their predecessors never had, to secure some uniformity in borough rule, liked to have the governments of the municipalities in the hands of men of substance. They encouraged the drift toward urban oligarchy which antedated the accession of Henry VII, since that drift tended to put the merchant above the craftsman, as in Tudor theory he should be.[1] It well comported with Tudor conceptions to concentrate the administration of the towns in the hands of the richer few, it did not comport with such conceptions for the central Government to repose blind faith in its chosen instruments. If according to Tudor theory it was a part of good policy to rely on the 'better sort' in ruling the towns, it was equally a part of good policy to suspect that the better sort would abuse the trust reposed in them, that they would become overbearing and tyrannical, acting in their own interest against that of the lesser folk. The Privy Council did not deal gently with middle-class oligarchs whose misconduct of local affairs was a grievance to the poor. Nor did it gladly suffer town councils which could not rule without faction and disorder, whatever the cause. Such councils were likely to find themselves under chilly scrutiny by a few of the neighboring gentry, bearing a special commission from the Crown to look into the situation with a view to bringing it to order.[2] Therein the Tudors indicated both the tentative character of their reliance on the middle class and the place they reserved for it in the structure of society.

In the good policy of the well-ordered commonwealth the middle class had a further role assigned to it. As a contemporary observer noted, the Government had 'policies to enrich the merchant and artizan by statute and law made for their benefits for which they give the prince a great sum of money and yearly rent and also get them great wealth thereby to be more able to contribute to the subsidies, taxes and wars'.[3]

To transfer the organic analogy to the barnyard, the Tudors regarded the middle class as the milch herd of the commonwealth. They

[1] James Tait, *The Medieval English Borough*, University of Manchester Historical Series, lxx (Manchester, 1936), 321–30. The preamble to the act transforming Leicester and Northampton into closed boroughs gives clear expression to the Tudor predilection in the matter of town government. *Rotuli Parliamentorum*, vi. 432*a*–433*a*.

[2] *The Official Papers of Sir Nathaniel Bacon*, pp. 16–17.

[3] Wilson, *State of England*, pp. 39–40.

had firmly grasped the sound lactogenic principle, propagated by a present-day American dairy, that contented cows give richer milk. They carefully tended their herd as long as it docilely did what was required of it, but woe to the milker that forgot its place and imagined that the attention it received licensed it to act like a bull in a china shop. We may close our investigation of the attitude of the Tudors toward the middle class with a tragi-comic illustration—the story of Henry VIII and the recalcitrant Londoner.

In 1544, with his finances groaning under the strain of war, Henry had asked for a benevolence for the prosecution of the campaign against Scotland. In the whole Court of Aldermen one man alone, Richard Reed, had the gumption or presumption to refuse to be benevolent despite all persuasion and reasoning. A milch cow was refusing to be milked, a habit Henry was loath to encourage. He had no taste for a merchant 'who for the defense of the realm and for the continuance of his quiet life . . . could not find in his heart to disburse a small quantity of his substance'. He felt that Richard Reed had better do 'some service for his country with his body whereby he might be somewhat instructed of the difference between sitting quietly in his house and the travail and danger which others do daily sustain'. So in the middle of January he dispatched the Alderman 'unto School' to the Warden of the Middle Marches, 'there to serve as a soldier . . . at his own charge' in the Scottish campaign. With fine didactic zeal Henry added that to insure Reed's education the Warden was to put him in positions of 'ordinary danger and in such a place in garrison as he may feel what pains other poor soldiers abide abroad in the King's service'. He was to be used 'in all things after the sharp military discipline of the northern wars'. At the end of this rigorous schooling the royal pedagogue had hopes that his recalcitrant pupil would at least know 'the smart of his folly and sturdy disobedience'.[1] The lesson seems to have been faithfully administered by the Warden, since the next we hear of Alderman Reed he is a prisoner of war of the enemy.[2] This unplanned extension course probably gave the unlucky London alderman ample opportunity during the long northern winter well to understand to what extent, in what sense, and for what purpose the Tudors relied on the commercial middle classes.

[1] *Illustrations of British History* . . ., ed. Edmund Lodge, 3 vols. (London, 1838), i. 99–100.
[2] Ibid. i. 124–5.

VII

We have tried to clear away the miasma of myth that surrounds the history of the middle class in Tudor England. We did so in the hope of diminishing the widespread faith in that myth in its wider provenance as the ultimate solution of all the problems of explanations in European history from the eleventh century on. For the sake of coherent discourse and mere common sense we have insisted on maintaining a fairly consistent definition of the group of men that comprised the middle class.

Now if we follow the actual history of this group from the eleventh century to the nineteenth in Europe, we can but be impressed at the irregular and sporadic character of its development in size, wealth, and effective power in relation to other groups. There are times and places where it absorbs wealth at a spectacular rate for decades and then relapses into political impotence, social insignificance and economic somnolence for centuries.[1] For a while its spokesmen lord it over the lords themselves; and then an alteration in the political climate, hard times, devastating war, reduce the significance of the group to its strictly economic limits of fulfilling a necessary function for the maintenance of society.

This curiously irregular development of the middle class, so little impelled from within, so much at the mercy of the shape of things beyond its control, should stand as a warning against the habit of thought which explains all the great alterations in European history in terms of its rise, the middle class thereby assuming the role of first mover self-moved. Like the development of theological conceptions, political and administrative institutions, and technology—to name but a few—through the centuries the development of social classes in general and the middle class in particular is sporadic, and discontinuous. Historical explanation resting on a conception so poor in content, so deficient in internal cohesion and historical dynamic as the role of the rising middle class cannot sustain a fabric so elaborate and complex as the civilization of the West over a period of seven hundred years.

It is by no means my intention to deny the historical importance of the rise of the middle class. In the war of words preceding the Reform Bill of 1832, one proponent after another of that measure argued that its peculiar merit lay in placing the borough franchise in the hands of

[1] The history of Flanders, the Upper Rhine and parts of Italy at various eras of their development illustrates this point.

those pre-eminently fit by their character and virtues to control the political destinies of England. The provisions for borough franchise in that bill did in effect transfer the power to choose a majority in the House of Commons to the group whose right to the designation of middle class I would not deny. Here indeed the spokesmen for the middle class demanded for it a sort of hegemony over English society. But in 1832 Henry VIII had been mouldering in his grave for nearly three centuries, Elizabeth for nearly two and a half. In the days of Henry and Elizabeth the urban middle class asked for no better place in society than that which it had enjoyed in the Middle Ages. Its new riches evoked from it no new social pretensions, no new unrest, no new ideology. The most conspicuous badges of success for a middle-class man were eminence at law, enjoyment of court office or royal favor, and the extensive purchase of land, by means of all of which he climbed out of his class. The stereotyped cultural attitude toward such climbing was disapproval. In literature this disapproval frequently found expression; but most of the writings scoffing at and denouncing the middle-class climber seem to be of aristocratic rather than bourgeois provenance and orientation. Tudor literature does not charge the climber with treachery for deserting his class in its struggle against its enemies after the fashion of later working-class attacks on complaisant rich trade union leaders. The literary jibe at the climber has as its context the hierarchical organic conception of society; it censures and sneers at him for thrusting his way in among his betters.[1] In literature and in life the landed aristocracy is abundantly self-confident. In literature and in life the only threat that gives it concern comes, not from the middle class, but from the peasantry and the rabble—Cade in literature, Kett in life. The only spectre it knows bears the image of Jacquerie, not of Jacobins. The Tudor middle class is no threat to aristocracy or monarchy because it has no ideology of class war or even of class rivalry. It does not seize on More's *Utopia* and the propaganda of the 'commonwealth' group of social critics, as the man of 1789 seizes on the writings of Rousseau and the *philosophes*, to claim in the

---

[1] The literature setting forth middle-class status pretensions in the Tudor age seems rather mild in its claims. It scarcely gets beyond the assertion that trade does not derogate from gentility, and that by Genoese and Venetian precedents great merchants in large-scale long-distance trading were not engaged in dishonorable transactions. In all this there is nothing of the tone of the trumpet blast against the monstrous regiment of aristocracy. This lack of robust assertiveness *vis-à-vis* the aristocracy is evident in the quotations from Elizabethan literature that Dr. Wright has included in the chapter on 'The Citizen's Pride' in his book *Middle-Class Culture*, pp. 19–42.

name of the people the right to power. To his own question, 'What is the Third Estate?' Abbe Sieyès answered, 'Everything'. His answer spoke the mind of the revolutionary middle class in France in the last days of the *ancien régime*. That answer would scarcely have occurred to the members of the middle class in Tudor England; indeed that answer would not even have been intelligible to them.

In nineteenth-century England an assertive, self-confident, politically alert, overwhelmingly rich social class, the middle class, was demanding its place in the sun of power and prestige. In the sixteenth century the most successful members of an amorphous congeries of non-agrarian economic groups, all modest in mien and modest in pretensions, were clambering out of their groups to the place where the sun was, and long was to remain, among the landed gentlemen and noblemen of England. It is not the purpose of this paper to explain the phenomenon of 1832, but only to say of Tudor England, it was not then, it was not there.

It could hardly be then or there as long as the middle class gave unwavering credit to a hierarchical organic conception of society, which placed the ultimate goal of middle-class striving not within the class but beyond it. The notion that the conception of society, surviving the economic cataclysm of the fifteenth century to be reasserted with renewed vigor in the sixteenth, could be destroyed by the economic revival and the rise in prices of the Tudor age indicates a failure to grasp the tenacity and elasticity of the hierarchical idea. It overlooks the fact that an effective reaffirmation of the conception was everywhere coincident with the revival. If we must find an explanation of the collapse of the hierarchical idea—and until it took place the consolidation and activation of a middle class was impossible—we had best look to those related movements, the Calvinist revolts and the development of absolutism. The relation between the two is intricate. Essentially we may say that on the theoretical side absolutist theory wrenched the idea of hierarchy from its context in the nature of things and made it a matter of the prince's will.[1] On the practical side it broke that complex

[1] The contrast between the old and the new can be seen by setting Claude Seyssel's *Grand Monarchie de France* against Hobbes's *Leviathan*. The two works were written a century and a half apart. For Seyssel, the social order itself is one of the main bridles on the King; along with religion and justice, it acts not to diminish the real power of the ruler but to bring his will in conformity to reason and right. In Hobbes all three bridles are expressly destroyed. The social order, religion, and justice are whatever the sovereign wills, and there is no external standard of reason or right in relation to which he can be judged. See especially Hobbes, *Leviathan*, part 2, Chapter 18.

of ties which bound court and country together in one commonwealth and thereby provided an impulse for a revision of the social order which was indissolubly linked with the commonwealth.[1]

From the other side, Calvinism, although socially conservative to the core and engaged in no direct assault on the hierarchical conception, nevertheless undermined the hierarchical structures. It did so not by attacking the theory, but by subordinating the practice to another and paramount consideration. That consideration was the *Regnum Christi*, and the chosen instrument for effecting the rule of Christ on Earth was the community of Saints, the fellowship of the Elect.[2] The Calvinist fellowship did not attack the hierarchical idea, but it spiritually transcended it and practically minimized it. In the heat of Holy War, Oliver Cromwell preferred 'a plain russet-coated captain that knows what he fights for, and loves what he knows' to 'that which you call a gentleman and is nothing else'.[3] And in the Kingdom where Christ ruled, King James himself, as Andrew Melville told him, was but 'God's silly vassal'.[4] 'This cause' a Puritan proclaimed in an Elizabethan Parliament, stretches 'further and higher than the monarchy of the whole world'. It is 'God's, the rest are all but terrene, yea trifles, call you them never so great, or pretend you they import never so much; subsidies, crowns, kingdoms, I know not what they are in comparison of this'.[5]

Finally the conception of hierarchy in society and polity was, as we have seen, ultimately linked with a world view, a universal vision, that saw the whole cosmos under the aspect of hierarchy—the great chain

[1] Some conception of the durability of institutions drawing part of their strength from the country rather than the court can be gathered from two recent studies of French government in the period of the new monarchy, Roger Doucet, *Les Institutions de la France au XVIᵉ Siècle*, 2 vols. (Paris, 1948), and Gaston Zeller, *Les Institutions de la France au XVIᵉ Siècle* (Paris, 1948). The complex network of relationships by means of which the so-called new monarchs harness court and country together in a princely commonwealth has not been adequately recognized or investigated. I have tried to touch on one aspect of this matter in 'The Education of the Aristocracy in the Renaissance', Essay 4 in this volume. In an introduction to a translation of Claude Seyssel's *Grand Monarchie de France* and in a comparative study of the French *gouverneur*, the Netherland *stadholder* and the English Lord-Lieutenant I hope in the future to deal with other aspects of it.
[2] Karlfried Frölich, *Gottesreich, Welt, und Kirche bei Calvin* (Munich, 1930).
[3] *The Writings and Speeches of Oliver Cromwell*, ed. W. C. Abbott, 4 vols. (Cambridge, Mass., 1937–47), i. 256.
[4] S. R. Gardiner, *History of England from the Accession of James I to the Outbreak of the Civil War, 1603–1642*, 10 vols. (London, 1883), i. 54.
[5] Pistor in the Parliament of 1571, *Journals of all the Parliaments During the Reign of Elizabeth*, collected by Sir Simonds Dewes (London, 1682), p. 166, col. B.

of being.[1] The more acute men of the seventeenth century believed that the insights of science and the arguments of Cartesian philosophy alike shattered that world view. With the passion for oneness and appetite for analogy that has been a persistent trait of Western thought men were soon shaping their ideas of human affairs after a cosmic model that knew no hierarchy. The graded social reality once deemed the reflection of natural law and the Will of God became a rank human deviation from the law of nature and Nature's God, who had created all men equal.[2]

Even after the hierarchical theory collapsed, the interests that it had sanctified survived, and its beneficiaries showed no inclination to surrender their privileges merely because enlightened minds considered them absurd and infamous. The eighteenth century was no doubt the twilight of the old regime, but only a bold prophet could have been certain that it was the moment before the dawn of the new. The middle class in Europe did not enter the Promised Land gently and gradually, by a sort of imperceptible oozing 'development'. It arrived in a holocaust, spattered with its own blood and the blood of its enemies. The only reason that could have convinced those enemies was the *ultima ratio*—the victorious exercise of force. Valmy, the great campaigns of the Army of the Republic, the blood-bath of the Terror, heralded the arrival of the middle class in a universal language that all Europe understood. And the history of those desperate years in the early 1790s, the series of near things and victories snatched from the jaws of defeat leave one with a sharp sense of how far short of inevitable that arrival was, how easily it might have been otherwise. Spiritually men are not islands, even an Englishman is not an island. So if we wish to understand the triumph of the English middle class in 1832, we may do well to think less on the rising middle class in Tudor England the better to remember that in 1789 there was a revolution in France.

[1] Arthur Lovejoy, *The Great Chain of Being* (Cambridge, Mass., 1936).
[2] An elaborate recent discussion of this development in Hiram Hayden, *The Counter-Renaissance* (New York, 1950).

6

Storm Over the Gentry *

I

HERE IS ONE story about the Great Rebellion.
In the hundred years between 1540 and 1640 England was swept by a durable economic tidal wave—the Price Revolution. Under the impact of that tidal wave prices rose at least threefold in about a century. On men with relatively fixed incomes and inflexible standards of consumption the rise in prices wrought havoc. Indeed it decisively altered the balance of property in England. The rural rentiers sank; the rural entrepreneurs came to the top. The crown lost property. More important, so did the aristocracy and some of the conservative landlords. Backward men by and large, medieval in their habits of thought and life, they spent beyond the shrinking yield of their unimproved estates, and soon those estates were feeding a hungry land market. What these living relics of a departed age lost, a new class gained. The new class was the rising gentry. Owners of estates of middling size, recruited from among the local landholders, the lawyers, and the merchants, they thrived by methods familiar to those merchants, with whom indeed they formed but a single social class. Estate management and especially cultivation of the demesne made them rich; rational farming practices enabled them to buy lands that for thriftlesssness and insouciance the aristocracy was forced to sell. To these 'economic realities', these 'social facts', these 'impersonal forces' of the age, 'political institutions' had to adapt themselves. When the days of reckoning came in the 1640s, they did not make a social change; they brought to completion and placed a political seal on a social change which had already taken place. The man who saw and set down the basic facts was the author of Oceana, James Harrington. His work epitomized the passing of the aristocracy and the rise of the middle-class gentry, and new rulers of England.[1]
So Professor R. H. Tawney, with an assist from Mr. Lawrence Stone.

* A shorter version of this essay without scholarly apparatus appeared in *Encounter*, X, no. 5 (May 1958), 22–34.

[1] See Bibliographical Note, Appendix A, p. 149. The writings listed there will hereafter be cited by the key words of their titles. The quoted phrases above are from Tawney, 'Harrington', p. 207.

Here is another story about the Great Rebellion.

In the hundred years between 1540 and 1640 England was swept by a durable economic tidal wave—the Price Revolution. Under the impact of that tidal wave prices rose at least threefold in about a century. On men with relatively fixed revenues and inflexible standards of consumption the rise in prices wrought havoc. Its most distinguished victims were the 'mere' gentry, those unfortunates whose sole source of income was the ownership of estates of small and middling size. Bound by country custom and the demands of status to extravagant consumption, they lacked the credit that might have enabled them, as it did the greater magnates, to limit their losses and to rebuild their fortunes in the shelter provided by borrowed capital. The mere gentry were doomed to disaster, to decline, or—even if they curbed their extravagance—to stagnation, for the way to wealth did not lie through agonized pennypinching in a dreary manor house. It lay through a risky gamble for favor at court. Those who won that gamble—court lawyers, court officials, court peers and royal favorites, even court merchants who battened on the commercial privileges that the court alone could bestow—comprised the rising class in the century before the Great Rebellion. From among those who lost the gamble, the mere gentry, came the recruits for several anti-Court rebellions which failed, and for the one—that of 1640—which succeeded. These impoverished squires are the true revolutionaries of the Puritan Revolution, wherein they appear as the Independent party. Their revolution is not one of hope but of disconsolate desperation. It is also a revolution of disaster, since, fundamentally hostile to state power, the mere gentry do not know what to do with state power when they have it. James Harrington is not their prophet, he is their self-hypnotized poet, singing them a fantastic song of a dreamer's day that never was and never could be, when the mere gentry ruled the land.

So Professor H. R. Trevor-Roper unassisted.

Thus two great winds blowing past one another through the pages of the *Economic History Review* have generated the storm over the gentry. That genial connoisseur of the idiosyncrasies of the historians' craft, Professor Edward Kirkland, has formulated the appropriate professional reaction to such a storm. Schooled in the strategies of historical discourse and aware that his fellow practitioners reserve an uncomfortable spot in the limbo of the trade for those who fall from the grace of ambiguity to the sin of positive assertion, the cautious historian says, 'On the one hand, *this;* on the other hand, *that.* It is premature to arrive at any conclusion. What we need is thirty-seven monographs, fifteen more years of investigation, a research institute, and a $200,000 grant from the foundations'. Pending the descent of this eleemosynary manna, however, we may tentatively venture an examination of the evidence offered by Professor Tawney and by Professor Trevor-Roper in support of their respective theses.

II

The evidence is of several different kinds. First, Tawney presents a good deal of comment from seventeenth-century writers, Trevor-Roper a little, intended to show that contemporary witnesses were conscious of the very social transformations which their mutually contradictory contentions allege to have been in process.[1] Second, Tawney and Stone on one side, Trevor-Roper on the other, offer a number of specific instances, observations on the careers and fortunes of sixteenth- and seventeenth-century individuals and families, to illustrate their conflicting general theses.[2] Here the similarity in kinds of evidence ceases. For Tawney and Stone support their arguments with a considerable mass of statistical data on the fortunes of whole social classes, while Trevor-Roper, though challenging the validity of his opponents' statistics, provides few of his own.[3] On the other hand Trevor-Roper offers a broad reinterpretation of the political history of England from the rebellion of the Earl of Essex to the Restoration, and Tawney, while ignoring his opponent's interpretation of that history, offers none of his own.[4]

Let us now examine these different kinds of evidence.

First, as to general statements by the men of the times, alleged by Tawney and Trevor-Roper in support of their divergent conceptions. A little caution suggests itself in dealing even with ostensibly pertinent contemporary remarks about the condition of this or that class. The human propensity to make a poor mouth knows no bounds of time or space; and on suitable occasions men of almost every era and almost every level of affluence have fed their discontent at the world's injustice and their sense of their own under-rewarded merit by invidiously comparing their degree of solvency with that of men richer than they.

[1] Tawney, 'Rise', pp. 2–6, 35–7; ibid. 'Harrington', pp. 216–17, 222; Trevor-Roper, 'Gentry', pp. 26, 40–1.
[2] Tawney, 'Rise', pp. 11–12, 16–18, 26–8; Stone, 'Elizabethan Aristocracy', *passim;* ibid. 'A Restatement', *passim;* Trevor-Roper, 'Anatomy Anatomized', *passim;* ibid. 'Gentry', pp. 6–24, 30, 33.
[3] Tawney, 'Rise', *passim*, esp. p. 33 and n. 3, pp. 35–6; ibid., 'Postcript', p. 94; Stone, 'A Restatement', p. 321.
[4] Trevor-Roper', 'Gentry', pp. 34–44; ibid. 'Oliver Cromwell', *passim.*

To this chronic human proclivity to conceive of oneself as in disgrace with fortune, there are sometimes added motives for pleas of poverty more immediately and materially pertinent to the private interests of the persons who advance them. Consider, for example, the claim of penury put in by Sir Edward Montague in behalf of the county of Northampton in the reign of James I. The claim is cited by both Tawney and Trevor-Roper as evidence of the impoverishment of that sector of the landed class which the exigencies of their respective and opposed arguments require them to impoverish.[1] Sir Edward complains that 'most of the ancientest gentlemens' houses in the county are either divided, diminished, or decayed', and that 'there hath been within these 3 or 4 years many good lordships sold within the county, and not a gentleman of the county hath bought any, but strangers, and they no inhabitants'.[2] The condition of the native Northamptonshire gentry may, of course, have been quite as parlous as Sir Edward's remarks indicate; but with only an *ipse dixit* to support his allegations, it seems pertinent to give some slight attention to the context of those allegations, to the circumstances and situation that elicited them. The observations are dated 1614, a year in which, Parliament having failed to pass a tax bill, the Government was pressing the gentlemen of every county for a benevolence—a free offering. The observations emanate from a gentleman with a considerable estate in Northamptonshire. They are addressed to the Earl of Exeter, the Lord-Lieutenant of the county, and therefore the semi-official link between the county and the Court. And they are headed, 'Reasons to satisfy some that think Northamptonshire a rich county and *underrated in subsidies and other charges*'.[3] In courts of law such testimony from such a source is usually described as self-serving; it does not and should not elicit absolute and unquestioning credence.

Moreover, the notion that one's own time is a brazen time, an epoch of decay, a mess, in contrast to some good old golden age is common enough in every era. Among the tropes appropriate for lamenting these dissolute latter days is the one that goes, 'Nowadays, alas, the rich get richer and the poor get poorer', and the other one that goes, 'Nowadays, alas, the rich get poorer and the poor get richer'. Since in most ages both processes described in the tropes are likely to be under way at once, a resolute Cassandra can draw double sustenance

[1] Tawney, 'Rise', p. 21; Trevor-Roper, 'Gentry', p. 40.
[2] *Historical Manuscripts Commission Reports*, Duke of Buccleuch MSS., iii. 82.
[3] Ibid. (Italics mine).

from her misery by passing insensibly from wringing her hands over the one process to wringing her hands over the other and opposite process. And writing at a later date the historian can find support for his thesis, whatever it may be, among contemporaries, because those contemporaries had dramatically before their eyes and generalized from the same sort of particular instances that the later historian has patiently dug out and generalized from. I am inclined to suspect that most of both Trevor-Roper's and Tawney's contemporary observers—in so far as they say anything relevant at all—are of the sorts described above. Such observers speak with profound cogency and insight only to those whose views their self-serving or fragmentary and tendentious assertions seem to support. Since this conclusion may seem rather arbitrary, the remarks of contemporary observers cited or referred to by Tawney and Trevor-Roper are printed as an appendix, so that any one who cares to may make his own assessment of them.[1]

We may quickly dispose of the evidence that consists of individual instances, tales of the fortunes of families, told by Tawney, Stone, and Trevor-Roper to illustrate the destinies of the classes to which those families belonged. In gross they constitute a magnificent but, I fear, misplaced deployment of erudition. For although, as each combatant has alleged of the other, some of the individual instances cited by both sides may be off the mark, some of the illustrations of both sides are no doubt right on the mark. They are indeed particular instances of what the writer who offers them takes to be crucial general processes. Then, if the individual instances sufficed to prove the general process, both Tawney and Trevor-Roper would have the better of the argument, and the conclusions of both as to the nature of the general trend of social change in seventeenth-century England would be validated. Since their conclusions are diametrically opposed, however, this is impossible.[2] Why individual cases can *illustrate* but cannot *demonstrate* either thesis is quite clear. The individual cases cited on both sides were in fact inherent in the structure of English society and polity in the period under consideration—and before and after. Surely at any time a hundred and fifty years either way of 1600 some landed families, both noble and gentle, because of recklessness, extravagance, or failure to adjust to economic changes had to sell land; some landed families, both noble and gentle, through good management, good marriages and good luck were able to buy land; and some families that owed a large increase in their fortunes to trade, or the practice of law, or office,

[1] See Appendix B, p. 153.   [2] See Appendix C, p. 160.

or royal favor, were purchasing estates or adding to their landholdings. All these things were happening between 1540 and 1640 too. That they were happening is all the particular instances set forth by Tawney, Stone and Trevor-Roper demonstrate and all they can demonstrate. In such circumstances the significance of the individual instance for both theories depends on the validity of the general argument, not the other way about. So we 'will have grounds more relative than this'.

III

Tawney provides such grounds in the form of statistics. His statistics are of two kinds: (1) casual statistics off-handedly dropped to lend artistic verisimilitude to large and bald assertions; (2) systematic statistics intended to provide a quantitative foundation for the general hypothesis that he is propounding.

In the first case, Tawney has not always been aware of the pitfalls that some of his casual statistics conceal, and consequently he has not always alerted his readers to the dangers. For example, in one of the most striking passages in 'The Rise of the Gentry', he writes of those 'splendid spendthrifts', the noble magnates:

> When, in 1642, all went into the melting-pot, the debts owed to the City by Royalists alone were put, in a financial memorandum, at not less than £2,000,000. Of the commercial magnates, who, a few years later, scrambled for confiscated estates, not a few, as Dr. Chesney has shown, were creditors entering on properties long mortgaged to them. It was discovered, not for the last time, that as a method of foreclosure war was cheaper than litigation.[1]

The estimate of Royalist indebtedness that Tawney cites may or may not have been an accurate one. The danger in the statistic has nothing at all to do with the accuracy of the estimate. It lies in the verisimilitude which the estimate lends to the notion that the finances of the Royalist (and therefore, in Tawneyese, feudal) aristocrats were in a very bad way by 1640—such a bad way that for those aristocrats the Civil War was scarcely more than a violent, but in any case inevitable, economic demise after a painful and lingering financial illness. But how precarious were the finances of land-owning Royalists by the 1640s?

After 1650 the Commonwealth and Protectorate sold the confiscated estates of fifty Royalists in eight southeastern counties. When we

[1] Tawney, 'Rise', p. 12.

learn that these fifty men were in debt to the tune of £140,000, the supposed £2,000,000 that Royalists owed in London seems plausible enough, and the notion of a general foreclosure on the Royalist aristocracy seems not farfetched.[1] But, alas, it turns out that fully four-fifths of the total debts of our fifty Royalist landowners was owed by just one man, the Earl of Cleveland.[2] That truly 'splendid spendthrift' was foreclosed right enough, properly sold up. His fate suggests two reflections. First, unless the security for his borrowing was remarkably good, we might want to withhold just one tear from the noble bankrupt in order to shed it over his bourgeois creditors. Second, a few such colossi of prodigality as the Earl of Cleveland would account for the whole of Royalist indebtedness in London and leave the rest of the cavaliers an astoundingly solvent lot. And when one considers that the average indebtedness of the forty-nine Royalist landlords who were *not* the Earl of Cleveland was a mere £500 apiece, such a conclusion would seem plausible.

Nevertheless, not all the Royalists repurchased their estates. Only one-third of the confiscated parcels sold in eight southeastern counties were bought back by their former owners—34 out of 100.[3] When we break these figures down, we get an interesting slant on Tawney's theory that the Revolution achieved the final liquidation of an unthrifty nobility and registered the triumph of the rising gentry. We omit the Earl of Craven who thought he knew a cheaper way than buying it to get his land back. Other Royalist peers were the former owners of twenty-four confiscated properties in the southeast that were sold after 1651. In 1656 the same peers were once more the owners of *twenty-three out of the twenty-four properties*. In this particular aspect of the process the foreclosure of the 'aristocracy' by war involved the loss of one life interest in a farm.[4]

When we take away the properties of the peers from the total of confiscated Royalist properties in eight southeastern counties, another curious fact emerges. Of the remaining properties, only fifteen per cent appear to have been repurchased by their former owners.[5] Unless we assume—what does not seem too probable—that those owners did not want to buy their property back, then it seems likely that most of them for lack of cash and lack of credit could not buy it back. Now

[1] Thirsk, 'Royalist Land', p. 199.
[2] Ibid.   [3] Ibid. p. 194.   [4] Ibid. p. 193.
[5] This follows by subtracting lands repurchased by Royalist nobles (ibid. p. 193) from the total of Royalist repurchases in the eight counties studied by Miss Thirsk (ibid. p. 194).

these impecunious owners were rural landlords, lesser gentry; and it begins to look as if these out-at-the-pocket Royalist gentlemen constitute a sort of subversive fifth column of declining gentry sneaked by Trevor-Roper into the southeast, the home territory of Tawney's rising gentry. Except, of course, that it would seem according to Trevor-Roper's theory that of all the mere gentry, the mere gentry of the Puritan counties of southern and eastern England should have come up Independent, not Royalist at all.

The fate of the Earl of Cleveland and of an almost anonymous clutch of Royalist gentlemen when their confiscated estates went on the market suggests a general reflection. It is quite likely that for every great and noble vessel that foundered conspicuously amid public acclaim or lamentation in the economic high seas of Tudor and Stuart times, dozens of small gentle cockle boats may have gone under, scarcely noticed by any but their unfortunate occupants. In any case it seems evident that the estimated £2,000,000 of Royalist debt in London does not help render intelligible the foreclosure of those 'splendid spendthrifts', the Royalist nobility, since not many Royalist nobles suffered foreclosure. Few statistics are more pathetic or less useful than the ones that render intelligible a course of events that did not happen. In the age of the Great Rebellion reports of the economic demise of the great landowning aristocracy of England were greatly exaggerated.

The second kind of statistics, the systematic ones which Tawney uses to support his general hypothesis concerning the rise of the gentry, are provided by the counting of manors, 2547 manors in six and one-third counties.[1] The count shows that the noble families which held a little more than thirteen per cent of those manors in 1561 held a bare six per cent in 1640. The count also shows that the gentry, which in 1561 owned but two-thirds of the manors, eighty years later owned four-fifths of them. Furthermore the statistics indicate that in 1560 almost one-fourth of the counted manors belonged to men who each held ten or more of them, fifty-seven per cent to men who held four manors or less. In 1640 less than one-sixth of the manors belonged to men who held ten or more of them, while men who held four or less owned sixty-four per cent of the manors involved. Now the tendency

---

[1] The statistics that Tawney derives from the counting of manors are tabulated in Appendix D, p. 162. The counties in which the count was made are Bedfordshire, Buckinghamshire, Hampshire, Hertfordshire, Surrey, Worcestershire, and the North Riding of Yorkshire (Tawney, 'Rise', p. 22, n. 1).

of these statistics is evident. While the gentry increased its holdings of manors by a substantial sixteen per cent in eighty years, the aristocracy lost a whopping fifty-four per cent. This presumably demonstrates with firm figures that while the aristocracy was suffering an abrupt economic decline, the gentry enjoyed a solid steady economic rise. This first set of statistics lays bare the facts; the second set points to the cause. While the holders of large estates dropped a full third of their manors between 1561 and 1640, the holders of small estates won a solid increment of fifteen per cent. This presumably demonstrates that the semi-feudal aristocratic rentiers with their vast ill-managed estates were too genially chuckle-headed or too thriftless to adjust to an increasingly commercialized economy their ways of land management and living. Therefore they were losing their landed property to middling and small owners, landed capitalist entrepreneurs, who ruthlessly applied business methods to the improvement and extension of their lesser holdings. If these statistics will bear analysis, we may write Q.E.D. under Tawney's argument, and close the book on the controversy over the gentry.

But the statistics will not bear analysis. For (1) they have imbedded in them a number of serious biases; (2) manors—the units of counting —are anything but homogeneous; and (3) the contrast between aristocracy and gentry that the statistics are supposed to reveal involves an arbitrary and largely false taxonomic assumption.

First let us look at the statistical evidence that is supposed to demonstrate the superior economic strategy of the small gentry. The basis of this evidence is a count of the manors held by men owning no more than four manors in six and one-third counties. If all such men held no manors at all anywhere else, the inference drawn from this evidence might be of some interest. But seventeenth-century English landlords did not conform their holdings to the statistical convenience of twentieth-century economic historians. A very considerable number of gentlemen with no more than four manors in the six and one-third sample counties owned manors in the remaining thirty-three and two-third counties in England, in Wales and in Ireland. Some of them, far from being small landowners, were very large landowners indeed. And of course any assertion about the total number of manors held by small landowners becomes meaningless when we actually have no notion how many of the landowners so classified really were small.

Tawney's estimate of a very heavy loss of manors by large landlords is open to a somewhat different criticism. The trouble in this instance is that one of the aristocratic large holders included in Tawney's statistics was too aristocratic and too large. He was the King. Between 1561 and 1640 the Crown divested itself of vast chunks of land; this is one fact that Tawney has established beyond all doubt. In his sample of six and one-third counties the Crown holding of nearly 250 manors in 1561 dwindled to about fifty manors in 1640. *This whole loss Tawney appears to have debited to the holders of ten or more manors.* When we remove the Crown lands from consideration, the loss of the large holders, men who owned ten or more manors in the sample counties, drops from the lordly thirty-three per cent that led Tawney to consign them to bankruptcy, to a somewhat less lordly one-half of one per cent, hardly a presage of impending economic catastrophe. With respect both to the rise of the small holder and the decline of the large, 'Professor Tawney's table maximizes errors in the direction of the trend that it is supposed to reveal'.[1]

What then does account for the losses of the nobility and the gains of the gentry, which Tawney's other set of statistics seems to reveal? For one thing the 'nobility' held fewer manors in 1640 than in 1561, because there were fewer 'nobles' in 1640 than in 1561. For in his first computations Tawney classified as noble only men who held peerages in 1560 and the inheritors of those peerages. But by 1640 one-third of such peerages were extinct, and extinct peers hold no manors at all. So some part of the loss of manors by the nobility, which Tawney ascribed to economic causes, was due to normal demographic attrition. Another part was due to circumstances unique to the peculiar status of the peerage. Some of the land of peerage families went to daughters in marriage settlements; some to provide for younger sons. When a peer died without a son, his *title* usually passed to his male heir, if there was one, but much of his *estate* might be divided amongst his heirs general. In the eight decades between 1561 and 1640 all these circumstances took their toll of the manors held by the successors in title to the men who were peers in 1561, and Tawney's statistics register that toll. Now dying without a son to inherit the family estate and making provision for a plethora of daughters and younger sons out of such an estate are not among the special privileges of the peerage. They are the sort of thing that happens to many an English gentleman, and they must have happened to the families of many who were gentlemen in 1561, extinguishing those families or wearing down their holdings. But such losses scarcely ever show in Tawney's statistics as a loss to the gentry.

[1] Cooper, 'Counting', p. 385.

They cannot show because *anyone but the inheritor of a peerage of 1561 who acquires the lost manors of the gentry is classified, merely in virtue of his acquisitions, as gentry*. Trevor-Roper rightly points out that while the group which Tawney classified as the aristocracy

> consists of a diminishing group of those families who happened to be noble at the beginning and still noble at the end of the period, his gentry consists both of the gentry who remained gentry throughout the period, and of those men who began as gentry and ended as peers, and of those who began as merchants, yeomen, or anything else, and ended as gentry, No wonder the gentry, thus calculated, appear to 'rise' at the expense of the peerage.[1]

A hypothetical biography of a grandson of a peer of 1561 may make clearer how Tawney's statistics worked. In this case our subject is a younger son, and his father generously settles five manors on him. Then the king ennobles him; he is now a peer. He marries the rich sole survivor of another noble family of 1561, who brings him twenty-five manors held in 1561 by the head of her family. In Professor Tawney's statistics all the thirty manors our man now holds will appear as a *debit* against the nobility, a *credit* to the gentry. Then gradually our man buys up twenty manors of needy squires. In Professor Tawney's table—where our man is classified as gentry—*these purchases do not register at all* since they are transfers within the gentry. So in 1640 this descendant of a noble family of 1561, himself a noble, holds fifty manors, twenty of which he bought from poor gentlemen; and Professor Tawney's table will score the effect of such a career on the balance of property as follows: *noble losses—30 manors; gentry losses—0 manors; noble gains— 0 manors; gentry gains—30 manors.*[2]

At this point our confidence in Professor Tawney's method of counting manors may have shrunk somewhat. It may shrink further if we consider what a manor is. Economically manors are not equivalent

---

[1] Trevor-Roper, 'Gentry', p. 5.

[2] Since this paper was written it has been publicly read twice and also read by several individual scholars. The experience has taught me that the first reaction to the above example is to point out that my statement of the result of Tawney's method of scoring must be in error. The answer is that my statement of the result is correct; it follows inescapably from Tawney's way of counting, described in the preceding paragraph. When Tawney recomputed his figures for noble holdings to include all families ennobled between 1561 and 1640, his statistics lost their oddity, but the peerage regained its manors (see Appendix D). What seems striking to me is the difference in the statistical result which would have followed from the death without successors of a half-dozen rich peers on the one hand, and a dozen well-chosen ennoblements on the other.

units like dollars or pounds or even bushels of wheat. They are incommensurate units of ownership like 'blocks' of stocks or the 'properties' of present-day real-estate parlance. In New York there is a property, a 125 ft. × 40 ft. lot with a two-story house on it in darkest Queens; I own it. There is another property, a somewhat larger lot at Thirty-fourth Street and Fifth Avenue with the Empire State Building on it; someone else owns it. A statistical study of the trend in real-estate transactions in which these properties appeared as equivalent units might lead to conclusions a little askew. So may a study of the trends of real-estate transactions from 1561 to 1640 where manors are taken as units, so that the manor of Writtle returning £922 6s. 10d. can appear as a unit equivalent to the manor of Matchings returning £2 10s. 6d. To know that the Petre family has sold one of these manors would not throw a brilliant light on their finances unless we knew which manor it was—Matchings or Writtle.[1]

Nor are we quite at the end of our difficulties. In quest of a new rising rural middle class and an old declining aristocratic class to contrast with one another, Tawney hit upon the gentry for the former role, the lay peerage for the latter. Tawney's scheme of classification, his identification of the peerage with the aristocracy and the gentry with the middle class, renders *all* his statistical findings irrelevant to the theory that they are intended to support. For, whether rising or not, the gentry did not stand to the peerage in the relation of a middle class to an aristocracy. Economically gentry and peerage were of the *same* class—the class that ordinarily drew the larger part of its income from the exploitation of proprietary rights in land. Although in theory peerage conferred on its possessor a status higher than that enjoyed by holders of any lesser honor, a peer of recent vintage and slender substance confronted by a many-acred gentleman of ancient lineage might discover that the theory was devoid of significant practical consequences. Time eroded too many ancient noble fortunes, the royal whim conferred peerages on too many persons of slight stature to allow of any precise equation of peerage with prestige. Neither a distinctive economic class nor a clear-cut prestige group, peerage was a legal status constituted as a consequence of the past favor of English monarchs. Collectively, but not individually, the peers were the first gentlemen of England in honor and wealth, clearly distinct from the rest neither in source of livelihood nor in way of life. So Professor

[1] I owe the example of Matchings and Writtle to W. R. Emerson of Yale University.

Tawney's numerical evidence is erected on an error in classification—a statistical mirage reared on a taxonomic illusion.

I can suggest no more fitting farewell to the peculiar terrain we have just traversed than that composed by Mr. Cooper whose guidance I have relied on almost all the way. 'The counting of manors seems to have effects dangerously similar to the counting of sheep. It introduces us to a dream world in which, as in our own dreams, reality may not be entirely absent, but appearances are often deceptive.'[1]

IV

Instead of statistics Trevor-Roper offers us a brief but brilliant sketch of his conception of the role of the 'mere' or declining gentry in the politics and society of England from the age of Elizabeth to the Restoration. Now Trevor-Roper's declining gentry are no figment of his imagination. *Grondeurs, frondeurs,* Adullamites sulking in their decaying, remote, rural lairs, always against the government, the *lumpenproletariat* and natural nihilists at the bottom of the landed heap, the chronic discontented second-lieutenants of the county hierarchy, envying their betters, despising their inferiors, detesting both, ready for trouble if they could find it—as Trevor-Roper describes them they sound like men we have met before somewhere. And indeed we have. They had found their poet centuries before in the Provençal troubadour Bertrand de Born. As *Raubritter* in Germany they had received the demolition that their passion for violence so well earned them when Franz von Sickingen's gang got blown out of the Landstuhl in 1523; and they had recently had joined to them their most distinguished English member, Sir John Falstaff. Surely we would find them among the barons in revolt before Runnymede and among the knights-bachelor that De Montfort led to disaster in Evesham. Surely later we would find them in the October Club and in the unruly gang of ultra-Tories that followed Lord Eldon out of preference and the Iron Duke out of awe and respect.

That this perdurable and undistinguished group was at large in England between 1540 and 1660 is evident. That its numbers may have been somewhat augmented and its collective temper somewhat exacerbated by the combined operations of adverse economic circumstances and Stuart indifference to its plight is quite probable.[2] That various

[1] Cooper, 'Counting', p. 388.
[2] Trevor-Roper, 'Gentry', *passim*, esp. pp. 35–42.

mere gentlemen had a hand in every attempted *coup d'état* from the rebellion of the Earl of Essex to the march of the New Model Army on London, Trevor-Roper has demonstrated beyond doubt.[1] That, after some of the mere gentry had stumbled toward power during the Interregnum and staggered from ineptitude to ineptitude under the burden of responsibility a few of them sought consolation in the pseudo-realistic Utopia of Harrington is quite likely.[2] So far what Trevor-Roper has to say seems plausible. But rather often he goes beyond these plausibilities to broad though somewhat vague assertions. Politically, he seems to indicate, there are really only two kinds of gentry—the fat court gentry and the depressed country gentry.[3] The Great Rebellion thus becomes 'the rising of the poor country gentry against the office holders'.[4] The Independents, who are mere gentry, convert the crisis of 1640 'from a series of political manoeuvers into civil war and social revolution'. It is they 'who more than any others make the Great Rebellion'.[5] At this point the scope of Trevor-Roper's generalizing brings one to an abrupt halt; for it certainly goes beyond the evidence he offers and it probably goes beyond the evidence anyone will ever offer. In the first place most of the Independents were not gentry, either rising or declining.[6] And however well the policy of the Independents may have mirrored their psyche, most of the declining

---

[1] Trevor-Roper, 'Gentry' pp. 38–9, 42–4.   [2] Ibid. pp. 45–50.

[3] Trevor-Roper is actually a little ambivalent on this point. See p. 132, n. 1, below.   [4] Trevor-Roper, 'Gentry', p. 22.   [5] Ibid. p. 33.

[6] The problems raised by religious groups and sects and their relation to political factions during the Civil War is a most perplexing one, made all the more difficult by the propensity of contemporary pamphleteers to use the names of religious groups as instruments of insult rather than as terms of description. See my following essay in this volume, 'The Problem of the Presbyterian Independents'. The temptation to cut the Gordian knot by firmly identifying the 'Independent' party with a single social group is very strong. Professor William Haller, however, has rendered this very attractive solution unfeasible. In *The Rise of Puritanism* (New York, 1938), and *Liberty and Reformation in the Puritan Revolution* (New York, 1955) he has shown how deeply imbedded in the psyches of Englishmen of many classes 'Independent' patterns of thought and conduct became in the century before the Puritan Revolution. To identify these patterns with an outlook confined to a segment of a segment of the landowning class is in one sense unduly to circumscribe Independency, in another unduly to expand it by incorporating into it the political and social outlook ascribed to that segment. To seek a way out of the confusion of tongues in which the use of the term 'Independent' is involved is both commendable and desirable; but it seems to me that the way Professor Trevor-Roper has chosen is too drastic and not subtle enough. In George Yule's recent detailed study, *The Independents in the Civil War* (Cambridge, Eng., 1958), he discerns no signs of unusual penury among the Independent members of Parliament.

gentry were not Independents. The gentry of the North and the West, regions that provided such superior facilities for going to pot on a stagnant rent roll, seem to have been predominantly Royalist.[1] Moreover a considerable number of the squires who sat in the Long Parliament, both Royalists and Roundheads, were in quite comfortable circumstances. They were neither overstuffed court gentry, nor starveling bankrupt mere gentry, but substantial, fully solvent country gentry. Dividing the English landlords of the century before the Great Rebellion between rising court and declining mere gentry is a little like dividing the participants in the French Revolution between aristocrats and *enragés*: it leaves out a lot of important people and makes it unduly hard to explain what actually happened.

V

This omission, neglect, or minimization of the role of one segment —the same segment—of the landed class is one of the few elements that the hypotheses of our two historians have in common. The hypnotic fascination that the rising lesser landholders have for Professor Tawney, the declining lesser landholders and the court folk for Professor Trevor-Roper, has prevented both writers from paying much attention to that third group of English landlords. Unlike Tawney's owners of small-to-middling estates, these men of the third group have large holdings. Unlike Trevor-Roper's rising court gentry, they draw a very great part of their incomes from land; and while—one, two, or three generations back—the fortunes some of them enjoy were built up through court favor, by 1640 the current possessors of those fortunes are under no present obligation to the current Court and receive little of its patronage. The logic of the arguments of both Tawney and Trevor-Roper puts this group of landlords in a bad way by 1640. Tawney appears to believe that the conservatism of such landlords in the turbulence created by the Price Revolution doomed them to disaster both economic and political.[2] Trevor-Roper suggests that at the

---

[1] For a study of real backwoods gentry in a western county see W. G. Hoskins, 'The Estates of the Caroline Gentry', in W. G. Hoskins and H. P. R. Finberg, *Devonshire Studies* (London, 1952), pp. 334–65. The assumption of a connection between the backwardness of the North and the military support that the King enjoyed in that region is of long standing, going all the way back to Gardiner. Samuel R. Gardiner, *History of England, 1603–1642*, 10 vols. (London, 1883–4), vii. 229. The causal relation implied is plausible, remains to be proved, and is difficult to prove.　　　　　　　　　　　[2] Tawney, 'Rise', pp. 7–12.

very least they faced creeping economic malnutrition consequent on inadequate access to royal bounty and courtly graft.[1] Denying themselves the bonanza of demesne farming, denied by the Crown the sustenance of court favor, these country magnates seem to have got themselves the worst of both worlds—Tawney's and Trevor-Roper's. As we shall see later, this shared depressing picture well comports with the divergent general conceptions of the historical process into which each of our twentieth-century historians seeks to fit the realities of the seventeenth century.[2] How well does the picture comport with the realities themselves?

The evidence available for answering this question is not all that one might wish.[3] There are, however, some clues. Recent investigation

[1] After an elaborate portrayal in the grimmest hues of the economic horrors suffered by men who relied for their income on land rather than the Court ('Gentry', *passim*, esp. pp. 26–44), Trevor-Roper rather grudgingly acknowledges that 'the improving gentry survived, . . . weathered the economic storm', and by the seventeenth century 'were once again prosperous as before. Sometimes they were perhaps even more prosperous' (ibid. p. 51). Yet these improving landlords play not even a minor role in Trevor-Roper's account of the revolution of the seventeenth century and of the events that precipitated that revolution. Having belatedly spared them from economic damnation he promptly consigns them to political oblivion. 'They were the solid substance of rural society, its soundest members, and, because sound, generally unobtrusive' (ibid.). Trevor-Roper produces no proof to validate his equation between economic vigor and political passivity in the countryside; and it is not the sort of equation whose face value is so evident as to impose acquiescence. It does not coincide with what Sir John Neale has to say throughout his work and in a special chapter on the subject about 'The Quality of the House' of Commons in Elizabeth's day: J. E. Neale, *The Elizabethan House of Commons* (New Haven, 1950), esp. pp. 301–20. And it fits no better with what, thanks to Mrs. Keeler, we now know about the members of the Long Parliament: Mary F. Keeler, *The Long Parliament 1640–1641: A Biographical Study of its Members*, Memoirs of the American Philosophical Society, xxxvi (1954), I, 20–1, 22–7. Mrs. Keeler's meticulous and painstaking studies of the individual biographies of all members of the Long Parliament in 1640–1 reveal two most widely shared traits. (1) The members were overwhelmingly local men. Eight out of nine members had local ties—mainly in the form of estates—in the region whence they came to Parliament (ibid. p. 20). (2) The members were extraordinarily rich. Of the four-fifths of the members on whom she has data sixty per cent had annual incomes of above £1,000; only ten per cent *may* have had incomes below £500. Even some of this group is underestimated, since it contains many lawyers who drew their incomes from fees and retainers, while the evidence on income comes principally from records of land-holdings (ibid. p. 27). It is hard to believe that so large a chunk of 'the solid substance of rural society' got itself elected to Parliament by being 'generally unobtrusive'.

[2] See below, pp. 140–142.

[3] The conclusions arrived at in the following paragraph are based primarily on the following studies listed with full title in Appendix A, section *b* (p. 150): Kerridge, 'Rent', Batho, 'Henry Percy', and Finch, *Wealth*. W. R. Emerson's paper on estate management was also useful, and I look forward to its early

seems to show that, without the benefit of either demesne farming or court favor, from the 1580s on, the large landlords may have been doing very well for themselves indeed. Around the 1580s the land market began to boom, and it seems to have continued to boom for the next half century. In those roaring days the annual rental on some estates climbed to a third of what those estates had sold for a few decades earlier. Income from new takings doubled, quadrupled, sometimes went up eightfold. Landlords who had earlier gone into debt to hold their estates now reaped a golden harvest. So did those who had sold outlying manors to concentrate their holdings into manageable blocks and to pay the costs of 'improving' their principal estates, that is, of renegotiating the terms of tenancy on them. The landed magnate rich enough and prudent enough to pay the high overhead costs of old-fashioned, tight-reined estate management now had his reward. This reward was not within the reach of smaller men who could not afford the expensive personnel that such management demanded. In this period of rising land values the more industrious and alert among the lesser gentry most likely enjoyed those small gains that were commensurate with their small holdings. But on the whole a general increase in land values is likely to be most profitable in gross to the men who have the most land to profit from, that is, to the very segment of the landed class which both Tawney and Trevor-Roper have consigned to economic debility. The neglect or misplacement of this segment by both writers leaves an unfortunate gap in their respective reconstructions of the socio-economic configuration of the English countryside between 1561 and 1660.

It leaves a political gap even more unfortunate. For the large landholders provided the realm with the more important part of that 'self-government at the king's command' which is the most significant trait of the English polity.[1] They were the deputy lieutenants. They were the sheriffs. They were the justices of the peace. They were the commissioners in the counties to look into the myriad of things that the Tudors and early Stuarts thought needed looking into, and the commissioners to do in the counties the enormous number of things that

publication. Miss Finch's detailed examination of the fortunes of five families from the same county is especially valuable. It abundantly illustrates the complexity of the web of circumstance that conditioned the rise and decline of family fortunes. It also makes clear the importance of the equity of redemption, a legal device developed at about the turn of the sixteenth century, in stabilizing the position of the mortgagor and giving him access to relatively cheap credit.

[1] A. B. White, *Self Government at the King's Command.*

the Tudors and early Stuarts thought needed to be done.[1] Such charge did not fall in the main to 'mere' gentry, out of sorts, out at the pocket, down at the heels. And although rising courtiers, rich in land, might appear on the rolls in the commission of the peace and on other local commissions, they could not afford to give much time to country matters. Rising at Court required above all a man's regular presence at Court; he had to be on hand when the auspices for levitation were favorable. It was to the local magnates, 'men of port and worship' in their neighborhood, that the pains and the prestige of local authority fell. And from before the accession of Elizabeth I it was these same men who came to Parliament from the counties and the boroughs to make up the larger part of the membership of the House of Commons. This majority of local magnates seem to have increased right up to 1640, so that in the House of Commons of the Long Parliament all other groups appear as auxiliaries—mere Balearic slingers and Nubian cavalry—to the close-packed legions of the rich much-landed country gentry.[2]

The close relation between the rich country gentry and the lower house of Parliament may help explain a rather puzzling feature common to Tawney's and Trevor-Roper's account of the century before 1640. This is their well-nigh sphinx-like silence with respect to the most celebrated activities of the House of Commons during that century. Such a silence is inevitably somewhat perplexing and perturbing to historians who, having approached the era from the constitutional side, have learned to think of the doings in the House of Commons as matters of some consequence in the days of the Stuarts. Yet the silence is natural enough. For whether the lesser landlords were rising with

[1] According to Mrs. Keeler, among the members of the House in 1640–1 there were over seventy men who were or had been deputy-lieutenants, 122 sheriffs, 219 justices of the peace and probably more, and 250 members of various local commissions. Keeler, op. cit. p. 18, table 3.

[2] For the Parliament of 1593 the computations of Neale, op. cit. p. 162, give forty-three per cent of the borough seats in the election of that year to 'foreigners', i.e. to men neither from the borough nor from the county in which the borough was located. With a somewhat more generous method of defining a local man (a man with a previous personal interest in the borough or its neighborhood), Mrs. Keeler finds only sixty-four carpetbaggers among all the members of the Long Parliament in 1640–1 (Keeler, op. cit. p. 20, n. 99). Therefore only fourteen per cent of these men were outlanders. This figure—arrived at by dividing the total membership *minus* the county members into the number of the carpetbaggers—errs, if at all, on the side of generosity. It is doubtful that the different ways in which the two writers define a 'foreigner' accounts for more than a small fraction of the discrepancy.

Tawney or declining with Trevor-Roper, they cut but a small figure in the affairs of Parliament before the Great Rebellion; and to Trevor-Roper's rising court gentry in the days of the early Stuarts the House was not a home. The men our two writers have selected as protagonists simply did not occupy what historians have long deemed the center of the stage in the political drama of the epoch. When we follow the guidance of Tawney and Trevor-Roper, we may occasionally feel that they have called on us to give close attention to the sporadic vaporings of the First Lord and the Second Lord or of Shallow and Slender, while the main plot is taking shape at the fringe of our vision or beyond our ken.

Not only does the personnel of the early Stuart House of Commons fall outside the orbit in which Tawney and Trevor-Roper ordinarily move; its political behavior does not reflect what they—and, I fear, a great many others—believe the purposes and aims of a powerful politico-social group must be. In short, from the accession of Elizabeth I to the summoning of the Long Parliament the rich country gentlemen who fill the House of Commons make no consistent or concerted effort to win permanent control and direction of the government. They do not claim or seek for the House of Commons a sovereign authority over the king. They do not even claim that the king-in-Parliament is always supreme over the king-out-of-Parliament. Their whole line of conduct is sure to be confusing to the point of unintelligibility to those who approach it with a simplicist conception of politics in mind. Tawney's picture of a power-hungry rural middle class moving inexorably toward domination over the ruins of a feudalism that the middle class itself destroyed seems peculiarly irrelevant to many of the utterances and actions of the rich country gentry in the Parliaments of the early Stuarts. In matters in which to us the issue of power seems to have been unmistakably and inescapably posed, in matters, too, in which they had the country strongly on their side, the Commons persistently encumbered their action by intricate arguments and manoeuvers to transform issues of present power into claims of ancient and traditional right. They did this despite the fact that making a case in law often presented well-nigh insuperable difficulties. They neither talked nor acted like would-be rulers of the realm.[1] Trevor-Roper's

---

[1] By far the best account of political attitude of the 'good Parliament men' under the early Stuarts is that of Margaret Judson, *The Crisis of the Constitution* (New Brunswick, N.J., 1949), pp. 44–106. 'During the whole first half of the seventeenth century very few men—moderate, radical, or conservative—faced up

presentation of the House as the politically befuddled and obtuse head of a rout of angry hard-pressed yokels is not very convincing either. For the leaders of the early Stuart Parliaments were an unusually well-educated group of men; and it is hard to believe that the members who so neatly, quickly, and effectively won the initiative in Parliament from the Stuarts were an inept gang of political Calibans.[1]

To construct an adequate account of the varied political attitudes and aims of the rich country gentlemen who crowded into the Parliaments of the first Elizabeth, James, and Charles is beyond the scope and purpose of this essay and beyond the ability of its author. It may be worth while, however, to make a few obvious points in the hope of clearing away some of the more persistent obstacles to such an account. In the first place it is *not* true that a political or social group occupying a strategic position in the power structure will necessarily and always use that position to seek supreme political power for itself. Such a group may instead seek to define certain terms and conditions within which the existing supreme authority shall be exercised. In the second place it is *not* true that all the purposes and interests which such a group tries to protect and advance are necessarily and always peculiar to that group. Some of those purposes and interests it may share jointly with other segments of the society; some, indeed, may be interests common to all the ruled as against the supreme ruling power. The way of wisdom, therefore, may not be always to seek for a particular interest behind every action of a powerful group nor to concentrate one's attention

squarely to the fact that the issue was more one of power than of law. Theories of government based on power and not on law never became popular with any group in this period' (p. 57; see also pp. 66, 86–7, 106). Miss Judson's study has received far less attention than it merits. On a much feebler and less adequate base of erudition I set forth conclusions similar to those of Miss Judson on the political ideology of the Commons in *The Reign of King Pym*, Harvard Historical Series, xlviii (Cambridge, Mass., 1941), 175–84, 214–16.

[1] For the education of the members of the House of Commons in the reign of Elizabeth I, see Neale, op. cit. pp. 302–6; for the education of the Commoners in the Long Parliament, Keeler, op. cit. pp. 27–8, and D. Brunton and D. H. Pennington, *Members of the Long Parliament* (Cambridge, Mass., 1954), pp. 6–7, 27. On the general question of upper-class education and service to the 'commonwealth', 'Education of the Aristocracy in the Renaissance', Essay 4 in this volume. Peter Laslett has shown that in Kent, at least, the gentry, instead of behaving in the appropriate vegetable fashion, were displaying a vigorous intellectual curiosity about very difficult and complex problems of political authority. P. Laslett, 'The Gentry of Kent in 1640', *Cambridge Historical Journal*, ix (1948), 148–64. On the capture of the machinery of the House by the opposition to the court, see Wallace Notestein, 'The Winning of the Initiative by the House of Commons', Raleigh Lecture, *Proceedings of the British Academy*, xi (1924), 125–75; also printed separately.

entirely on those actions in which the particular interest of that group is clearly evident.

These strictures are readily applicable to the House of Commons in the early seventeenth century. If we do not confine our attention to the affairs in which the rich country gentry of the day had an obvious particular interest—for example, wardships, purveyance, distraint of knighthood, enclosure, breach of forest law, concealed lands—we may note that the House of Commons was also concerned with such matters of joint and common interest to many Englishmen as the independence of the judiciary, the survival of representative institutions, freedom from arbitrary arrest, defense against arbitrary exactions by the State, and preservation of the rule of law. If we incline to regard the latter common interests as of greater consequence than the former particular ones, we may fortify our conviction from the record of the seventeenth-century House of Commons, for on the face of that record it is clear enough that the rich country gentry who dominated the House of Commons shared our conviction. The duration and intensity of their discussion of issues of common concern considerably exceed the time and effort they devoted to dealing with their particular group interest.

Finally, if we do not insist that the seventeenth-century House of Commons aimed at supreme power, we can spare ourselves explaining away the inordinate amount of backing and filling the House engaged in when it found itself confronted with the problem of power. We hardly need be surprised that the House showed itself indecisive and uncertain in the face of the question of the nature and locus of supreme authority in the realm, for that, after all, is the toughest of all problems of power. But the same rich country gentlemen who did not know exactly what they wanted for themselves in the way of power knew very well what they did not want for the king in the way of power; and throughout the seventeenth century they showed remarkable skill both in country charges and in the House of Commons in seeing to it that the king did not get what they did not want him to have. In this respect there is no obscurity or confusion whatever in the course pursued by the rich country gentry from the accession of James I to the accession of William III. From the Apology of the Commons in 1604 to the Declaration of Right in 1688 their line of action is consistent, clear, and effective. And the latter document is not an assertion of the social supremacy of the middle-class gentry or of the political supremacy of the House of Commons; it is precisely what on the face of it it appears to be: a charter of liberties of free Englishmen in the right line of Magna Carta, the Confirmatio Cartarum, and the Petition of Right. Such a notion of the role of the House of Commons in the seventeenth century may seem most naive to those to whom that century is the era of the rise of the English rural middle class or of the decline of the English country gentry. It may appear somewhat less naive to those to whom the seventeenth century is the era of the consolidation of the bureaucratic monarchical despotisms on the European continent—the age of the Great Elector, of Richelieu, Mazarin, and Louis XIV. The author of the above words cannot help being aware that to give them utterance is to invite the allegation that he is a fautor of the currently odious and heretical Whig interpretation of history. To any cries of 'Whig! Whig!' that his remarks may elicit he can only reply, adapting a famous riposte of a fellow-countryman, 'If this be Whiggery, make the most of it'.

VI

Supposing the analysis, presented above, of the data put in evidence by Tawney and Trevor-Roper to be well-founded, what then is the present standing of the controversy over the gentry? With respect to Trevor-Roper's part in it, in fairness we need to add a little to what we have previously had to say. We have hitherto been more concerned to criticize what appear to be errors than to render due praise to merit. Yet in Trevor-Roper's studies there is substantial merit to praise.

(1) A very considerable part of Trevor-Roper's contribution to the controversy has taken the form of an all-out assault on the interpretive structures reared by Professor Tawney and Mr. Stone. Up to now we have paid little of the tribute due to his magnificent if terrifying work of destruction. Tawney has indicated his feeling that Trevor-Roper's way of dealing with those with whom he disagrees is somewhat *fortiter in modo*.[1] Setting aside any impulse to propose rules to govern the amenities of intellectual strife and postponing the summing-up on Trevor-Roper's theories, in an academic generation a little over-addicted to *politesse*, it may be worth saying that violent destruction is not necessarily of itself worthless and futile. Even though it leaves doubts about the right road for London, it helps if someone rips up, however violently, a 'To London' sign on the Dover cliffs pointing south.

[1] Tawney, 'Postscript', p. 97.

(2) In insisting on the Court-against-country element in the crisis of the seventeenth century and in giving substantial content to the otherwise evanescent conception of 'Court', Trevor-Roper has performed a service of inestimable benefit to historians of the period. For in the crisis of the seventeenth century the Court in conflict with the country was certainly one of the vital spots, and of all the vital spots the one whose morphology and physiology has been least studied and least understood. When treated at all, the Court has usually been relegated to the status of a secondary and derivative phenomenon, a mere adjunct to a class conflict which it is presumed to reflect. Trevor-Roper treats the Court—as it should be treated—as primary, one of the irreducible elements of the crisis of the age. This is pioneering, and important pioneering, too. Like most pioneers, Trevor-Roper may have made mistakes here and there; that is the price that a breaker of new ground must always pay for his venturesomeness. But a minor error or two will scarcely diminish the solid value of Trevor-Roper's treatment of the Court as an effective historical entity.

(3) For the rest of Trevor-Roper's interpretation of the crisis of the seventeenth century we may take our stand on the grounds afforded by our previous criticism of his argument. He has provided us with a study of a social group, the declining gentry, that historians of the period from 1540 to 1660 have hitherto neglected. He has discerned some of the forces that may have molded the outlook of that group and has related the political conduct of some of the declining gentry to the outlook he ascribes to them. A trifle exalted perhaps by his discovery, he has claimed for the declining gentry of the seventeenth century a somewhat larger historical role than a calmer and fuller analysis is likely to attribute to them—a sin, possibly, but a venial one. Under the circumstances historians who for decades have been blandly and blindly overvaluing the role of the middle class during six centuries of Western history might properly hesitate to cast the first stone. At any rate, there is little danger that Trevor-Roper's more exorbitant claims will achieve orthodox status. The danger is rather that, attracted to the pleasant and easy work of deflating his claims, when our work is done we may not notice that there remains much solid substance to many of his contentions.

It is otherwise with the theory espoused by Tawney and Mr. Stone. As Mr. Stone himself has recently written: 'It is now something of a commonplace that the collapse of the *ancien régime* in 1640 was an event that must be related to a shift in the social balance, the transfer of a section of the national income away from the Crown, some of the Peerage, and the Episcopacy to the middle class of gentry, officials, and lawyers that took place in the preceeding century.'[1] It does indeed seem that the hypothesis of Tawney and Stone is on the verge of enshrinement in the pantheon of historical commonplaces. What else can be said for it? Only that it is an interesting theory, that the evidence thus far adduced in its support is unconvincing, that the data underlying that evidence is in large part misleading, ambiguous, irrelevant or merely erroneous. It is not wholly certain that the transformation of Professor Tawney's thesis into a commonplace will prove an immeasurable boon to the cause of historical enlightenment.

VII

When historians as able as Professor Tawney and Professor Trevor-Roper pile on their evidence a burden of hypothesis heavier than that evidence can sustain, we may suspect that their judgment has been clouded by over-addiction to some general conception of the historical process. Professor Tawney is sufficiently explicit about the incentive for his fascinating redrafting of the historical picture of the gentry and for his singular view of their social orientation. In the manner of which he is a master he has made it easier to swallow his sharp-edged conclusion by encapsulating it within a suave and disarming apology.

> To speak of the transition from a feudal to a bourgeois society is to decline upon a *cliché*. But a process difficult to epitomize in less hackneyed terms has left deep marks on the social systems of most parts of Europe. What a contemporary described in 1600 as the conversion of 'a gentry addicted to war' into 'good husbands' who 'know as well how to improve their lands to the uttermost as the farmer or countryman', may reasonably be regarded as an insular species of the same genus.[2]

The English gentry, that is to say, must be transfigured into a *bourgeoisie* to maintain the view that the rise of the *bourgeoisie* is the indispensable framework for almost a millennium of history. The necessity becomes the more pressing if one is committed to the belief that socially the Reformation was a bourgeois revolution. For then between

[1] Lawrence Stone, *An Elizabethan: Sir Horatio Palavicino* (Oxford, 1956), p. xvii.   [2] Tawney, 'Rise', p. 6.

the bourgeois revolution of the sixteenth century and the bourgeois revolution that broke out at the end of the eighteenth century in France, the English Revolution of the seventeenth century is egregiously out of line unless it, too, is bourgeois. But from the beginning of that revolution to the end the men with decisive power were landed folk not city folk, not *bourgeoisie* in the inconvenient etymological meaning of the term. Surely then the most expeditious means of bringing the English Revolution into line with the other revolutions is to rechristen the seventeenth-century gentry and call them henceforth *bourgeoisie*, on the ground that that was their right name all along. Tawney not only rebaptizes the gentry, he recharacterizes them. Those who recall the magnificent and ambivalent sketch that Marx draws of his hero-villains, the *bourgeoisie*, in the *Communist Manifesto* will hardly fail to recognize the lineaments of his old acquaintances in Tawney's description of 'the agricultural capitalists . . . who were making the pace, and to whom the future belonged', the rising gentry revolutionizing the relations of production in the countryside in their ruthless single-minded drive to appropriate the surplus value of England's largest industry.[1] Recently Tawney has had some second thoughts on the free-wheeling use of such terms as aristocracy, gentry, merchant, and especially middle class. With the humility that is part of his greatness he has acknowledged the occasional peculiarities in his own use of those words.[2] And yet one may suspect that it was not a technical problem of nomenclature that stirred the storm over the gentry; that at the eye of the storm there is an issue not of names but of substance, and that the issue is that of the dynamic of social change, the framework of social history.

The general conception that dominates Trevor-Roper's studies also finds the source of human action in the circumambient economic configuration. But for him the motor of history is not the great impersonal secular movements of economic change; it is simpler than that. Groups of men in similar market situations are driven to common action and a common outlook by the similar way in which the same events impinge on their identical economic interests. The motor of history for Trevor-Roper is a sort of behavioristic reflex system of stimulus and response triggered by twinges in the pocketbook nerve. This is a kind of economic determinism; but it is the motives of groups, not, as in Tawney's case, the patterns of history, that are economically determined. The rising court gentry act the way they do because they

[1] Tawney, 'Rise', pp. 12–18.   [2] Tawney, 'Postscript', p. 97.

have got their snouts into the rich swill box of court favor and intend to keep them there. The declining country gentry join conspiracies, become Puritans, and disport themselves in other unseemly and disruptive ways because they cannot muscle their way to the trough. The great crisis of the seventeenth century is the consequence of a certain lack of empathy between the little piggies that went to Court and had roast beef and the little piggies that stayed home and had none. On a slightly broader view Trevor-Roper's protagonists and antagonists do not seem quite of a stature to bear the historical burden he imposes upon them. Perhaps that is why he pares down the burden, reducing that fairly magnificent upheaval, the Puritan Revolution, to the dimensions of a foolish farce that could conceivably have been brought off by the lowgrade louts and sharpers who people his stage. In the squalid setting of this farce there is not enough room for William Chillingworth or Richard Baxter, for Edward Coke or Francis Bacon, for Thomas Wentworth or Oliver Cromwell, for John Selden, or John Lilburne, or John Hampden, or John Pym, or John Milton. In such a setting men of such stature and others like them would poke their heads right up through the ceiling; for with all their limitation they stood high enough to see a little beyond the deedbox and the dinner table. Somehow without these men I find the age of the Puritan Revolution a little dull. What is worse, without some understanding of what such men stood for in their own minds and in the eyes of others, I find that age not very intelligible.

VIII

We are still left with the problem that started Tawney on his quest. The problem may be defined in the following fashion. In medieval England effective leadership of the 'country' opposition to the policies of the Crown had almost always rested in the hands of the great lords, the territorial magnates. Throughout the decades of growing estrangement from royal policy that preceded the Great Rebellion, however, it was not great lords who organized and directed the 'country' opposition. In this crucial period of English history the burden of leading that opposition was borne mainly by a cluster of prosperous country gentlemen and successful common lawyers. Why at this particular historical juncture did the 'country' find its leadership in social strata beneath the top? Why among the gentry rather than among the nobility? Why instead of hearing of the Earl of This and Baron That do we mostly hear of Sir Edward Coke and Sir Thomas Wentworth and Sir John Eliot, of Edward Dering and Edward Hyde, of John Hampden and John Pym, of the Five Knights and the Five Members? Cleared of subsequent and extraneous complications this is the problem that Tawney faced. In the sense set forth in the preceding paragraph the rise of the gentry is not a hypothesis to be verified; it is a simple fact, a fact that requires explanation.

When Tawney sought to explain the fact of the rise of the gentry, he was guided by the prepossession which we have already examined to look for the explanation in one particular direction. He assumed that the solution to his problem must be sought in some transformation in the *economic* situation of the gentry on one hand, of the great magnates on the other—in the economic rise of the gentry, the economic decline of the 'aristocracy'. We have learned to regard with some reservations the evidence which Tawney adduced in support of his solution to the problem of the gentry. But the reservations are directed toward the *solution*, not toward the *problem*. The problem remains— real enough and challenging enough. And we cannot turn to Trevor-Roper for a solution. For him the problem does not exist. His aristocracy is divided among Royalist aristocrats who are 'in', 'Presbyterian' aristocrats who are 'out', and Independent mere gentry who, like Huck Finn's father, are just 'agin the guv'ment'. This procedure really involves turning one's back on the problem and acting as if it were not there. But it is there all right.

If we reject Tawney's own solution of the problem that lay at the beginning of his quest, do we have any clue as to the direction in which we might seek a solution? We do have such a clue, I believe; and oddly enough, Tawney provides it. Among the quotations from contemporaries on which he relies—quotations which, it seems to me, do little to support his argument—there are several that point clearly to a line of inquiry that he disregards. First Sir Walter Raleigh:

> The lords in former times were far stronger, more warlike, better followed, living in their countries, than they now are. There were many earls could bring into the field a thousand barbed horses; whereas now very few of them can furnish twenty to serve the King. . . . The justices of peace in England have opposed the injustices of war in England; the King's writ runs over all; and the Great Seal of England, with that of the next constable's, will serve to affront the greatest lords in England, that shall move against the King. The force therefore by which our Kings in former times

were troubled is vanished away. . . . [In those troublous days] the noblemen had in their armories to furnish some of them a thousand, some three thousand men, whereas now there are not many that arm fifty.

Then Sir Francis Bacon:

Touching the [powers of] command [of the magnates], which is not indeed so great as it hath been, I take it rather to be a commendation of the time, than otherwise: for men wont factiously to depend upon noblemen, whereof ensued many partialities and divisions, besides much interruption of justice, while the great ones did seek to bear out those that did depend upon them. So as the Kings of this realm, finding long since that kind of commandment in noblemen unsafe unto their crown, and inconvenient unto their people, thought meet to restrain the same by provision of laws; whereupon grew the statute of retainers; so as men now depend upon the prince and the laws, and upon no other.

Finally John Selden:

When men did let the lands under foot [i.e. for less than its full current value], the tenants would fight for their landlords, so that they had their retribution; but now they will do nothing for them, nay, help the first, if but a constable bid them, that shall lay the landlord by the heels; and therefore 'tis vanity and folly not to take the full value.[1]

Now all these men seem to be saying much the same thing about the noble magnates; but what they are saying is not that the nobles are bankrupt, or even much poorer than they used to be.[2] They are saying very emphatically that *the magnates do not directly control arms and men as they once did*, that the old relation between high status or great landed wealth and a great *military* following no longer subsists. On the face of it, then, all the observations set out above direct our attention not to the economy but to the organization of armed forces. And if we follow

---

[1] For the sources of the above quotations, see Appendix B, p. 153.

[2] Only Bacon suggests any decline in the fortunes of the nobility. He says, 'There have been in ages past, noblemen . . . of greater possessions . . . than they are at this day. . . Possessions are less . . . because certain sumptuous veins and humours of expense, as apparel, gaming, maintaining of a kind of followers, and the like, do reign more than they did in times past. Another reason is, because noblemen now-a-days do deal better with their younger sons than they were accustomed to do heretofore . . .'(see Appendix B, p. 153).

their leading, we discover that in the century and a half between Henry VI and the death of Elizabeth there was indeed a radical transformation in the structure of England's military reserve. In the middle of the fifteenth century the larger part of the battle-ready military reserve was made up of the retinues of the magnates. Besides the magnates' tenantry, lesser landlords bound themselves to the great men of the realm by 'writing, oath, or promise'; [1] in return they often received from their lord a sort of uniform, his livery, which they wore as a sign of their clientage. They also usually received a money fee which conjoined them to the lord's band of retained men, his retinue.[2] Most fee'd retainers were bound to come at the call of their lord, prepared to fight under his command and in his quarrels. In return, besides fee and livery, the magnate gave his follower 'goodlordship', which might mean anything from using his influence at Court to gain for his retainer some office that the latter coveted to overawing a jury that might otherwise take a strait-laced, provincial and unsympathetic view of his retainer's propensity toward trespass or homicide. Involvement in the system had its dangers. During a time of turmoil they included death in battle or in a local brawl, or attainder when the faction one's lord followed lost out in the struggle for control of the throne. Even in the mid-fifteenth century a squire might avoid the entanglements of the retaining system and its attendant risks; but the price of disengagement was high. In that turbulent age, when the support of a great man was a needful help amid ever-present troubles, such support was doled out meagerly and with much delay to the man who dallied on the edges of the retaining system, reluctant to let it engulf him. Even such a one was impelled for his own protection to seek from some magnate the less formal clientage of 'goodlordship' and to become that magnate's 'well-willer'.[3]

At the end of the sixteenth century the bare form of the retaining system survived; but it was a shell, a feeble shadow of its former self. The squirearchy no longer rose in arms at the behest of the great lords,

[1] *Statutes of the Realm*, 8 Edward IV, c. 2.

[2] The term retainer has survived in the legal profession to describe a payment giving one a claim on the services of a lawyer.

[3] The whole history of retaining in the fifteenth and sixteenth centuries has been clarified in W. H. Dunham's excellent monograph, 'Lord Hastings' Indentured Retainers, 1461–1483: The Lawfulness of Livery and Retaining under the Yorkists and Tudors', *Transactions of the Connecticut Academy of Arts and Sciences*, xxxix (1955), 1–175. The conclusions in this portion of my essay are largely the result of reflections on Dunham's study. For the troubles of Sir John Paston, who did not become a magnate's retainer, see Dunham, pp. 41–4.

although for show they might ride about the country in some personage's train. In 1628 Parliament repealed almost every statute passed during the preceding 250 years to regulate, control, or suppress the evil practices that flourished under the protection of the retaining system. In so doing Parliament did not aim to reinvigorate a living institution by giving it legal sanction but only to provide a decent and honorable interment for an institution long since dead.[1]

In their reflections on the great alteration of the political and social structure of the landed class that the collapse of the retaining system entailed, all three of the observers whom we previously quoted went at once and unerringly to the root of the matter. Thus Bacon: 'The kings of this realm thought meet to restrain [retaining] by provision of laws; whereupon grew the statute of retainers; so as men now depend upon the prince and the laws, and upon no other.' Even more to the point, Selden: 'Tenants ... now ... will do nothing for [their landlords], nay, help the first, if but a constable bid them, that shall lay the landlord by the heels.' And Raleigh: 'The Great Seal of England, with that of the next constable, will serve to affront the greatest lords in England that shall move against the King. The force, therefore, by which our Kings in former times were troubled is vanished away.' In effect by 1600, and indeed long before that date, a whole range of human relations among the landed classes, once subject to the retaining system and to the wider ramifications of goodlordship, were regulated by the administration of the law in the King's courts. That law also firmly repressed any move by any magnate that might seem to have as its purpose the restoration of the retaining system to its former function and power.[2]

Between the maintenance of smooth, constant, knowable rules for social interchanges, which is the concern of men of law, and the maintenance of personnel and material in readiness for use in the deployment of massive violence, which is the concern of men of arms, there always has been and probably always will be some conflict. In the fifteenth century the balance—or imbalance—of society heavily favored the men of arms to the detriment of the men of law. Under the Tudors that balance shifted far in the opposite direction. Military needs still gave retaining a short lease on life, but it was an enfeebled

[1] *Statutes at Large*, 3 Charles I, c. 4, sec. 27.

[2] Only during the brief reigns of Edward and Mary was there any serious threat of a revival of the retaining system during the sixteenth century. Dunham, op. cit. pp. 109–13, 151–6.

sort of retaining, closely regulated, carefully scrutinized, and well policed by the three great Tudors. Fully to account for the shift in English society that crippled the retaining system lies beyond the scope of this essay and transcends the capacities of its author. Certainly one major element in the process was the institution of the Lord-Lieutenants and the formation of the county trainbands. When county militia under the command of Crown officers replaced private retinues under the command of territorial magnates as the reserve of its armed forces, England advanced with giant strides toward domestic tranquillity and military incompetence. With its cement of retaining fatally weakened the whole framework of goodlordship, from which the fifteenth-century magnate derived his power, loosened up. To have the good will of the neighboring great lord was no doubt still advantageous, but at no major peril lesser landlords could get along without it. Consequently the gentry of the Tudor period acted with greater independence than their predecessors in the days of Lancaster and York; and a plain Elizabethan country gentleman, not even a knight, could successfully press the election of his candidate to a county seat in the Commons against the efforts of a peer—who was also the Lord Chamberlain, a Privy Councillor, and Lord-Lieutenant of the county—to secure the seat for his own eldest son.[1] Elizabeth further reduced the capacity of noble magnates to function as centers of 'country' discontent by keeping most of the magnates who were of any account enmeshed in the transaction of her own and the realm's affairs. Nor must we forget that the only intransigeant 'country' opposition during the reign of Elizabeth came from the Roman Catholics—poor and dangerous material out of which to construct a clientage, as the Earls of Northumberland and Westmorland learned to their cost.

Edmund Burke once remarked that the function of great properties was to serve as a rampart for lesser properties.[2] Whatever the value of this observation as a sociological generalization, the tendency of the owners of lesser landed properties in England to gravitate into the political orbit of the greater landed proprietors is beyond doubt. Through the centuries from the eleventh to the eighteenth this tendency manifested itself in a variety of institutional forms adapted to the varied historical transformations that England underwent during the

<hr/>

[1] Neale, op. cit. pp. 42–5.
[2] Edmund Burke, 'Reflections on the Revolution in France', in *The Works of Edmund Burke*, Bohn's Standard Library Edition, 6 vols. (London, 1890–4), ii. 324.

span of seven hundred years.[1] Its last medieval manifestation was the armed retainer band of the fifteenth century. The crystallization of the landowning strata into power blocs, each dominated by one or a few great landed lords, began again after the Restoration; and this new form of an old social fact attained its consummate perfection during the eighteenth century in the golden age of the Whig oligarchy.

But in the years of crisis in the early seventeenth century no serried arrays of gentle henchmen of noble houses took their political orders from the heads of those houses. I have touched lightly on one reason why this was so: at that time, having lost their vocation for commanding retinues of armed squires, the magnates had not yet found their vocation for commanding solid phalanxes of borough members sitting in Parliament for the rotten and pocket boroughs that the magnates controlled. The result was a power vacuum in England during the very years when a concurrence of fiscal, constitutional, political, and religious grievances evoked widespread opposition to the crown and made it necessary for that opposition to achieve some measure of co-ordinated action. Into the vacuum created by the temporary incapacity of the magnates poured the country gentry—not the brisk hard-bitten small gentry of Professor Tawney, nor yet the mouldy flea-bitten mere gentry of Professor Trevor-Roper—but the rich, well-educated knights and squires who sat in the Parliaments of James I and Charles I. There they do not seem to have formed tight well-knit 'interests', as their successors a few decades later were to do.[2] Rather, they—especially those among them who came back to one Parliament after another— formed inchoate groupings, loose 'connections', occasionally joined but not, as far as I can judge, controlled by one or another opposition peer.[3] Into such invertebrate groupings the rich gentry of England organized themselves to oppose the activities of the King during the most severe constitutional crisis in English history. It is not an accident that when at last the opposition rallied under one 'overmighty subject', that subject for the first time in the annals of England was not a great territorial magnate but a substantial squire, a House of Commons man, John Pym.

[1] A study of the varied institutional arrangements by means of which the territorial magnates maintained their dominant position through the vicissitudes of the ages would seem to be a desideratum. See 'A New Framework for Social History', Essay 2 in this volume.

[2] For a meticulous analysis of the 'interests' in the last Parliament of William III, see Robert Walcott, *English Politics in the Early Eighteenth Century*, Harvard Historical Monographs, xxviii (Cambridge, Mass., 1956), 34–69, 198–215.

[3] J. H. Hexter, *The Reign of King Pym*, pp. 73–88.

IX

And now one final word before we emerge at last from the storm over the gentry. The two scholars whose combined but clashing efforts raised that storm have at least one thing in common. It is the main purpose of both Professor Tawney and Professor Trevor-Roper to show that the seventeenth-century revolution in Britain was closely related to prior shifts in the personnel of the landowning classes and shifts in the dimensions of their estates, their incomes, and their economic prospects. That a revolution prepared by conflicts over Parliamentary privilege, royal prerogative, judicial independence, arbitrary arrest, power of taxation, and the rule of law in England, triggered by a religious upheaval in Scotland, and traversed by the complex lines of fission that separated Anglican from Puritan, courtier from country man, was indeed closely related to the matters that have especially engaged their attention, neither Tawney nor Trevor-Roper has proved. And what such masters of the materials of seventeenth-century history and of historical forensics cannot prove when they set their minds to it, is not likely ever to be proved. Yet the destruction left in the wake of the storm over the gentry need not enduringly depress us. At least one amateur of seventeenth-century history observes the havoc with a sense of relief, even of emancipation. He takes faith and freedom rather seriously himself; and he has not felt that in so doing he is necessarily eccentric. He is inclined to think that a good many men in the mid-seventeenth century took them seriously too. For such a one it is something of a relief to feel that the outcome of the storm over the gentry licenses him to turn part of his attention from rent rolls, estates accounts, and recognizances of debt to what a very great scholar calls *Liberty and Reformation in the Puritan Revolution*.

APPENDIX A

Bibliographical Note (see p. 117, n. 1)

The materials bearing on the controversy over the gentry which appeared before the publication of 'Storm over the Gentry' in *Encounter* fall into two categories, those directly concerned with the controversy and those bearing indirectly on it.

(a) *Works directly involved in the controversy*. The two studies by Professor Tawney that lie at the heart of the controversy over the gentry are a part of that reinterpretation of the era between the Reformation and the Glorious Revolution which forms the substance of Tawney's historical work. That reinterpretation is to be found in an integrated group of writings which include the Introduction to Wilson's *Discourse on Usury*, *The Agrarian Problem in the Sixteenth Century*, and *Religion and the Rise of Capitalism*. The studies that precipitated the storm over the gentry were 'Harrington's Interpretation of His Age', Raleigh Lecture, *Proceedings of the British Academy*, xxvii (1941), 199–223, also separately printed; and 'The Rise of the Gentry, 1558–1640', *Economic History Review*, xi (1941), 1–38. Published reaction, positive or negative, to the thesis Tawney set forth in these articles was slow in coming, perhaps on account of the Second World War; but his arguments made a deep impression and were propagated through classroom and tutorial instruction. The first confirmation of Tawney's argument was Lawrence Stone's article, 'The Anatomy of the Elizabethan Aristocracy', *Economic History Review*, xviii (1948), 1–53. Stone's study complemented the studies of Tawney. It purported to show a decline in the aristocracy to coincide with the rise of the gentry that Tawney believed he discerned in the period he had under consideration. The first assault came three years later. It was a flank attack directed primarily at Stone rather than at Tawney. It was made in Professor (then Mr.) Trevor-Roper's article, 'The Elizabethan Aristocracy: An Anatomy Anatomized', *Economic History Review*, 2nd ser., iii (1951), 279–98. Mr. Stone replied to Professor Trevor-Roper's assault in a rejoinder entitled, 'The Elizabethan Aristocracy—A Restatement', *Economic History Review*, 2nd ser., iv (1952), 302–21. A year later in 'The Gentry, 1540–1640', *Economic History Review*, Supplement 1 (1953), Trevor-Roper delivered a full-scale frontal attack on the position maintained by Professor Tawney. In 'The Rise of the Gentry: A Postscript', *Economic History Review*, 2nd ser., vii (1954), 91–7, Professor Tawney came to the defense of the statistical data on the distribution of manors which had appeared in his essay on the rise of the gentry. This data—previously impugned by Trevor-Roper in 'The Gentry'—was then subjected to minute and adverse analysis in an article by J. P. Cooper, 'The Counting of Manors', *Economic History Review*, 2nd ser., viii (1956), 377–89. Up to the moment Mr. Cooper's critique closes the list of writings immediately directed toward the controversy over the gentry.

(b) *Works bearing on the controversy but not directly involved in it.* While the central controversy over the position of the gentry and the aristocracy between the Reformation and the Great Rebellion was in progress, a number of studies appeared that bore on the issues of that controversy. The extent to which they bore on those issues varied from the writings of Trevor-Roper, who obviously had them very constantly in mind, to the writings of Professor Campbell and Miss Thirsk, whose researches, undertaken independently of the controversy, happen to throw light on one aspect of it. A list such as that which follows cannot pretend to completeness, since one's conception of what is relevant will depend on the context in which one considers the controversy. The list includes only those studies that have come to my attention, the relevance of which to the issues in controversy seemed to me clear and unmistakable. Mildred Campbell, *The English Yeoman under Elizabeth and the Early Stuarts*, Yale Historical Studies, no. 14 (New Haven, 1942). Joan Thirsk, 'The Sales of Royalist Lands during the Interregnum', *Economic History Review*, 2nd ser., v (1952), 188–207. Eric Kerridge, 'The Movement of Rent, 1540–1640', *Economic History Review*, 2nd ser., vi (1953), 16–43. Joan Thirsk, 'The Restoration Land Settlement', *Journal of Modern History*, xxvi (1954), 315–28 H. R. Trevor-Roper, 'Révolution Anglaise de Cromwell', *Annales: Économies, Sociétés, Civilisations*, 10e année (1955), 331–40. H. R. Trevor-Roper, 'Oliver Cromwell and his Parliaments', in *Essays Presented to Sir Lewis Namier*, ed. R. Pares and A. J. P. Taylor (London, 1956), pp. 1–48. Perez Zagorin, 'The English Revolution, 1640–1660', *Cahiers d'Histoire Mondiale*, ii (1955), 668–81, 895–914. A. R. Batho, 'The Finances of an Elizabethan Nobleman: Henry Percy, Ninth Earl of Northumberland', *Economic History Review*, 2nd ser., ix (1957), 433–50. M. E. Finch, *The Wealth of Five Northamptonshire Families 1540–1640*, Northamptonshire Record Society Publications, xix. Christopher Hill, 'Recent Interpretations of the Civil War', in *Puritanism and Revolution* (London, 1958), pp. 3–31. The very enlightening paper, on estate management during the period here under consideration, read by Prof. W. R. Emerson at the meeting of the American Historical Association in 1956, has unfortunately not yet been published. Finally, I am indebted to Professor Emerson for a thorough and enlightening critique of the first draft of the present essay.

* * * *

Notoriously the way of the peacemaker is hard. With the best of will thrusting himself between two well-armed adversaries, he is all too likely to get himself efficiently clobbered by both. Such was the short sad history of the irenic exercise entitled 'Storm over the Gentry'. Its appearance in *Encounter* was not, alas, the occasion for a general lying down of the lions with the lambs or even with the other lions. It evoked or provoked an outpouring of letters to the editor so voluminous that the mere sample published almost equalled the original article in length. One or two replies were nearly vitriolic enough to burn a hole in the paper they were printed on. Letters appeared in the 1958 issues of *Encounter* for July (XI, i. 73–7), August (XI, ii. 75–6), September (XI, iii, 73–4), October (XI, iv. 68–70), and November (XI, v. 81). The letters in the July issue along with Mr. Cooper's letter in September and Miss Wedgwood's in November have been of particular interest to scholars. The interest they have attracted has provided me with a sound lesson in humility, since they seem to be cited with considerably greater frequency than the article that was their first occasion.

Several studies bearing on the storm over the gentry appeared either after the publication of my essay or too late for me to consider them in writing it. Two of these are fully cited elsewhere in this book: Lawrence Stone's 'The Nobility in Business' (see p. 85, n. 1), and George Yule's *Independents in the English Civil War* (see p. 184, n. 1). Mr. Stone has also published a most impressive investigation, 'The Inflation of Honours, 1558–1641', *Past and Present*, xiv. 45–70. In 'The General Crisis of the Seventeenth Century', *Past and Present*, xvii. 31–64, Professor Trevor-Roper has projected his views on to a broad European background. Those views are scrutinized and criticized by six historians in *Past and Present*, xviii. 8–42. In three articles in *The Listener* (7, 14, and 21 April, 1960), Peter Laslett has again emphasized how extensively the lines of class and status were traversed and in some measure blurred by an all-pervasive familism.

Three American scholars have recently published articles bearing on the problem of the relation of the gentry to the English revolution. Wilson Coates, 'An Analysis of Major Conflicts in Seventeenth-Century England', in *Conflict in Stuart England*, ed. W. A. Aiken and B. D. Henning (New York, 1960), pp. 17–39. Judith Shklar, 'Ideology Hunting: The Case of James Harrington', *American Political Science Quarterly*, lii (1958), 662–92. Perez Zagorin, 'The Social Interpretation of the English Revolution', *Journal of Economic History*, xix (1959), 376–401. Finally, too late for me to assimilate its results or to grasp its implications the massive work of G. E. Aylmer, *The King's Servants: The Civil Service of Charles I, 1625–42* (London, 1961), reached me just as I was correcting proofs on this book. At first glance its conclusions, tangential to those expressed in 'Storm over the Gentry', do not seem to conflict with them.

APPENDIX B

The 'Contemporary Witnesses' (see p. 121, n. 1)

In presenting the contemporary witnesses to the social processes that Tawney and Trevor-Roper believe they discern in the period before the Civil War, I have omitted those, cited by Tawney, who wrote during the period of the Commonwealth and Protectorate and after the Restoration (Tawney, 'Rise', pp. 36 and 36, n. 1, 3 and 4; pp. 37 and 37, n. 3). In the first place they are not contemporary; in the second place a number of them—as Trevor-Roper correctly indicates ('Gentry' pp. 45–50)—are not offering independent observations but are reflecting the common dogma of a single group, the Rota. The truly contemporary witnesses fall into two groups—those emitting general observations on the trend of events and those making specific comment on local situations.

(*a*) The General Observers:

Professor Tawney's general observers ('Rise', p. 5, n. 1; p. 6, n. 1), whose remarks are supposed to reflect among other things the *economic* rise of the gentry, in part at the expense of the aristocracy, offer certain difficulties. The passage from Thomas Wilson is too long for complete citation, so I have had to select only the statements that seem to bear on Professor Tawney's argument. It is necessary to warn the reader that in reading the first statement (Wilson, p. 18), he may deceive himself if he translates Wilson's 'gentlemen' into Tawney's 'gentry'. In the context of Wilson's scheme of social classification the term may include gentlemen only (Wilson, p. 17), esquires and gentlemen (ibid. p. 23), or the whole class that lived from the profits of agriculture without working the land with their own hands (ibid. p. 17). Since in citing the Venetian Calendar, Tawney, referring to long *relazioni*, has only given the document number, I have had to guess at what statements in those *relazioni* he deemed relevant. The passages cited or summarized below were the most nearly germane that I found, and if I missed any more pertinent sections, it is the result of obtuseness not sloth. Because I was unable to see a copy of the edition of Bacon used by Tawney, I am not sure I have found the right quotation there either.

Calendar of State Papers, Venetian (*Relazioni* of the Venetian Ambassadors). 1603–7, no. 739.

[p. 504] James I spends a great deal on his accession to the throne and, showing 'the liberality of his nature', gives away £2,000,000. 'The consequence is the crown is in debt, but not deeply. . . .When he

[James] wants to reward anyone, he lets out part of the Crown land at the old rent; and the tenant raises the rent three or four times over. In this way the King rewards his servants without putting his hand in his pocket.'

1617-19, no. 658.

[p. 388] Comment on the impoverishment of the treasury through James I's lavish gifts and on the extravagance of the royal household.
[p. 391] More on the King's debts. 'Gold and silver . . . [are] leaving this Kingdom owing to the excessive expenditure of the nobility upon clothing. . . .'

1621-23, no. 603.

[p. 435] Low yield to Crown on land granted for years. 'The revenues of wards, no longer farmed out but recovered for his Majesty, are borne better by the subjects because of so little advantage to him.'
[p. 437] On James I: 'His liberality and munificence flow like rivers and seas, and continually fatten his favorites.'

'The aims of his Majesty and of the Parliament are diametrically opposite. The former leans to absolute monarchy; the latter leans to liberty, with constant commotion like mingled elements which contend to overcome each other.'

'In the lower house of over 400 members, all less concerned in the court than those of the upper house and mostly unaccustomed to any authority, they use it, when they possess it, with great vainglory and vigor, and desiring to order everything that comes into their hands. Thus one will hear a semi-rustic oppose the King and government. . . .'

[p. 438] 'Although his Majesty has frequently punished some of them, yet as they are adored by the populace, they constantly multiply like the hydra's heads.' More on the fiscal feebleness of the Crown in face of Parliament.

[p. 440] James's policy of selling titles. 'He has thus raised to the highest rank men of the lowest birth to the exasperation of the old nobility who, with reason, cannot endure to see some rich merchant or some simple gentleman, who may at one time have served them or their ancestors, become equal or superior to themselves.'

[p. 444] 'The magnates are mostly hated for their vain ostentation, better suited to their ancient power than their present condition. Thus the troop of malcontents do not know whom to approach.'

1629-32, no. 374.

[p. 302] 'I am assured that a certain cavalier has taken a farm, and for lack of money the treasurer has assigned some crown lands to him.

They have made alienation of these on previous occasions to such an extent that what was formerly worth £200,000 does not now amount to half that sum.'

Historical Manuscripts Commission Reports, Earl Cowper MSS. [i, 129]. J. Coke to Buckingham, 12 February 1622 [3].

With respect to an earl's effort to get the inheritance of Bristol Castle: 'Whether it be safe and fit to put it in so great a subject's hands, how faithful soever, I humbly leave to his Majesty's wisdom.' With respect to a noble seeking grant of Kingswood Forest where Coke sees a chance of income for the Crown, 'The crown will necessarily grow less in honor and power as others grow great.'

Sir Walter Raleigh, Works (1751).

[p. 9] *Maxims of State*. 'State mysteries are of two sorts.

'1.) General; that pertain to all states; as first, to provide by all means that the same degree or part of the commonwealth do not exceed both in quantity and quality. In quantity, as that the number of the nobility or of great persons be not more than the state or commonwealth can bear. In quality, as that none grow in wealth, liberty, honors, etc. more than is meet for that degree; for as in weights the heavier weights bear down the scale: so in commonwealths that part that excelleth the rest in quality and quantity overswayeth the rest after it, whereof follow alterations and conversions of state. Second to provide that the middle sort of people exceed both extremes; viz. of nobility and gentry and the base, rascal and beggarly sort. For this maketh the state instant and firm when both extremes are tied together by a middle sort, as it were with a band.'

[pp. 206–7] *The Prerogatives of Parliaments*. Justice of the Peace: 'The lords in former times were far stronger, more warlike, better followed, living in their countries, than they now are. Your lordship may remember in your reading that there were many earls could bring into the field a thousand barbed horses . . . whereas now very few of them can furnish twenty to serve the king. . . . The justices of peace in England have opposed the injustices of war in England; the King's writ runs over all; and the Great Seal of England, with that of the next constable's, will serve to affront the greatest lords in England, that shall move against the King. The force therefore by which our Kings in former times were troubled is vanished away, but the necessities remain. The people therefore in these late ages are no less to be pleased than the peers; for as the latter are become less, so by reason of the training through England, the Commons have all the weapons in their hand.'

Counsellor of State. 'Was it not so ever?'

J.P. 'No, my good lord, for the noblemen had in their armories to furnish some of them a thousand, some two thousand, some three thousand men, whereas now there are not many that can arm fifty.'

C. of S. 'I hold it not safe to maintain so great an armory or stable; it might cause me or any other nobleman to be suspected, as the preparing of some innovation. . . . Such a jealousy hath been held ever since the time of the civil wars over the military greatness of our nobles, as made them have little wills to bend their studies that way. . . .'

J.P. 'The power of the nobility being now withered, and the power of the people in the flower, the care to content them would not be neglected, the way to win them often practiced, or at least to defend them from oppression.'

Francis Bacon, *Works* (1884).

[ii. 252] 'First, concerning the nobility; it is true, that there have been in ages past, noblemen, as I take it, both of greater possessions and of greater command and sway than they are at this day. One reason why the possessions are less, I conceive to be because certain sumptuous veins and humours of expense, as apparel, gaming, maintaining of a kind of followers, and the like, do reign more than they did in times past. Another reason is, because noblemen now-a-days do deal better with their younger sons than they were accustomed to do heretofore, whereby the principal house receiveth many abatements. Touching the command, which is not indeed so great as it hath been, I take it rather to be a commendation of the time, than otherwise: for men were wont factiously to depend upon noblemen, whereof ensued many partialities and divisions, besides much interruption of justice, while the great ones did seek to bear out those that did depend upon them. So as the kings of this realm, finding long since that kind of commandment in noblemen unsafe unto their crown, and inconvenient unto their people, thought meet to restrain the same by provision of laws; whereupon grew the statute of retainers; so as men now depend upon the prince and the laws, and upon no other; a matter which hath also a congruity with the nature of the time, as may be seen in other countries; namely, in Spain, where their grandees are nothing so potent and so absolute as they have been in times past. But otherwise, it may be truly affirmed, that the rights and pre-eminencies of the nobility were never more duly and exactly preserved unto them, than they have been in her majesty's time; the precedence of knights given to the younger sons of barons; no subpoenas awarded against the nobility out of the chancery, but letters; no answer upon oath, but upon honour; besides a number of other privileges in parliament, court, and country. So, likewise, for the countenance of her majesty and the state, in lieutenancies, commissions, offices, and the like, there was never a more honourable and graceful regard had of the nobility; neither was there ever a more faithful remembrancer and exacter of all these particular pre-eminencies unto them; nor a more diligent searcher and register of their pedigrees, alliances, and all memorials of honour, than that man [Lord Burleigh], whom he chargeth to have overthrown the nobility; because a few of them by immoderate expense are decayed, according to the humour of the time, which he hath not been able to resist, no, not in his own house. And as for attainders, there have been in thirty-five years, but five of any of the nobility, whereof but two came to execution; and one of them was accompanied with restitution of blood in the children: yea, all of them, except Westmoreland, were such, as, whether it were by favour of law or government, their heirs have, or are like to have, a great part of their possessions. And so much for the nobility.'

John Selden, *Table Talk*, *s.v.*, 'Land'.
'When men did let the lands under foot [i.e. for less than their value], the tenants would fight for their landlords, so that they had their retribution; but now they will do nothing for them, nay, help the first, if but a constable bid them, that shall lay the landlord by the heels, and therefore 'tis vanity and folly not to take the full value.'

s.v., 'Knight's Service.'
'Knight's Service in earnest means nothing, for the lords are bound to wait upon the King when he goes to war with a foreign enemy, with, it may be, one man and one horse, and he that does not is to be rated so much as shall seem good to the next parliament. And what will that be? So 'tis for a private man that holds of a gentleman.'

Godfrey Goodman, *The Court of James I* (1839).
pp. 290–1] Reporting a conversation at court: 'Nothing did grieve him so much as that the King's officers who should buy land for the King, or at least preserve the King's land, that they should be purchasers to buy the King's land as usually they were.'

p. 311] Reporting a discussion that goes on between James I and Lord Treasurer Cranfield while the gentlemen waiters call James three times, My lord told the King that he did wish that they (the gentlemen waiters) would eat up all the meat and leave him the reversion, for so they had done with his estates; they had culled out all the best things, and left him to live upon projects and fee-farms.'

Thomas Wilson, *The State of England, 1600, Camden Miscellany*, xvi (1936).

[pp. 18–19] 'It cannot be denyed but the Common people are very rich, albeit they be much decayed from the States they were wont to have, for the gentlemen, which were wont to addict themselves to the warres, are nowe for the most part growen to become good husbandes and knowe as well how to improve their lands to the uttermost as the farmer or countryman, so that they take their farmes into their handes as the leases expire, and eyther till themselves or else lett them out to those who will give most; whereby the yeomanry of England is decayed and become servants to gentlemen, which were wont to be the glory of the Country and good neighbourhood and hospitality; notwithstanding there are yett some store of those yeomen left who have long leases of such Landes and Lordships as they hold, yea I know many yeomen in divers Provinces in England which are able yeerly to despend betwixt 3 or 5 hundred pound yeerly by theire Lands and Leases and some twise and some thrise as much; but my younge masters the sonnes of such, not contented with their states of their fathers to be counted yeoman and called John or Robert (such as one), but must skipp into his velvett breches and silken dublett and, getting to be admitted into some Inn or Court or Chancery, must ever after thinke skorne to be called any other than gentleman; which gentlemen indeede, perceiveing them unfitt to doe them that service that their fathers did, when there leases doe expire turne them out of their landes, which was never wont to be done, the farmer accounting his state as good as inheritance in tymes past, and lett them to such as are not by their badd peniworths able to gentleman it as others have done.'

[p. 23] 'These are the States of the Nobility, both Clergy and laye which are called *nobilitas maior*; there rests to touch those of the meaner nobility, which are termed *nobilitas minor* and are eyther knights, esquyers, gentlmen, laweyers, professors and ministers, achdecons, prebends, and vicars.'

Trevor-Roper ('The Gentry', p. 26) quotes only one contemporary observer, Sir John Oglander, but he is a contemporary who does indeed describe the situation of the mere gentry precisely as Trevor-Roper describes it.

'It is impossible for a mere country gentleman ever to grow rich or raise his house. He must have some other vocation with his inheritance, as to be a courtier, lawyer, merchant or some other vocation. If he hath no other vocation, let him get a ship and judiciously manage her, or buy some auditor's place, or be vice-admiral in his county. By only following the plough he may keep his word and be upright, but will never increase his fortune. Sir John Oglander wrote this with his own blood, June the 24th, 1632, then aged 48 years.'

(b) The Specific Commentators:

Several of the specific contemporary commentators I was unable to run down. It is worth noting with respect to a number of the commentators on specific areas that both Tawney and Trevor-Roper cite them (Tawney, 'Rise', p. 21; Trevor-Roper, 'Gentry', pp. 40–1; ibid. 'Revolution Anglaise', p. 334). This seems to be the case with Berkshire, Northamptonshire, Staffordshire, and possibly Bedfordshire and Nottinghamshire. Unless one or the other of these two scholars egregiously confused the meaning of what he read, it is unlikely that a contemporary cited by both Trevor-Roper and Tawney provides very firm confirmation for the argument of either.

Publication of the Harleian Society, xix (1884).

[pp. 206–8] 'A catalogue of the names of gentlemen of quality that have sold their estates and are quite gone out of *Bedfordshire* within less than the space of fifty years, and a known truth by Sir Robert Chernock of Hullcott.' One hundred and four names follow. Then, 'This list was taken in February 1667/8. February 14, 1667/8 was taken a list of the gentlemen now remaining.' Sixty-five names follow.

Thomas Fuller, *The Worthies of England* (1840).

i. 140, *Berkshire:*

'Sure I am that ancient gentry in this country, sown thick in former, come up thin in our, age. . . . I behold the city of London as the cause thereof.' Refers to the convenience of part of the county to London.

i. 162, 'Lands in Berkshire are very skittish and often cast their owners . . . I desire that hereafter the Berkshire gentry may be better settled in their saddles.'

ii. 95, *Hereford:*

'I am credibly informed that the office of Under-Sheriff of this county is more beneficial than in any other county of the same proportion; his fees, it seems increasing from the decrease of the state of the gentry therein.'

Historical Manuscripts Commission Reports, Duke of Buccleuch MSS, iii. 182.

[1614] 'Reasons to satisfy some that think Northamptonshire to be a rich county and underrated in subsidies and other charges. . . .

'Ninthly, most of the ancientest gentlemens' houses in the county are either divided, diminished, or decayed.

'Tenthly, there hath been within these 3 or 4 years many good lordships sold within the county, and not a gentleman of the county hath bought any, but strangers, and they no inhabitants.

'In (Sir Ed.) Montagu's hand and endorsed by him. Reasons delivered to [the] Earl of Exeter that Northamptonshire is not so rich.'

APPENDIX C

An Individual Case: Sir Thomas Tresham (see p. 160, n. 2)

Some intimation of the inadequacy of particular instances as a foundation for our authors' general arguments may be gained from the fact that on occasions Tawney and Trevor-Roper seek sustenance for their opposed hypotheses in the career of one and the same man. Both historians, for example, use the career of Sir Thomas Tresham as a particular instance confirmatory to their general contentions. To Tawney, Tresham is the beau ideal of the rising gentry, the economically rational country gentleman on the make, ruthlessly trampling on all beneath him and pulling down all above him in his rush toward the wealth he could realize from the land—a calculating rackrenter, encloser, and depopulator ('Rise', p. 16). To Trevor-Roper, who includes much, but not the whole, of the history of the family in his purview, the Treshams are a nearly perfect instance of declining mere gentry (Trevor-Roper, 'Gentry', pp. 20-1). Deprived of the royal largesse on which the family fortune had depended, and committed to a scale of building and spending beyond their curtailed means, they fell into the habits of anti-government religiosity and conspiracy characteristic of the hard-pressed mere gentry—witness the lethal involvement of Francis Tresham, Sir Thomas's son, in the Gunpowder Plot. They finally came to an appropriate end in the 1640s with the almost simultaneous economic and biological extinction of the male line.

In Miss Finch's recent study the history of the Tresham family fortune is set out in full detail (*Wealth*, pp. 66–99). From her narrative we learn how it happened that two able historians, technically correct in their statements of fact, could be seriously misled in the inferences they drew from the facts. Her account shows how far Sir Thomas Tresham actually was from conforming to Tawney's conception of rising lesser gentry.

1. Sir Thomas can hardly pass muster as a small, newly-risen landlord of the sort that, according to Tawney, was inheriting the earth from 1558 to 1640. His great-great-grandfather in the mid-fifteenth

century already held land in twenty-five manors. His great-grandfather, his grandfather, and his father all added to the estate that they inherited. Judged merely by the extent of his acres and not by Tawney's typology of the agrarian capitalist spirit, Sir Thomas really cannot pass muster as lesser gentry.

2. Even though on the income side Sir Thomas conducted himself —in congruence with Tawney's typology—like the very model of a 'modern' minor gentleman, on the outgo side he was thoroughly 'feudal'. He spent considerably on building, and much more on keeping up an excessive number of houses and an inordinately large household, and on maintaining a lavish hospitality in the old style.

3. Sir Thomas displayed an extraordinary proficiency in the shadier transactions of the new landlordism; but at the time when he was performing his most remarkable feats along these lines he was not rising at all; he was going broke fast. It was by the pressure of debt that he was led to his merciless expedients for grinding the faces of his tenantry, although in Sir Thomas's case necessity may have been happily mated with inclination.

Confronted with Miss Finch's array of data, Trevor-Roper's facts about the Treshams also came short of supporting his general contentions.

1. Although cut off from the nutrient of court handouts, Sir Thomas Tresham was quite successful in increasing his income entirely from the proceeds of estate management. In fifteen years he improved his rental revenues by one half and doubled the size of his flock to about 6000. Sir Thomas was a declining gentleman; but he was a declining gentleman with an income of about £3500 a year.

2. The Treshams were Catholic, and one of them got involved in desperate doings—the Essex rising and Gunpowder Plot. But Francis Tresham did not become a Catholic and a plotter because the family estate failed to yield enough to support him. Rather the estate failed to yield enough to support him because the Treshams were Catholic and Francis a Catholic and a ne'er-do-well; he became a plotter because he was a fool, to boot.

3. Although Sir Thomas Tresham was lavish in matters of household and hospitality and spent a bit on building, none of these outlays would have ruined the Treshams. What brought them low were (1) the succession of heavy mulcts they suffered from their Popish proclivities and activities, (2) the over-generous provision that Sir Thomas made for an excessively large family—three sons and six daughters, (3) the fecklessness and incompetence of Sir Thomas's heir, and (4) the extremely high cost of loan capital to landlords through the sixteenth century and the early years of the seventeenth.

APPENDIX D

Professor Tawney's Statistics (see p. 124, n. 1)

Economic History Review, 2nd ser., vii. 94.

The Ownership of 2547 Manors in Seven Counties in 1561 and 1640.

		Crown	Peers	Gentry	Other
1561		242	335	1709	261
		9·5%	13·1%	67·1%	10·2%
1640	(Assigning to gentry manors owned by families ennobled 1561–1640)	53	157	2051	286
		2%	6·1%	80·5%	11·2%
1640	(Assigning to peers manors owned by families ennobled 1561–1640)	53	343	1865	286
		2%	13·4%	73·3%	11·2%

Economic History Review, xi. 33

	Manors belonging to owners who held four manors or less		Manors belonging to owners who held five to nine manors		Manors belonging to owners who held ten or more manors	
	Number	%	Number	%	Number	%
1561	1445	56·7	490	19·2	612	24·0
1601	1457	57·2	544	21·3	648	21·4
1640	1638	64·3	488	19·1	421	16·5
1680	1684	66·1	556	21·8	347	13·6[1]

[1] Professor Tawney's percentages for 1680 are very slightly off (totaling 101.5 per cent) because in arriving at them he used 2,547 as a divisor. The sum of manors for 1561, 1601 and 1640 is 2,547. For 1680, however, it is 2,587.

7

The Problem of the Presbyterian Independents *

PATTERNS SANCTIFIED BY great historiographic traditions tend to become fixed. Frequently these patterns are neither logical nor coherent, but the sanction of use and wont behind them is so powerful that researchers tend to force new materials into the time-honored molds. In this way the Germanist tradition imposed itself on Bishop Stubbs,[1] and the Whig interpretation of eighteenth-century politics was not completely overthrown until Sir Lewis Namier finally destroyed it through his patient work on the Newcastle papers.[2] An even more famous case, perhaps, is that of Cromwell, rescued only after two centuries of nearly unanimous obloquy and set on a pedestal by the hero-worshiping Carlyle.[3]

The school of historians which followed Carlyle in the rehabilitation of Cromwell riveted an already venerable theory of Civil War politics on to the history of the Interregnum. That theory is somewhat as follows. In the beginning of the war the parliamentary party was united in its opposition to the autocratic pretensions of Charles I and the popish tendencies of the High Anglican group in the Church. As long as the royalists remained a threat, the factions in Parliament held together. When royalist pressure slackened, Parliament and its adherents split along religious lines. On one side, the Presbyterians tried to impose on England a tyrannical church uniformity after the Scottish pattern. On the other side, the Independents, a majority in the New

*An earlier version of this essay appeared in the *American Historical Review* in October 1938.

[1] William Stubbs, *Select Charters and other Illustrations of English Constitutional History* (Oxford, 1870), Introductory Sketch.

[2] Lewis B. Namier, *The Structure of Politics at the Accession of George III* (2 vols., London, 1929) and *England in the Age of the American Revolution* (London, 1930).

[3] Thomas Carlyle, *Oliver Cromwell's Letters and Speeches with Elucidations*, ed. S. C. Lomas, 3 vols. (London, 1904); Wilbur C. Abbott, 'The Fame of Cromwell' in *Conflicts with Oblivion* (New Haven, 1924), pp. 151–80.

Model Army but a minority in Parliament, set the doctrine of religious toleration against the persecuting aims of the Presbyterians. When in 1647 the army leaders realized that in order to establish Presbyterianism, the parliamentary majority was ready to sacrifice the gains of the Civil War, they impeached eleven Presbyterian commoners and marched on London to save the revolution from intolerant reaction. In 1648 the Scots invaded England, pledged to restore Charles I to his throne. While the army was fighting off this invasion, the Presbyterians in Parliament again opened negotiations with the King. By this time the Independents had decided that there could be no peace while Charles lived. In Pride's Purge they used the army to lop off the Presbyterian majority in Parliament. They also lopped off the House of Lords [1] and the head of the King. For the next four years the Independent Rump Parliament ruled England. Then it quarreled with the Independent army to its own detriment. Its dissolution by Cromwell in 1653 paved the way for the Protectorate. The death of Protector Oliver in 1658 brought on an anarchy that ended only with the restoration of the Stuart dynasty in 1660.[2]

The traditional picture of the early years of the Interregnum makes a sharp distinction between the Presbyterians and the Independents, treats the two groups as mutually exclusive, and resolves the parliamentary history of those years into a struggle between them. The material of fact at our disposal for testing the 'mutual exclusion' theory, or any other theory of parties in the Long Parliament, is scanty. Division lists there are none, and lists of members indicating a political preference on a specific issue are few. One period of crisis, however, has left us with fragments of information from which we can construct the rough equivalent of a division list. On 6 December, 1648, Colonel Pride's troop purged the House of Commons of those so-called Presby-

[1] *Acts and Ordinances of the Interregnum, 1642–1660*, eds. Charles H. Firth and Robert S. Rait, 3 vols. (London, 1911), ii. 24. Cited hereafter as *A.O.I.*

[2] Gardiner and Shaw do not draw the line of religious cleavage so sharply as it is drawn in the foregoing sketch; Samuel R. Gardiner, *History of the Great Civil War, 1642–1649*, 4 vols. (London, 1893), ii. 66–7. William A. Shaw, *A History of the English Church during the Civil War and under the Commonwealth*, 2 vols. (London, 1900), i. 206–319. The contemporaries and successors of Gardiner and Shaw overlooked their distinctions, which were indeed neither completely nor clearly set forth. The above sketch is a fair summary of the opinions of Carlyle, Firth, Trevelyan, Montague, and Buchan. Carlyle, i. 225; Charles H. Firth, *Oliver Cromwell and the Rule of the Puritans in England* (New York, 1923), pp. 144–63; George M. Trevelyan, *England under the Stuarts* (London, 1914), pp. 225–91; Francis C. Montague, *The History of England, 1603–1660* (London, 1907), pp. 322–45; John Buchan, *Oliver Cromwell* (London, 1934), pp. 229–47.

terian members who wished to continue peace negotiations with the King. Seven weeks later a packed high court of justice declared Charles Stuart, King of England, guilty of treason. On 30 January he was beheaded. During the next few months the 'Independent' remainder of Parliament cleaned away the debris of the monarchy, and England was declared a kingless commonwealth by legislative fiat of the Rump.

From three sources it is possible to compile a reasonably complete list of the men who actively participated in the destruction of the monarchy and the governing of the Commonwealth: (1) The warrant for the execution of Charles I contains the signatures of those who inflicted the death penalty on him.[1] (2) William Prynne set down in a pamphlet the names of those members of the House of Commons who took the engagement to support the Commonwealth.[2] (3) Scattered through the journal of the House of Commons from mid-December 1648 to April 1653 are the names of the members who helped to rule the new republic.[3] Eliminating duplications, these three lists contain in all about two hundred names.

Here we have the two hundred staunch Independent commoners, the sheep who are separated from the goats. Some Presbyterians, perhaps, supported the New Model Army while the war lasted; some, perhaps, drew off to that army in 1647 and engaged to live and die with it.[4] But in the era of the Rump waverers must needs have recoiled in face of the burning question, 'Will you pay the price for religious toleration; will you by word or deed countenance the execution of the King?' The men who signed the death warrant of Charles Stuart, who repudiated his legitimate successor, swore allegiance to the Commonwealth, and acted in the supreme legislature of the new government, these regicides and rumpers could not be Presbyterians; they were the gold tried in the fire, the ultimate and essential Independents.

It is so obvious that the two hundred regicides and rumpers must have been Independents that it is disconcerting to discover among them at least thirty-nine men who allowed their names to be enrolled among the elders of the parliamentary Presbyterian Church.[5] Distressing to

---

[1] Gardiner, *Civil War*, iv. 309, n. 1.

[2] *A Remonstrance and Declaration of Several Counties, Cities and Burroughs* (London, 1648), pp. 4–5.

[3] *Journal of the House of Commons*, vi. 96 *ad fin.*, vii. 1–272; hereafter cited as *C.J.*

[4] For a list of the Engagers see *An Engagement of the Lords and Commons that went to the Army, 4 Aug., with their Names thereunto Subscribed* (London, 1647).

[5] These thirty-nine Independents in presbyteries, given in vol. ii of Shaw are: Francis Allen, p. 403; John Ash, p. 415; Nathaniel Bacon, p. 426; William Ball,

the lover of symmetry as is the presence of all these 'Independents' in a place where they do not belong, it is easier to believe that they were members of presbyteries than to explain their inclusion in the lists as accidental. The early ordinances on ecclesiastical affairs, antedating the official erection of any presbyteries, provided for a Presbyterian hierarchy of church courts from congregational elderships through classis and provincial synods to the national assembly.[1] So the 'Independents' who allowed their names to appear on eldership lists must have done so with full knowledge that the national church was to be Presbyterian in form. They were not obliged to offer their services. No penalty in law lay against a man for refusing to act as an elder. On the contrary, one qualification for the eldership, prescribed by the first ecclesiastical ordinance which Parliament passed, was willingness to 'undergo the ... office'.[2] Nor can the presence of so many 'Independent' names be attributed to a superfluity of zeal on the part of local Presbyterian ministers anxious to make a brave show on their lists. In the compiling of the lists the local clergy and the local gentry acted only as advisers to

p. 403; Sir John Barrington, p. 382; Robert Blake, p. 421; Sir William Brereton p. 435; Peter Brook, p. 395; Robert Brewster, p. 425; John Corbett, p. 407 William Ellis, p. 404; Thomas Fell, p. 390; John Goodwyn, p. 434; Robert Goodwyn, p. 434; Brampton Gurdon, p. 429; John Gurdon, p. 423; John Harrington, p. 415; Edmund Harvey, p. 426; William Heveningham, p. 425 Roger Hill, p. 421; Lislibone Long, p. 417; Sir William Masham, p. 380; William Masham, p. 380; Sir Henry Mildmay, p. 375; John More, p. 415; Sir Roger North, p. 426; John Palmer, p. 420; Alexander Popham, p. 415; Edward Popham p. 415; Edmund Prideaux, p. 404; John Pyne, p. 421; Robert Reynolds, p. 428; Alexander Rigby, p. 397; George Searle, p. 420; George Snelling, p. 403; George Thompson, p. 403; Benjamin Weston, p. 435; Henry Weston, p. 434; Sir Thomas Wrothe, p. 421. It is possible, of course, that the names in the presbytery lists in some cases coincide with those of the Members of Parliament by mere accident For instance, John More who sits in Parliament is not necessarily the John More whose name appears on the presbytery list. To reduce the chance of error to a minimum I have included in the above list only those members whose names occur in the lists of elders for the particular county for which they sat in Parliament (twenty-four in number) and those who can be shown to have had some other special connection with the county where their names appear on the list of elders. Fifteen members in the above list did not sit in Parliament for the counties where they were elders. Twelve of these fifteen, however, were active on the committees for those counties, as can be seen in *A.O.I.*, volume i: Francis Allen, p. 746; John Ash, p. 68; Nathaniel Bacon, p. 639; William Ball, p. 970; Sir John Barrington, p. 91; Sir William Brereton, p. 44; Robert Goodwyn, p. 116; Edmund Harvey, p. 537; Roger Hill, p. 235; John Pyne, p. 170; Robert Reynolds, p. 235; Benjamin Weston, p. 624. William Heveningham of the Dunwich classis was a landowner in Suffolk (Alfred Suckling, *History and Antiquities of Suffolk*, 2 vols., [London, 1847], pp. 384–90). The two 'Independent' tryers of elders at the Inns of Court, Prideaux and Ellis, were important Interregnum lawyers.

[1] *A.O.I.*, i. 749–54.   [2] Ibid. p. 749.

the county committees,[1] who certified the final drafts to the Houses of Parliament.[2] The 'Independents' on the eldership lists were members of the very county committees that drew them up and of the House that ratified them. If they had any scruple about serving in a church organized along Presbyterian lines, they could easily keep their names off the lists either by refusing to allow the county committees to include them or by demanding in the house or in the Committee on Scandalous Sins, which finally approved the county lists, that their names be struck from the roster of elders.[3] A particularly flagrant example of an 'Independent' who failed to do anything of the sort is Sir William Masham. He was a member of the county committee for Essex, the committee which drafted the eldership list for the shire, and he was one of the ten members of the joint Committee on Scandalous Sins who signed the order approving the Essex eldership lists *on which his own name appeared*. Both law and circumstance militated against the enrollment in presbyteries of Members of Parliament who did not care to belong. We can only conclude that the thirty-nine 'Independents' enrolled in presbyteries were there because they wanted to be there, or at least had no objection to being there.[4] Against this statement the fact that on most of the eldership lists the elders are certified merely as 'fit to serve' cannot be urged. It is true that they were so certified, but the fact is of no significance. As pointed out above, fitness to serve depended in part on willingness to serve. The form of certification simply meant that the men listed were fit and willing to serve subject to the approval and ratification of Parliament or of the joint Committee on Scandalous Sins.[4]

At first glance this conclusion seems to leave us in a curious dilemma, and as we look further the dilemma grows 'curiouser and curiouser'. Our thirty-nine 'Independents' serving in elderships are about one-fifth of the two hundred regicides and rumpers in the House of Commons. If we stop there, if only one-fifth of our true-blue Independents turn out to be Presbyterians, our problem is puzzling enough. But the more rigorously we examine our data on the English Church during the Interregnum the more suspicious we grow. For a rigorous examination shows that probably far more than one-fifth of the 'Independents' were Presbyterians.

All of the thirty-nine Presbyterian 'Independents' are listed as elders in one or another of seven counties. These seven counties are the only

[1] Shaw, ii. 6.
[2] Ibid. ii. 392, 421.
[3] *A.O.I.*, i. 91; Shaw, ii. 380, 392.
[4] Shaw, ii. 374, 392, 412.

ones whose complete classis lists are extant.[1] We have positive evidence, however, of the existence of more or less complete Presbyterian organizations in twelve other counties.[2] And although positive proof is lacking, it is probable that some counties had presbyteries which disappeared, leaving no trace behind them. Otherwise, how are we to account for the fact that in the eastern tier of Puritan counties the only ones which left no evidence of a Presbyterian establishment were Norfolk, not the least in zeal among them, and Cambridgeshire, the seat of the university which the Presbyterians regarded as peculiarly their own? Why should we assume that in the center of western Puritanism and surrounded by counties with presbyteries, Dorset had none and that, while Warwickshire had a full classical ordinance, neighboring Northamptonshire, a focal point of early English Presbyterianism, had none?[3] Far from assuming that our thirty-nine members include all the 'Independents' who co-operated or connived in the establishment of Presbyterianism, we must admit that they are probably only that fraction of the whole group of equivocal 'Independents' who happened to live in or be associated with the seven 'list' counties.

Although returns for some counties are lacking and for others are useless because of their fragmentary character, we are singularly fortunate in the distribution of these seven 'list' counties that did make full and complete returns. We have Essex and Suffolk in East Anglia, Surrey in the southeast, Somerset in the southwest, Shropshire in the western midlands, and Lancashire in the north.[4] Only the central and eastern midlands are not represented. Moreover, among the members for the 'list' counties at the time of Pride's Purge a little less than three-eighths become regicides or rumpers, and a little more than three-eighths of the total membership of the House followed the same course.[5]

[1] See Shaw, vol. ii, for them: Essex, pp. 374–92; Lancashire, pp. 393–8; London, pp. 399–404; Shropshire, pp. 406–12; Somerset, pp. 413–21; Suffolk, pp. 423–31; Surrey, pp. 431–5.

[2] Shaw, vol. ii: Cheshire and Derbyshire, p. 373; Devonshire and Durham, p. 374; Hampshire, p. 393; Lincolnshire, p. 399; Northumberland, p. 405; Sussex and Warwickshire, p. 436; Wiltshire, pp. 437–8; Yorkshire, pp. 438–40; Westmorland, p. 369.

[3] Shaw, ii. 436; Roland G. Usher, *The Reconstruction of the English Church*, 2 vols. (New York, 1910), i. 252, 256.

[4] London cannot be said to be typical of any area in England but its own. As metropolitan capital its situation was unique.

[5] Although thirty-nine regicides and rumpers belonged to presbyteries in the 'list' counties, altogether only thirty-two rumpers and regicides sat for those counties. A considerable number of the 'Presbyterian' Independents did not

The proportion of regicides and rumpers representing the seven counties was thus almost the same as their proportion in the House at large. And since there was a modicum of sectional homogeneity in seventeenth-century England, we may study the seven shires for which our data are adequate, if not as perfectly typical of the whole kingdom, at least as acute cases of a chronic and pandemic condition.

So we shall seek to arrive at a reasonable estimate of the amount of Presbyterianism among the 'Independents' by studying its prevalence among the Members of Parliament representing the seven 'list' counties. Altogether these seven counties returned eighty-eight members to the House of Commons—Essex 8, Lancashire 14, Middlesex (including the borough of Southwark) 10, Shropshire 12, Somersetshire 16, Suffolk 16, Surrey 12. From the eighty-eight we may, however, strike out four who apparently had no connection with the local politics or the social and economic life of the counties where their parliamentary constituencies were located.[1] The remaining eighty-four members do have such connections.[2] Twenty-three who were not elders in their county presbyteries owned land or were active in politics in the shires where

represent in Parliament the counties where they served as elders (see p. 165, n. 5). Of the eighty-eight members who sat for the 'list' counties the thirty-two rumpers and regicides comprise thirty-six per cent. At the beginning of the Long Parliament there were altogether 513 members of the House of Commons. The number was greatly reduced by the defection of the royalists and by death. In 1645, however, the house began to issue writs for new elections to refill the vacant seats. By the time of Pride's Purge the membership was nearly back to its original size. About two hundred of the commoners sitting at that time became regicides or rumpers—that is, forty per cent.

[1] I have been unable to find any evidence of the association of Sir Charles Legrosse, a Norfolk man, with Suffolk (*Norfolk Archaeology*, iii. 90), of Walter Strickland, a northerner, with Somerset, of Sir Edward Spencer with Middlesex, or of Sir Richard Wynne with Lancashire. In 1647 there was a movement to expel Legrosse from Parliament on grounds of malignancy. Strickland spent most of his time in Holland as parliamentary agent. Spencer was returned from Middlesex some time after the first eldership list for the county was published. Wynne, an old courtier from Wales (G. E. C. [Cockayne], *Complete Baronetage*, 5 vols. [Exeter, 1900] i. 64–5), was seated for Liverpool on the Molyneux-Stanley interest (J. A. Picton, *Memorials of Liverpool*, 2 vols., London, 1875, i. 83). It is perhaps best therefore to eliminate all four from our present consideration.

[2] On a strict interpretation eighty-two might be a more accurate number; but although Sir John Clotworthy (member for Maldon, Essex) and William Masham (member for Shrewsbury, Shropshire) had no connection with the places which returned them as members, nevertheless they resided in 'list' counties, Clotworthy in Middlesex (*Accounts and Papers*, 1876, lxii, pt. 1, 488, 'Members of Parliament') and Masham in Essex (*A.O.I.*, i. 91). Since they were thus just as available as the other eighty-two for service in 'list' county elderships, we may include them in our study.

they had their parliamentary seats.[1] The rest, sixty-one in all, were listed in their county elderships. Of these sixty-one members of their county presbyteries, twenty-four were regicides or rumpers, thirty-seven others were not.[2] Now the very best we can hope for is that these twenty-three non-Presbyterians will turn out to be regicides and rumpers. If this is the case, the regicides and rumpers, that is to say, the 'Independents', are still a bastard breed, nearly half Presbyterian. Such a mongrel Independency does violence to our old conception of party

[1] William Langton was of an old Lancashire family (Edward Baine, *History of the County . . . of Lancaster*, 4 vols., London, 1836, iv, p. 409). Anthony Bedingfield's family had land in Suffolk, where he was returned from Dunwich (John Burke, . . . *History of the Commoners of England*, 4 vols., London, 1836, iv, p. 409). For Sir John Clotworthy see the above note. For the other members not connected with the county presbyteries see *A.O.I.*, vol. i: James Ash, p. 974; William Bell, p. 114; Sir Robert Bindlose, p. 707; William Carent, p. 1243; Humphrey Edwards, p. 447; Sir Gilbert Gerard, and John Glynn, p. 536; Thomas Grove, p. 974; Thomas Hodges, p. 1091; John Holcroft, p. 1239; Capel Luckyn, p. 1237; Thomas Mackworth, p. 1091; William Lord Monson, p. 1093; Sir Poynings More, p. 1094; Sir Robert Parkhurst, p. 1095; Isaac Pennington, p. 1087; Thomas Sandys, p. 976; Sir Thomas Soame, p. 1087; Samuel Vassal and John Venn, p. 1087. [In her indispensable register of members, *The Long Parliament 1640–1641: A Biographical Study of its Members* (Philadelphia, 1954), M. F. Keeler has mistakenly indicated (e.g., s.v., Gerard, Sir Gilbert) that I classified the twenty-three men in the foregoing list as Independents. The confusion may have been the consequence of a youthful ineptitude at exposition on my part, which I have tried here to rectify. In any case the twenty-three members listed in this note actually correspond to the seven 'Independents' and sixteen 'Presbyterians' not in presbyteries of the first table on p. 172, n. 2. The seven 'Independents' on the list were Ash, Carent, Edwards, Mackworth, Monson, Pennington and Venn. The rest were 'Presbyterians'.]

[2] The number twenty-four is used here instead of thirty-nine because, although thirty-nine regicide and rumper members of Parliament had elderships in the seven 'list' counties, fifteen of the thirty-nine did not sit in Parliament from these counties. See p. 165, n. 5 above.

For the thirty-seven members of Parliament from the seven 'list' counties who were not regicides or rumpers but who belonged to the presbyteries of their respective counties, see Shaw, vol. ii: Sir Ralph Ashton and Ralph Ashton, p. 394; William Ashurst, p. 395; Francis Bacon, p. 426; Sir Nathaniel Barnardiston, p. 429; Sir Thomas Barnardiston, p. 429; Maurice Barrow, p. 428 (there spelled Batrow); Alexander Bence and Squire Bence, p. 425; Edward Bishe, p. 434; Sir Humphrey Briggs, p. 409; Sir Ambrose Brown, p. 433; Sir Robert Charlton, p. 411; Sir Thomas Cheke, p. 375; Robert Clive and Sir John Corbett, p. 410; Sir Simond Dewes, p. 428; George Evelyn, p. 433; Sir John Evelyn, p. 434; Harbottle Grimston, p. 391; George Horner, p. 417; Sir Richard Houghton, p. 396; Thomas Hunt, p. 407; Sir Martin Lumley, p. 384; Thomas More, p. 412; Sir Richard Onslow and William Owfield, p. 434; Sir Philip Parker, p. 423; William Pierpont, p. 409; Sir William Playters, p. 426; John Sayer, p. 388; Richard Shuttleworth, sr., and Richard Shuttleworth, jr., p. 394; Sir William Spring, p. 428; William Strode, p. 417; Esay Thomas, p. 412; Clement Walker, p. 415.

divisions in the Long Parliament. The actual situation, however, does considerably more violence to that conception. For as a matter of fact only seven of these twenty-three commoners not included in the presbyteries are regicides and rumpers.[1] This gives a total of thirty-one 'Independent' members for the seven 'list' counties, and *over seventy-five per cent* of them are Presbyterians. The remaining fifty-three members, who were neither regicides nor rumpers, did not, politically speaking, survive Pride's Purge. They were the 'Presbyterians'. But of these 'Presbyterians' *only seventy per cent* belonged to their county presbyteries. Our study moves toward a most outrageous conclusion. As we naturally expect, a rather high percentage of 'Presbyterians' are Presbyterians; but as we most assuredly should not expect, an even higher percentage of 'Independents' are Presbyterians.

This analysis may encounter an objection. It may be said that it is unfair to jumble all the members who were not regicides or rumpers together and label them Presbyterians, that those only should be called Presbyterian who were excluded or arrested in Pride's Purge. On the theory that Presbyterians and Independents were mutually exclusive groups this is a very dubious distinction. Instead of objecting to this distinction, let us make it, however, and study the results. Twenty-five arrested or excluded members sat for the seven counties and had local interests in those counties besides representing them in Parliament. Only about five-eighths of these twenty-five 'Presbyterians', i.e. sixteen, were enrolled as elders in their several counties. More than six-eighths of the 'Independents' who sat for these counties were so enrolled.[2] So our dubious distinction has done us no good. However we wrestle with our data we come to the same absurd result. Among the members who sat for the 'list' counties the proportion of 'Independents'

---

[1] James Ash, Humphrey Edwards, Thomas Hodges, Thomas Mackworth, William Lord Monson, Isaac Pennington, John Venn.

[2] That is, twenty-four of the thirty-one 'Independents'. See the tables, p. 172, n. below. The twenty-five members from the seven counties, purged by Pride and not returning to the House, were distributed as follows: in presbyteries—Sir Ralph Ashton, Maurice Barrow, Sir Ambrose Brown, Sir John Corbett, Sir Simond Dewes, Harbottle Grimston, George Horner, Sir Martin Lumley, Sir Richard Onslow, William Owfield, Sir Philip Parker, Sir William Playters, Sir William Spring, William Strode, Esay Thomas, Clement Walker; not in presbyteries—Sir Robert Bindlose, Sir John Clotworthy, Sir Gilbert Gerrard, John Glynn, Thomas Grove, John Holcroft, Thomas Sandys, Sir Thomas Soame, Samuel Vassal. For lists of excluded and arrested members see William Prynne, *The True and Full Relation* (London, 1648), p. 11; *The Second Part of the Narrative* (London, 1648), pp. 3–8; *The Parliamentary History of England to 1803* (36 vols., London, 1806–20), iii. pp. 248–9.

who were Presbyterian was greater than the proportion of 'Presbyterians' who were Presbyterian. And since we may consider these counties as roughly typical of the rest,[1] the same proportion is true for Parliament as a whole. That is to say, *there was a larger proportion of Presbyterian 'Independents' than of Presbyterian 'Presbyterians' in the Long Parliament*. The use of quotation marks in our discussion of the 'Presbyterians' and 'Independents' as political parties stands as a barrier between us and sheer nonsense.[2]

If the bulk of the parliamentary 'Presbyterian' party lagged behind the 'Independents' in enthusiasm for joining presbyteries, it might be

[1] See p. 168, above.

[2] The statistical results of our study may be represented county by county in this tabular form:

	Independents in presbyteries	Presbyterians in presbyteries	Independents not in presbyteries	Presbyterians not in presbyteries	Not connected with the place from which they sit	Totals
Essex	2*	4	0	2	0	8
Lancashire	4	6	0	3	1	14
Middlesex	2	0	2	5*	1	10
Shropshire	2	7	2	1	0	12
Somerset	8	3	2	2	1	16
Suffolk	4	10	0	1	1	16
Surrey	2	7	1	2	0	12
TOTALS	24	37	7	16	4	88

* For the inclusion of William Masham and John Clotworthy in the numbers indicated see above, p. 169, n. 2.

	No. in presbyteries	% in presbyteries	No. not in presbyteries	% not in presbyteries
Independents	24	77	7	23
Presbyterians	37	70	16	30
Members secluded or arrested 1648	16	64	9	36

thought that the former party acquired its label through the superior orthodoxy of its leaders. The leaders of the 'Presbyterian' party, at least according to the idea of the Independent army, which had good cause to know, were the eleven members impeached by that army in 1647. By the time of the Restoration three of them were dead,[1] and two received no honors from the returned Stuart.[2] But among the rest were distributed three knighthoods and a knighthood of the Bath, a baronetcy, a barony, and a viscounty.[3] One of the eleven, who became a knight and also a king's sergeant, had been lord chief justice under Oliver Cromwell, and the viscount had served on one of the Protectorate commissions for the settlement of Ireland. Another of the impeached members sat in all of the Protectorate parliaments.[4] Of course, the skill of so many of the eleven members at trimming their sails to shifts in the political wind does not prove that they were not staunch Presbyterians. It does leave one wondering, though, about the intensity of their zeal for orthodoxy.

What we can discover about the religious opinions of the eleven confirms our suspicion of their Presbyterian ardor. Specific evidence as to the theological preferences of four of them is lacking, while a fifth is a doubtful case.[5] Of the remaining six Sir John Maynard seems to have been a 'real' Presbyterian.[6] Massey, on the other hand, was ready to betray Gloucester to the king at the very time that negotiations were under way for an alliance between Parliament and the champions of the godly discipline from Scotland.[7] Waller dreamed of a latitudinarian Puritanism altogether incompatible with the divine right of presbyteries,[8] and Edward Harley at the Restoration became a regular

[1] Sir Philip Stapleton, Sir John Maynard, Anthony Nicholas.

[2] Sir William Lewis, Sir William Waller.

[3] Edward Massey and John Glynn, knights; Edward Harley, knight and K.B.; Walter Long, baronet; Denzil Holles, Baron Holles; John Clotworthy, Viscount Massareene.

[4] In the same order, Glynn, Clotworthy, Nicholas.

[5] Stapleton, Nicholas, Lewis, Long. Clotworthy may or may not have been a zealous Presbyterian; see *Dictionary of National Biography*.

[6] Siranniho [John Harris], *The Royal Quarrel* (London, 1647). Harris's distinction between 'real' and 'royal' Presbyterians is illuminating.

[7] Gardiner, *Civil War*, i. 198, and n. 2. Clarendon says of Massey that he was 'not intoxicated with any of those fumes which make men rave and frantic in the cause', *History of the Rebellion and Civil Wars in England*, ed. W. Dunn Macray, 6 vols. (Oxford, 1888), bk. VII, sec. 158.

[8] 'There may be different characters of parties in the church . . . Episcopians . . . Presbyterians and . . . Independents; and yet all be Israelites indeed.' Sir William Waller, *Vindication of the Character and Conduct of Sir William Waller* (London, 1793), p. 228.

communicant of the Church of England.[1] John Glynn, whose feline talent for landing on his feet brought him unscathed through one political crisis after another, conducted one of the earliest recorded filibusters in the House of Commons. A 'Presbyterian' leader, he filibustered against a bill that would have freed presbyteries from political regulation.[2] His is not the most startling case. In March 1646, the Commons passed a church bill which Baillie, the Scottish commissioner to the Westminster Assembly of Divines, attributed to the joint machinations of the Erastians and Independents and considered so entirely evil that he doubted whether the Presbyterian ministers would consent to perform their offices under it.[3] By way of contrast the commoner who carried the bill to the Lords celebrated the date of its passage as 'the dawning of a glorious day which our ancestors hoped to have seen but could not'.[4] This enthusiast for a measure hated by true Presbyterians was certainly not an Independent; he may have been an Erastian, and he was indisputably the acknowledged leader of the 'Presbyterian' party in the house. His name was Denzil Holles. To the question, 'How Presbyterian was the "Presbyterian" party?' the true answer seems to be, 'Not very'.

Dr. William A. Shaw has shown that the Presbyterianism of the parliamentary Presbyterian Church was as equivocal an affair as the Independency of the 'Independents'.[5] To complete the record let us review briefly the history of the establishment of the parliamentary church during the Civil War.[6] Presbyterianism is rather difficult to define. It is not simply Calvinism. Archbishop Whitgift and John Cotton were both orthodox Calvinists without being Presbyterians. Presbyterianism is Calvinism operating under a specific form and substance of church government. The form of Presbyterian church government is a hierarchy of ecclesiastical tribunals beginning with

[1] *Letters of the Lady Brilliana Harley*, T. T. Lewis, ed. Camden Society Publications, old ser., lviii (London, 1853), p. 241.

[2] Bulstrode Whitelocke, *Memorials of the English Affairs* (London, 1732), pp. 110–11.

[3] Robert Baillie, *Letters and Journals . . . 1637–1662*, ed. D. Laing, 3 vols. (Edinburgh, 1841–1842), ii. 360–1.

[4] *Journal of the House of Lords*, viii. 202; see Clarendon's statement (bk. VIII, sec. 248), that Holles confessed that he was merely using the Presbyterians to oppose the Independents.

[5] Shaw, vol. i.

[6] For the most important ecclesiastical ordinances see *A.O.I.*, vol. i: regulating the election of elders, 19 August, 1645, pp. 749–54; concerning church government and suspension from the sacraments, 20 October, 1645, pp. 789–93; amending previous ordinances, 5 June, 1646, pp. 852–5.

the congregation and ending in the national synod. That hierarchy existed in law in England during the late forties of the seventeenth century.[1] The substance of Presbyterianism is the jurisdiction, independent of the state, exercised by the ecclesiastical courts over the whole nation in all questions of morals. This is the 'godly discipline' of Geneva and Scotland, abhorred by Charles I.[2] Without it the Presbyterian tribunals are courts without jurisdiction, empty and impotent.

For a year and a half, from January 1645 to June 1646, the Long Parliament labored at the ecclesiastical settlement. The Grand Committee on Religion of the House of Commons debated the problems of the settlement, often three times a week, for a year after the battle of Naseby.[3] There is no question here of unconsidered emergency legislation hastily adopted because of the exigencies of war. Throughout eighteen months the pressure on Parliament to establish the godly discipline never relaxed. The Scots commissioners, the assembly of divines, the City of London, the clergy of London—four of the most powerful of Parliament's allies—united to force Parliament to grant the substance of jurisdiction to the presbyteries.[4] At one point the assembly threatened a clerical sit-down strike unless they had their way. The unremitting hammering to which the Commons were subjected finally brought out a statement of their position so explicit as to leave no possible doubt as to their intentions. 'We cannot', they declared flatly, 'consent to the granting of so arbitrary and unlimited jurisdiction to near ten thousand judicatories to be erected within this kingdom . . . by necessary consequence excluding the power of the Parliament in the exercise of that jurisdiction'.[5] When the time for action came the Commons proved that they had meant precisely what they said; they had no intention of turning England over to the tender mercies of the elderships. The scheme of ecclesiastical discipline ultimately adopted by Parliament was anything but the answer to a Presbyterian's prayer. Instead of granting 'arbitrary and unlimited jurisdiction' to the presbyteries, it gave them a regulated jurisdiction over a limited group of scandalous sins. In all cases not enumerated in the ordinance appeal lay not through the hierarchy of church courts but directly from the congregational eldership to a committee of both Houses of Parliament.[6] The final determination of the power of the

[1] *A.O.I.*, vol. i., pp. 749–54.

[2] *Charles I in 1646*, J. Bruce, ed. Camden Society Publications, old series, lxiii (London, 1856), pp. 22–3.

[3] E.g. *C. J.*, iv. 266–72.   [4] *L.J.*, vii. 558–9, viii. 105, 232, 258.

[5] *C. J.*, iv. 513.   [6] *A.O.I.*, i. 852–5.

presbyteries lay not between them and God, as the Presbyterians would have had it, but with a Parliament that had already manifested its sympathy with John Selden's war cry, 'Chain up the clergy on both sides'.[1] Several months after Parliament had passed the basic ordinance on church discipline, King Charles contrasted the true Presbyterian system of Scotland, where 'the clergie will depend on none', with the pseudo-Presbyterianism of England, where the clergy depended on the two houses without the King.[2] Charles knew whereof he spoke. As Baillie, the Scottish Kirk commissioner, bitterly observed, the English ordinance set up merely 'a lame Erastian presbyterie'. Fully conscious of what it was doing, Parliament established the outer shell of Presbyterian church government in England; then, still fully conscious of what it was doing, Parliament refused to breathe into that shell what alone could give it real life and power—'arbitrary and unlimited jurisdiction', the substance of Presbyterian discipline.[3]

We thus emerge from our investigation with 'Independents' who were not Independents adhering in a larger proportion than 'Presbyterians' who were not Presbyterian to a 'Presbyterian Church' that was not really Presbyterian. Such a conclusion has a certain destructive value. If in the Long Parliament many 'Independents' were members of presbyteries and many 'Presbyterians' were not members of presbyteries, if the leadership of the 'Presbyterian party' was hardly Presbyterian at all, and if the Presbyterian Church was to some degree Erastian, then the Long Parliament could not have been simply the arena for a titanic struggle between real Presbyterians and real Independents. This statement is painfully negative and has no constructive value. It explains nothing; the anomaly of the Presbyterian Independents remains as anomalous as before. It is possible either to leave the whole problem in the air or to suggest an explanation for which evidence cannot be given within the limits of this article. Accepting the latter alternative and hoping at a future time to present the supporting proofs, we offer some generalizations.

John Pym dominated the House of Commons in the first year of the Civil War. During the time of his hegemony no religious issues of any consequence emerged in Parliament, and in many instances party

[1] John Selden, *Table Talk* (London, 1906), p. 30.

[2] *State Papers collected by Edward, Earl of Clarendon*, Richard Scrope and Thomas Monkhouse, eds. (3 vols., Oxford, 1767–86), ii. 260.

[3] The Presbyterianism described above is of course Reformation Presbyterianism, not the twentieth-century variety.

divisions in the houses cut clean across sectarian lines.[1] In the twelve-month that followed Pym's death it was the intensity of a man's religious ardor rather than the nature of his favorite brand of church government that determined his party allegiance. All the fiery and militant Puritans, regardless of their sectarian preference, were united in a single alliance—the *soi-disant* 'godly party'. It was not for an ultimate common end that the militant Puritans worked together. For the time being they all despised the same things and the same people with such intense fervor that they did not need a constructive program to bind them together. Hostile to all members of Parliament more moderate and more peace-loving than themselves, distrustful of the military skill and the devotion to the 'cause' of the Lord General, the Earl of Essex, the 'godly party' set out to harass the moderates and discredit the Earl. They attained their second objective when Essex's army surrendered to the royalists at Lostwithiel. Immediately there-after, toward the end of 1644, the 'godly party' was torn asunder. Since its internal cohesion was destroyed by the emergence of the religious issue in an acute form, we must briefly analyze the religious situation in the Civil War Parliament.

Shrewd John Selden once remarked: 'The House of Commons is called the Lower House in twenty acts of Parliament; but what are twenty acts of Parliament among friends?'[2] The Commons were the tail that wagged the dog, and since the outbreak of hostilities the Commons had been overwhelmingly Puritan. They could be satisfied by no mere half-hearted changes in the Church. In contrast to the moderate Anglicans and the out-and-out Erastians, who wanted only a read-justment or diminution of ecclesiastical power, the Puritan mass in the Lower House insisted on the need for a fundamental spiritual reform of the Church. The minimum of reform acceptable to all the Puritans involved the abolition of ritualism and drastic revision of the prayer book, the reaffirmation of pure Calvinist doctrine, an increased em-phasis on the preaching of the Word, radical alterations in the existing church government, and the embodiment of these reforms in a unified national Church. Probably the aspirations of the bulk of Puritan com-moners were no more specific than this. Differences lay in the intensity rather than in the form of aspiration. There were in the House, how-ever, men with clear and distinct ideas as to the best or the only form of Church government suitable to carry out the reforms commonly

---

[1] J. H. Hexter, *Reign of King Pym*, Harvard Historical Series, xlviii (Cambridge, Mass., 1941).   [2] Selden, p. 31.

desired. Unfortunately their ideas were not identical; they were divided into three separate groups. All three groups either antedated the Long Parliament or could point to ideological predecessors earlier in the seventeenth century. The Erastian Puritans felt that the desired reforms could best be achieved through a sharp reduction of clerical power in general and of the power of the bishops in particular and through the transfer of part of the king's ecclesiastical prerogative to Parliament. The Presbyterians, on the other hand, would have no truck with the bishops. They wanted to displace episcopacy altogether for the only form of church government plainly set forth in Holy Scripture—Genevan-Scottish Presbyterianism. The Independents also wanted to abolish episcopacy for the only form of Church government plainly set forth in Scripture—the congregational form based on New England models. Now the very soul of the 'godly party' had been its Presbyterian and Independent leaders, and in 1645 the question of church government divided these leaders and thereby destroyed the spiritual unity of the 'godly party'. As a consequence of this split the Puritan religious settlement was the result of a series of bewilderingly shifting coalitions among the three doctrinaire religious groups. By 1645 episcopacy was a dead issue. It had been destroyed by the Solemn League and Covenant, the work of Presbyterians, Independents, and nonsectarian Puritans, two years before. Now, *faute de mieux*, the Erastians[1] and the mass of Puritans united with the Presbyterians to set up the form of Presbyterian government and then, quickly putting about, united with the Independents to prevent the establishment of a real Presbyterian discipline. The resulting ecclesiastical settlement, recorded in legislation between 1645 and 1648, may not have been perfect in the eyes of most Puritan members of Parliament, but it probably represented a rough approximation to what they wanted. If it had not, we would not find nearly three-quarters of them joining up in our seven 'list' counties.

While the members were settling the Church a curious and complicated set of crosscurrents developed in Parliament. In 1644 young Henry Vane and Oliver St. John, the leaders of the Independents, foresaw the imminent breakdown of the 'godly party', and they worked out a clever scheme to prevent the balance of power from falling into the hands of the Presbyterians. The conduct of the military campaign of 1644 had profoundly disappointed the high hopes of the militant Puritans, and consequently the Independents had no trouble in swinging

[1] i.e. Puritan Erastians like Sergeant Maynard and Whitelocke and non-Puritan Erastians like Selden (if there was anybody else like Selden).

them in favor of a general army reform. The Independent leaders so manipulated the reform as to displace a high command actually or potentially hostile to them with an officer group friendly to them. At the same time the reforms gave the new force a unified command and reasonable assurance of regular supply and pay. The result was the great New Model Army, of which Gardiner somewhere says that it was not the army of a party but the army of the nation. But really the unique fact about the New Model was that it was both the one and the other and something else besides. In the pay of the Long Parliament, it represented the nation in so far as the will of the nation and the will of the majority in that Parliament coincided. Moreover, its commanders were closely united to the parliamentary Independents by bonds of sympathy, friendship, and obligation. Soon, however, it developed an *esprit de corps* and aims and purposes of its own, not always congruent with the aims of the parliamentary Independents or the will of the nation. As long as it kept busy beating the royalist enemy and insuring the departure of the Scots army from England, it enjoyed a broad general support among the Puritans. When, however, it deviated from its national ends and began to develop distinct political and religious tendencies of its own, and when its military work was accomplished, most of the Puritans thought that the time had come to get rid of it. The minority that sympathized with some of the army's political or religious objectives stood by it, and the parliamentary Independents, unable to muster a majority in either House under any circumstances without the threat of force, naturally followed the course set by the army that they could no longer control.

Meanwhile the split in the 'godly party' had had a further influence on the development of parliamentary politics. Throughout 1644 the Independent chiefs, young Vane and Oliver St. John, had acted in closest conjunction with the real leaders of the real parliamentary Presbyterians, the Scottish commissioners in London. When, because of the religious schism in the 'godly party', they could no longer use them, the Independent leaders were ready to throw the Scots to the wolves. They turned on them as before they had turned on Essex, and, playing on the old English distrust of a traditional enemy, tried to destroy them. This policy of the Independents and the obvious hostility of the New Model to Presbyterianism drove the Scots and their English followers into the waiting arms of the Earl of Essex and the moderate, pacific Members of Parliament. Many of the moderates were Erastians with no special affection for Presbyterianism and no special antipathy to reformed Episcopacy. To retain the support of these men for the parliamentary Presbyterian Church the Scots and their friends accepted the conservative political program of the moderates and in so doing subordinated their former zeal for radical political reform to the quest for peace. Most of the Presbyterians and many of the less radical Puritans joined with the old 'peace party' in an effort to get rid of the army, while on the other side the friends of the New Model rallied to its defense. The conflict reached its climax in 1647, when the army saved itself from being disbanded by overawing the hostile majority in Parliament. Thenceforth the men at Westminster had to face the problem of the relation of the military force to the civil government. In December 1648 the army itself effected an arbitrary solution of this and many other problems by forcing out of Parliament all members who would not implicitly sanction its violent method of dealing with a recalcitrant king.

The general situation just outlined is undeniably complex, but it is nonetheless a drastic simplification of the actual development of political groups in the Long Parliament. In the complexity of this development lies our key to 'the problem of the Presbyterian Independents'. The average Puritan commoner who, more or less willingly, joined the parliamentary Presbyterian Church never had a chance to choose between Presbyterianism and Independency, between persecution and toleration, between war and peace. Instead of having his choice between an ideal black and an ideal white he had to pick his way among an infinite variety of grays—shifting, unstable, uncertain. He could not choose between real Presbyterianism and real Independency because those alternatives were never offered him.[1] He had to choose, rather, between the flaccid, trussed-up Presbyterianism that Parliament had established and the continually fluctuating program of the Independents, who shifted from Presbyterianism with toleration of dissent to Episcopacy with toleration of dissent to an undefined form of church government with toleration of dissent. Moreover at various times the Puritan member would find questions not immediately germane to the religious issue influencing his attitude on church government. Might the establishment of Presbyterianism by Parliament involve

[1] In the early months of 1646, during the excommunication controversy, Parliament did have a choice between real Presbyterianism and something else, but that something else was not real Independency or any other kind of Independency. Indeed as a part of their campaign to prevent the establishment of real Presbyterianism men like St. John accepted the form of a Presbyterian church government.

moral obligations to the Scottish foreigner? Was Presbyterianism worth the sacrifices of political principle that the moderates expected as the price of their co-operation? Could one conscientiously submit to the surrender of some of Parliament's political demands in order to induce the king to accept Presbyterianism? How far could one trust the king to fulfill any promise he might make with regard to the settlement of the Church? How good was the king's word? And if his word was worthless, what securities had Parliament and the Puritans against his treachery? Might it not be better to cast him off altogether and remodel both Church and State nearer to the heart's desire? But how would such a violent act consort with the Covenant that Parliament had made with the Scots, before God, 'to protect the King's person?' So a member might start to examine his belief on the proper organization of the Church and end by examining his belief on the proper organization of the State. Or he might start with the State and end with the Church. Or he might start with either one and end with the question of the limits of religious toleration or of the danger of military dictatorship or democracy. On any issue that came to vote in Parliament a member had to give his yea or his nay; but on a single issue twelve men might give their yeas for twelve different reasons. Their overt act would be identical, their underlying motives diverse.

To this rule the question of allegiance to the Commonwealth was no exception. Every member, Puritan or non-Puritan, had to decide whether to give his allegiance; but each man had his own reasons for his decision, and the number of permutations and combinations of possible reasons is enormous. The desire for religious toleration doubtless impelled many Independents to support the Commonwealth; but to argue that because many Independents were Commonwealthmen, therefore all Commonwealthmen were Independents is to indulge in a *non sequitur*. One could as well reason that because many grafters and profiteers were Commonwealthmen, therefore all Commonwealthmen were grafters and profiteers. In fact there were republicans in the Rump who cared little for Independency or toleration and Independents who cared little for republicanism. There were also officers playing the old army game of follow-the-leader, and radical Puritans who felt that the Stuart dynasty was hopeless although they had no prepossessions in favor of Independency or republicanism or toleration, and light-fingered gentlemen mainly concerned to get their hands on any money that was going. As in every other considerable political group, so in the Rump there were men who had taken the path of least resistance and men too cowardly to defy superior force, men who, having no principles, always turned up on the winning side and men whose principles bore a regular functional relation to their profits.[1] Most of the rumpers were, of course, Puritans. They believed in a national church, Puritan in doctrine and spirit. The Church established by Parliament in 1645-8 met these specifications. It might be a little too Presbyterian for some and not quite Presbyterian enough for others, but still it would do; only papists, prelatists, and fanatics could find no place in it. Accordingly, many members who later sat in the Rump served as elders in the parliamentary Presbyterian Church. There was no reason why they should feel guilty of inconsistency because, in fact, they were not so.

Having suggested why, in our opinion, so many Commonwealth-men were members of the Presbyterian Church, we may attempt briefly to explain how the polymorphous group of regicides and rumpers came to be called Independents. To a generation that has observed the multiple and indiscriminate uses of the words 'fascist', 'communist', and 'liberal' this explanation should present no serious difficulties. As soon as the Civil War got properly under way gentle-men on all sides started calling their opponents ugly names and them-selves pretty ones. To hurl opprobrious epithets at the enemy was as integral a part of the combat as to slit the enemy's throat or pillage his wine-cellar, stable, and pig-pen. Indeed the fabrication of epithet is the only technique of warfare in which the Industrial Revolution has wrought no perceptible improvement. Among the labels, honorific and comminatory, which the factions pasted on themselves and each other during the Interregnum were Cavalier, Malignant, Delinquent, Papist, Loyalist, Royalist, Puritan, Roundhead, Brownist, Rebel, Common-wealthman, Republican, Cromwellian, Presbyterian, Independent, Anabaptist, and Neuter. Some of these labels had meaning only with reference to the contemporary conflict. A 'Rebel' was anybody fight-ing on the side opposite to you. 'Neuter' was the name which, what-ever side you were on, you would apply to anybody who did not share

---

[1] Professor M. M. Knappen has brought to my attention a passage from Mrs. Hutchinson's biography of her husband which seems to bear out my hypothesis of the complex structure of the Rump parliament. She says: 'Most of the Presby-terian faction, disgusted at this insolence [Pride's Purge], would no more come to their seats in the House; but the gentlemen who were of the other faction or of none at all, but looked upon themselves as called out to manage a public trust for their country, forsook not their seats while they were permitted to sit in the House.' Lucy Hutchinson, *Life of Colonel John Hutchinson* (London, 1899), p. 331.

your enthusiasm for disemboweling the kingdom for the greater glory of God and the king, or God and the Parliament. Other epithets, however, had besides their objurgatory value a permanent meaning. If you were a parliamentarian, a 'Papist' would mean to you one on the king's side with a strenuous dislike for Puritanism, but a papist was at the same time and specifically a communicant of the Roman Catholic Church. As a parliamentarian you would have no scruple about labeling Walter Montague and the Duke of Newcastle as 'Papists'; but in fact while Montague was really a papist, Newcastle in a vague sort of way was a good Anglican.[1] What is true of the word 'Papist' is equally true of the words 'Presbyterian' and 'Independent'. In theological discussion a Presbyterian was a Calvinist believing in a specific form of church government and a specific method of ecclesiastical discipline. An Independent was a Calvinist who supported another specific form of church government and another specific method of ecclesiastical discipline. But if you were a Member of the House or a pamphleteer during the Long Parliament and wanted to call somebody a bad name, you probably would not let fine-spun theological distinctions hamper you. If, for example, the somebody to be vilified had opposed the disbanding of the New Model army, got a job for his uncle through the good offices of Sir Henry Vane the younger, and voted to sequester the estates of your royalist brother-in-law, like as not you called that man 'Independent' without examining too closely his religious position. Such an examination might have revealed that doctrinally the man was a reasonably orthodox Presbyterian. By calling him an 'Independent' you would have made a small contribution to the general confusion about the nature of parties in the Long Parliament.

For the pamphleteer the supposititious division of the Long Parliament into two distinct parties may have served a useful purpose. One who has already divided the world into the forces of good and the forces of evil always finds it convenient to paste the same black label on all men and all things he dislikes, to seek God on one side and the Devil on the other and in between a great gulf. The purposes of the historian are not—or should not be—identical with those of the pamphleteer. He should be less concerned to fix guilt than to understand the complex of forces that creates the form, the substance, and the texture of what

[1] For Walter Montague, see *Dictionary of National Biography*; for Newcastle, Margaret, Duchess of Newcastle, *Memoirs of William Cavendish, Duke of Newcastle* (London, 1886), p. 185.

he is examining. A historian studying the Civil War Parliament, free from the prepossessions inflicted on him by the pamphleteer will see an almost anarchic hurly-burly of men, in which all but the most doctrinaire are pulled in many different directions by many forces varying in their intensity as the circumstances vary. He will see these fluctuations in aspiration, belief, interest, and prejudice actualized in the forming, disintegrating, reforming, and shifting majorities in the House of Commons. Eventually he may reach some conclusion as to the significance and relative importance of the various forces. That conclusion is not on the whole likely to be that the Civil War Parliament was primarily the arena in which two closely matched religious groups, the Presbyterians and the Independents, struggled for supremacy.[1]

[1] In the twentieth year of its life—if it can be called that—the above study along with H. R. Trevor-Roper's 'The Gentry, 1540–1640', became at once the inspiration and the target of a monograph, George Yule's *The Independents in the English Civil War* (Cambridge, Eng., 1958). Yule discovered several errors or evidential weaknesses in my lists of 'Presbyterians', Presbyterians, and 'Independents'. These errors and weaknesses, however, were not of sufficient dimension significantly to affect the statistical basis of the argument in the above article. Moreover, in his study, Yule insisted that a fundamental religious issue did separate the true Presbyterians from the true Independents—the issue of toleration. In reviewing the book, I observed that in this matter 'where Yule's conclusion stands in flat contradiction to my own, Yule almost certainly has the matter right, and I had it wrong' (*American Historical Review*, lxii [1959], 362). Without seeking to limit the above acknowledgment of error, I should like to emphasize that probably the majority of the 'Presbyterian' party in Parliament were not true Presbyterians and that on Yule's own showing the majority of the 'Independent' party in Parliament were not true Independents.

Personal Retrospect and Postscript

I

TO DESIGNATE AS personal any portion of a work which has pretensions to being scholarly, is to court misunderstanding and opprobrium. Nowadays, for some reason or other, the term 'personal' seems to evoke in people's minds such other terms as intuitive, emotional, and romantic in their most invidious sense: that is, bereft of both actuality and reality. And if it be identified with or assimilated to those other three, the personal has no place in a book with scholarly pretensions. But the identification and assimilation seem to me somewhat arbitrary. Judgments and opinions arrived at after wrestling with the evidence and investigating contrary judgments and opinions are no less personal than emotional reactions or intuitive hunches. Indeed to me they seem in a sense more personal; I have lived with them longer and more intensively; they more fully belong to me and I to them.

The 'Retrospect and Postscript' that follows is personal, then, only in the sense that the views there expressed will be those that I have come by more or less honestly and in the hard way, through a consideration as careful and rational as my capabilities permit of the appropriate evidence and the alternative views. The extent to which this 'Retrospect and Postscript' was personal was not evident to me until I had written a sizable part of it. Out of a decent respect for the opinion and custom of scholars I had sought to avoid the first person singular, referring instead to 'the present writer', and 'the present author'. Soon, however, the pages became so densely packed with 'present writers' and 'present authors' that out of a decent respect for the amenities of English expression it was necessary to jettison the whole cargo and put the first person singular in its place. The substitution made it quite evident that the 'Retrospect and Postscript' *was* personal; in precisely what sense, I have tried to indicate above.

II

Retrospects at the ends of books often suffer from one or the other of two common flaws. There is on the one hand the retrospect in name only. Far from being a detached examination of the course and movement of his thought, it is continually in the writer's mind as he composes his work. It is a brooding and directive omnipresence determining, all along, the ways in which the writer's mind shall tread. The retrospect that will here follow avoids such artificiality not through any particular virtue of mine, but simply because the preceding content of this book was almost complete as it here appears before I thought of composing a retrospective conclusion for it. An unintended escape from one common defect of the retrospect, however, only exposes a writer the more dangerously to the other defect. In a series of studies the oldest of which was completed more than two decades ago, the temptation retrospectively to find a continuity in one's conceptions and a firm directional purposefulness in one's labors throughout the intervening years is powerful. One is very strongly driven to discern in the child the father to the man, and to leave the impression that all one's effort has followed the lines of a precocious but masterly plan. Such a self-image is not perhaps as flattering as it appears at first sight, since it tends to imply that between intellectual nonage and maturity one has really learned nothing of any serious importance. This implication is quite agreeable to me since it does not touch my own case. Although not a broad and deep learner, I certainly have been a very slow one, and therefore during the past quarter century have continued to extend my historical interests and to add stray bits here and there to my understanding. Thus some of the views expressed in this retrospect are different from those I held at the time I composed the chapter on the 'Presbyterian Independents' in 1937. Moreover, several of my studies omitted from this book are so wholly irrelevant to those published here that not on the most latitudinarian view could they be brought into a semblance of unity with them or fitted into some unified and gradually unfolding plan of my (purely imaginary) synthesizing intellect. There is some hope, then, that this concluding chapter may be a fairly honest retrospect, in which after rereading the preceding essays I draw implications not too clearly visible on the face of them.

III

A few general notions about history, however, have carried forward from my apprenticeship in the historian's craft to the present, three principally; and those three notions have played a considerable part in my thinking and writing about history. They have left their mark on this book. Stated in the fairly crude way in which they were held by a beginner in the trade almost a quarter of a century ago, they run somewhat as follows:

1. When you read history for a while with a little good sense you end up by knowing more about the past and understanding it better than you did before you started. To this only one condition is attached: that you do your reading and studying in order to know about and understand the past, and not to make a case for some kind of action in the present or to make some kind of prediction about the future.

2. The only way you can fit history into what is roughly described as the economic or class interpretation is to leave out half or three-quarters of what happened and not ask any very bright questions about the remnant.

3. A good part of the troubles of the historian results from the way people use words. The people whose writings are the main contemporary sources of information about the period which concerns the historian often used words carelessly. So do many of the historians who have written about that period—any period whatever.

There is no need to point out to readers of this book that the sharpening of these early dim perceptions and their application to particular historical problems has been one of my serious concerns.

What is less evident is the peculiar situation in which two of my perceptions left me a quarter of a century ago. Among historians in America two intellectual fashions were dominant in the mid-thirties. One was Marxism or its less austere congener, the economic interpretation of history. The other was historical relativism, a position then especially modish as a consequence of the brilliant Presidential Address which Carl Becker delivered at the meeting of the American Historical Association in 1931, 'Everyman His Own Historian'. To repudiate both relativism *and* the economic interpretation of history was automatically to exclude one's self from the world of historical fashion. There were, of course, and in great abundance, historians who were out of fashion intellectually, the historians of an earlier generation and their too-faithful disciples. They took pride in being what they called 'scientific', and they indicated that if one were scientific, one did not care about theories and ideas, but just found and reported the facts. From any comforting communion with them I was barred by my third notion, the one about the carelessness with which historians tended to use words. It seemed to me that the members of this group had very little notion of what they meant by 'scientific', or 'theory', or 'idea', or 'fact', and that an accurate translation of all that they said on the subject was: 'We do not terribly mind collecting historical data, but we detest thinking very hard about them.' Thus I felt somewhat isolated from both the new-fangled and the old-fashioned historians of the thirties and early forties. This sense of isolation, of fumbling in the dark without any very useful clues as to which way to go, seems to have afflicted a good many of the historians of my generation. As much as the Second World War, it may account for the relatively low output of studies by those historians. Certain it is that 'magisterial volumes' and 'definitive works' have not flowed freely or in large number from our pens.

While wandering in the outer darkness, I felt that it might be useful—and would certainly be pleasant—to pelt the children of light, the historians *à la mode*, with whatever missiles came my way in the course of my groping about. This kind of destructive criticism is sometimes lamented in the profession; but, setting aside its congeniality to one's temperament, it is defensible on less subjective grounds. The worship of idols is as stultifying to the historian's work as it is elsewhere; and efficient iconoclasm at least has the virtue of turning the thoughts of former idol worshippers in directions where truth perhaps may be found instead of where it surely may not. Moreover in stating one's negations of an orthodoxy one frequently finds oneself drawn not merely to agnostic denial but to the formulation in positive terms of a small heresy. The process may seem like making a molehill out of a mountain; but then, if the molehill is quite solid and the mountain was very shaky, there is gain, however trifling, in the operation.

Earlier I tried to state in the rough form in which I held them at the time three fundamental convictions with which I started work as a professional historian. In the preceding essays the reader will have found much fuller and more precise formulations of those convictions. A few additional remarks will bring up to date my notions about the points in question.

IV

The fad of historical relativism left its mark on more than a generation of historians: whether they accept the arguments of the relativist or not, there are many historians today who would feel it gauche or naive or somehow improper to say that what they were concerned with was the attainment of truth about history. (Such historians might also be somewhat embarrassed to say what they were concerned with, if not the attainment of truth about history.) In fact, truth about history is not only attainable but is regularly attained. It is true, for example, that at Waterloo on 18 June 1815 Napoleon I and his army were decisively defeated by a coalition army commanded by the Duke of Wellington. This is true in the simple sense that it is an *accurate* description of something that happened in the past, and the accurate description of things that happened in the past is one of the ends of history writing. But is it an adequate description? The answer to that question is another question: 'Adequate for what?' The statement as it appears is quite adequate for a dictionary of dates. It is not adequate for a historical study of the era of Napoleon; and if by 'adequate' is meant a narration of everything thought and said and done at Waterloo that June day, no historical account of any event can ever be adequate. The whole issue has been confused by a failure to make some rudimentary distinctions, the most important being that between knowing something and knowing everything. To prove that there is nothing about which a finite mind can know everything, is not to prove that there is nothing about which a finite mind can know something; and to demonstrate that all human knowledge is incomplete and all human truth partial is not to demonstrate that all human knowledge is ignorance and all human truth false or some ambiguous thing between true and false. That this is the working conviction of historians as contrasted with their inept excursions into theory is easy to demonstrate. After reading a book on a subject, one can know more or less or just as much about the subject as one did before reading the book; one can understand it better or worse or as well. Has there ever actually existed a historian, who, after a first reading of Marc Bloch's *Société Féodale* would seriously assert that he knew less about Europe between 900 and 1200 than he did before, or only as much about it, that he understood the Europe of that time worse or only as well? But if no historian would seriously give such an answer, then all historians must believe, whatever in flights of epistemological fancy they profess to believe, that by reading *La Société Féodale* they know more about the past and understand it better. And this is to assent to the possibility of a positive increment of knowledge and understanding, that is, of truth, about the past, which is their concern.

Historians have concealed this assent from themselves by failing to make another distinction. Some of the conceptions current and widely accepted in the period in which they live may have an impact on historians, and no historian is likely to be wholly immune from such impact; it is also evident that some of these conceptions are ephemeral. The historical relativists have managed to confuse themselves and a good many less self-conscious historians by overdrawing on the implications of these facts. A paraphrase of Abraham Lincoln may indicate what has happened. Some historians seem to base everything they write on ephemeral conceptions of the time they live in. And all historians base some of what they write on these ephemeral conceptions. But all historians do not base all they write on such conceptions. Moreover, with respect to the more distinctly time-bound conceptions, a shaking-down process takes place. They get sifted out after a while; but a considerable residue, not contaminated by them, remains. The fact that Bishop Stubbs believed in the Germanic historical myth of his day did not invalidate the whole, or even a very large part, of the *Constitutional History of England*.

There is a final point worth making on this whole matter. Certainly a historian thinks within the limits of what is known and believed during his lifetime. If one conceives it to be the proper goal of the historian to find out what actually happened in the past and to make what he finds out as intelligible as possible, then no doubt some beliefs current in some places at some times can militate against the attainment of this goal. For example, the belief in inevitable evolutionary progress did so in the West during the nineteenth century and the Marxian dialectic does so in the Communist countries today. But one belief, if quite firmly held—and it has been so held by many historians—very much helps one forward toward that goal. It is simply the belief that the first and only irrevocable commitment of men who write history is to find out what happened in the past and to render it intelligible. Here again historians, particularly in the United States, have tended to subscribe in the abstract to a view which they would at once repudiate in a properly selected concrete instance. Would any of them seriously assert that as an account of the life and teaching of the historical Jesus, *The Man Nobody Knows*, by Bruce Barton, can be equated with Professor S. J. Case's life of Jesus? But what are the roots of the difference? For one thing, Barton was quite ignorant of the best efforts of previous historians to know about and understand the historical Jesus, while Case knew all about them. For another, although the minds of Mr. Barton and of Professor Case were furnished at about the same time, from the historian's point of view the mind of the former was full of junk while that of the latter had excellent equipment, including as a key piece that very prime commitment to know and understand which is so useful for learning the truth about history.

V

The vogue of relativism in history writing has not been as noxious as at first thought it might seem. This is because relativism does not actually provide any clear and positive directives as to how historians should go about wrestling with evidence. So when historians who professed to be relativists got down to writing history, they assessed evidence, drew inferences, and arrived at conclusions in much the way their daddies used to do; and that was not a bad way, all in all. The only real loss was that a few historians wrote so much about being historical relativists that for a while they did not write much about history.

The second approach to history, fashionable for a very long time both in America and England, the approach which under whatever name explained most of the history of the West since the eleventh century as the consequence of the decline of feudalism and the rise of the middle class, was far more of a nuisance than historical relativism. Claiming to be scientific, it imposed on historians a specific canon for the selection and weighting of evidence. That canon was at once arbitrary, extraordinarily rigid, and peculiarly insipid. Nevertheless it commanded assent explicit or tacit from so many historians that it became a serious obstacle to the advancement of historical understanding. This wide assent may justify the pertinacity with which in several essays in this book I have hammered away at the foolish historical doctrine which commanded it. Because of my own earlier pertinacity only a point or two remains to be cleared up here. The first point is that I do not for a moment doubt that conflicts of interest among groups seeking what they conceived as their own advantage have had a most important place in history for centuries—indeed, for millennia. The second and crucial point is that the conventional economic interpretation makes wholly unintelligible many of the conflicts of interest which in fact were going on between 1450 and 1650, the age that has most interested me. Here at the very center of its concern, that interpretation betrays its inadequacy.

There are several causes for this inadequacy; but for the early-modern historian one of them seems to have been outstandingly catastrophic: the primary classification of economic groups almost universally adopted by those addicted to the economic interpretation of history makes it impossible to apply that interpretation to the actual conflicts of economic groups in the Western World between 1450 and 1650. The classification referred to divides the entire population of the West into three groups, or to use the term preferred by the interpreters themselves, classes. The classes are declining-feudal, rising-middle, and exploited-working. The above hyphenation is not casual or accidental; it is of the very essence of the classification. No historian of the early modern era who has attempted an economic interpretation of it has so much as conceived of the possibility of a rising feudal or working class, and an exploited or declining middle class.

Now anyone who, without wearing the blinkers of the taxonomy just set forth, has studied any of the more important economic complexes of the early modern age—coal or woollen cloth, for example—knows that the group interests involved were very numerous indeed, and that several bases of classification are indispensable in order to sort those interests out. One, of course, is relation to the factors of production. In the woollen industry this basis itself requires care in its use, since in some textile areas a man might own the instruments of one of the two main processes (weaving), without owning the raw material, the instruments of the preliminary processes (cleaning, carding or combing, dyeing), the instruments of the finishing processes (fulling and shearing), or even enough instruments of the other main process (spinning) to keep his own loom busy. In some regions the organizer of the industry, the clothier, might own nothing but the wool at the beginning and the cloth at the end, or he might own several of the instruments for preliminary and final processing. Elsewhere the weaver was quite likely to own the raw material, the finished product, and a loom, but few or none of the other instruments of production. Moreover, the clothier might also be a grazier, and the interest of such a man with respect to the market price of wool would not be identical with that of the clothier who was not a grazier. Indeed, it is evident that an incredible variety of arrangements of ownership were possible in the woollen-industry complex, and that a very considerable number of these variations in fact existed at one place or another in the complex.

But we are not at the end of our difficulties here, for an adequate classification of economic interests must concern itself with more than formal relationship to the instruments of production. Besides the making, one must consider the taking; besides the production of the goods, the distribution of income. The interests of the petty operator did not always coincide with that of the large dealer or those of the lesser landlords with those of the greater, a difference in quantity at some point becoming a difference in quality or kind, as a well-known sage once remarked. Legislation intended to restrict the size of enterprises reflected public awareness of this particular conflict of economic interest. Legislation also reflected awareness of similar conflicts between urban and rural working men in the same industry. The growth of the village cloth industry feeding the Antwerp market undermined the older cloth industry of the Flemish and Brabant cities, as the growth of the village cloth industry in England sapped that of the urban centers. Village industry threatened the urban workers with unemployment and starvation; and the crushing or subjection of their fellows in the country long stood high on the agenda of the woollen-cloth workers of the towns. This geographical basis of economic group interest did not affect workers alone. The interests of the outport merchants and of the London merchants often were in conflict during the sixteenth century; and the London merchants were quite willing to stack the deck against their provincial brethren.

All these interest groups and many, many more, separately and in coalitions of varying density and dimension created the actual economic conflicts of the early modern era. One would think that the description and analysis of these actual conflicts might have a high priority among the adherents of the economic interpretation of history. Actually in English economic history the pioneering work in such analysis was done by men with no commitment to that interpretation: Unwin, Lipson, Nef, and Heaton. The orthodox adherents of the economic interpretation have failed to deal with one of their primary problems because they have been kept busy by the hopeless tasks imposed on them by their taxonomy of interest groups, the three-class system previously described. Inordinate amounts of energy and considerable reserves of ingenuity have been brought to bear on the utterly footling attempt to fit the intricate actualities of the early modern era to a crude, adamantine framework contrived for the exigencies not of historical investigation but of nineteenth-century social politics. Under such circumstances it is scarcely a matter for wonder that this colossal effort has produced a minimal and wholly incidental yield.

As these words are written, the signs multiply that—barring reimposition by political authority—this ridiculous way of investigating the past is about to be interred with the speed and silence by means of which historians minimize embarrassing confrontation with past error.

In a decade or two it may even have lost its hold on the subconscious level where historians store and sometimes issue for use conceptions that they consciously reject and deplore. But suppose this to be the case, where do we go from here? Granted that disorder is better than wrong order, must we give up the quest for a better order? To move toward an answer to this question we ought first to take a look at the course followed by most historians of recent decades who did not get deeply enmeshed either in relativism or in the economic interpretation.

VI

By and large the historians who avoided the pitfalls of the economic interpretation did so by following rather closely in the footsteps of their predecessors, the scientific historians of an earlier day, whose ur-father was not Marx but Ranke. At the same time they extended an old method of organizing historical investigation, or rather of disorganizing it. They split the past into a series of tunnels, each continuous from the remote past to the present, but practically self-contained at every point and sealed off from contact with or contamination by anything that was going on in any of the other tunnels. At their entrances these tunnels bore signs saying diplomatic history, political history, institutional history, ecclesiastical history, intellectual history, military history, economic history, legal history, administrative history, art history, colonial history, social history, agricultural history, and so on, and so on. At first glance one might think that these kinds of history came into being as a consequence of a rational attempt at an exhaustive classification of what is knowable about the past, and that history continues to be written under these headings *because* the classification represents the best way to deal with the past. Nothing could be further from the truth. Whether or not the current classification provides the best means for exploring the past, it did not come into being as a result of any conscious aiming at the best on the part of historians.

What mainly determined the way historians split up history during the past century was a ridiculously adventitious set of circumstances: the way in which public authorities and private persons tended to order the documents which it suited their purposes to preserve. The basis of constitutional history was the preservation and segregation of the commands of the superior public authorities, of administrative history the care with which accountable public servants preserved the documents for which they were responsible, of intellectual history the irrepressible urge of intellectuals and literary folk to hand on their maunderings to posterity and to display their erudition by references to the writings of other intellectual and literary folk, and so on. The supreme illustration of the artificial basis on which these kinds of history rested is the existence side by side of diplomatic history, military history, and naval history. No one has ever much improved on Clausewitz's definition of warfare: 'War is a mere continuation of policy by other means'. So if ever three human activities were inextricably bound together, scarcely intelligible save when conjoined, they are diplomacy, land warfare, and naval action. Yet only rarely did historians write about them together. The archives and publications of source materials on these three matters tended to be separated; and historians simply adapted their classifications of and concern with the past to the convenience of dead bureaucrats. At times this procedure was carried over from monographic studies into works dealing with the general history of a nation; and instead of a coherent account of the interrelated uses of all the instruments of policy and power by which that nation defended or expanded itself, we got a chapter marked 'Foreign Affairs', another marked 'The Army and the Wars of . . . and . . .' and a third marked 'The Navy'. Thus was attained the *reductio ad absurdum* of a mode of dividing the past that never made sense and was never intended to do so.

Nevertheless, historians following the tunnel method often produced solid results. They went deep into sources that earlier generations of historians had not investigated at all. Frequently, of course, the limitations that the tunnel historian imposed on himself concealed from him and from his readers as well many of the insights that might have been theirs had he undertaken his work with a somewhat broader view of its scope and a fuller sense of what it impinged on. But such limitation was usually the consequence of lack of imagination. To a historian with keen vision and a ranging imagination the mere form of tunnel history was no impenetrable obstacle. After all, Maitland's *History of English Law*, the greatest of all books on medieval England, was, formally at least, tunnel history.

VII

Our consideration of tunnel history brings us, somewhat circuitously as we shall see, to the matter of 'factors' in history. For several decades now historians and others have been lending a new intensity of murkiness to the already obscure region called historical explanation by their use of the term 'factor'. What the history of the term itself in this connection is I do not know; I only know that it was already there when my interest in history began about three decades ago, that it is still there, and that its use there may some day make an entertaining chapter in the history of historical thought, provided that the author of the chapter has a sufficiently macabre sense of humor. At the moment it is not even known where the historians picked the term up. It sounds as if it comes from mathematics. If this is so, and if the use of the term 'factor' in historical discourse conjures up in the reader's mind any analogy with mathematics, then that use becomes doubly disastrous intrinsically meaningless and extrinsically confusing. For a factor in mathematics is exactly the opposite of a factor in history. It is itself precise, and it stands in a precise relationship to the precise number of which it is a factor. Of any such number there are a determinate and readily determinable number of factors. Historical factors are models of imprecision; it is never entirely clear what they are factors of, and their number seems to fluctuate at the whim of the historian. At the moment the confusion about historical factors is so unutterably utter that, short of arduous researches, one can only guess at what happened to create it. My own guess is that the confusion has partly arisen from the sources whence historians have drawn their factors and partly from the way in which they and others have used them.

There seem to be two (or perhaps two and a half) sources of historical factors. The first and most abundant source has been the tunnel history earlier described, and that source has by no means yet run dry. The procedure here is to take each kind of history that the tunnel historians have dreamed up and turn it into a factor relevant (or irrelevant) to the explanation of some constellation of happenings: the First World War, the French Revolution, the Reformation. Of course the number of such factors is quite indeterminate. It is open to any reasonably ingenious historian to dream up a new tunnel—marital history, technological history, ecological history—and thus to add a new factor to the explanation of almost every constellation of events already unsatisfactorily explained by the combination (addition? multiplication? integration?) of all the tunnel-history factors previously deemed relevant. In this system (if that is the right word) of historical explanation the historian is at the mercy of the scheme of classification of European archives and of the temperamental quirks of colleagues in quest of new fields to conquer or just to browse in.

The second source of factors has been the organization of the faculties of American universities. The social-science divisions of such faculties used to include only the departments of History, Political Science, Economics, and Sociology. And by an odd coincidence, when economists, political scientists, and sociologists wrote about factors in history there often turned out to be only three factors: economic, political, and social. This remarkable restraint, almost barrenness, in the creation of factors, contrasted with the wondrous fecundity of tunnel history in producing them, almost leads one to suspect some sort of contraception. And there seem to be grounds for such suspicion. For with a few exceptions tunnel history has stayed safely within the Department of History; so historians, their vested interests untouched, have remained hospitable, free of cost, to most kinds of tunnel history and to the factors to which they gave birth. For the other academics in the division of social sciences, the situation was quite different. To add a factor to those already used in explaining what happened might suggest the need of a new social science department to deal with that factor. And one can see to what a horrid carving up of academic empires such a procedure might lead.

The restraint of the other departments of the social sciences has had consequences even more eccentric than has the abandon of historians. One might wonder, for example, on what rational grounds matters concerned with population should be deemed, as they usually are, elements in the economic factor. The answer is there are no rational grounds; that they are so deemed is simply a historical accident. It just happened that Thomas Malthus, who more than a century and a half ago made all literate men conscious of some of the problems of population, was one of the fathers of political economy; and ever since his day population has been mainly in the economic preserve. Another peculiarity of the restraint above referred to has been the eccentric but prodigious expansion of the social factor. Among the so-called systematic social sciences the economists first delimited their area of concern, and then the political scientists. The remainder was left to the sociologists and to the social factor. Fifty or sixty years ago this remainder did not seem to amount to so much; but with the increase of curiosity about men's doings, it has undergone an enormous growth. And the sociologists have not let a bit escape their jurisdiction. For a while, in the 1940s, it appeared that the anthropologists might break loose and hack out an anthropological factor for themselves; but their prospects seem to have dimmed. So in the second or social-science way of treating factors the social factor is still the Pooh-Bah, the Lord-High-Everything-Else.

Those who deal with factors in this second way seem regularly to admit only one intruder, the ideological factor. It got in as a consequence of a fierce, if futile, controversy between Marxist and non-Marxist social scientists, the former alleging that in historical development ideology was mere superstructure, the latter insisting that it was not superstructure. Or slightly reformed Marxists would say that only the economic factor was really basic in the long run, while non-Marxists would say that the ideological factor was basic in the long run, too. Consequently it would not be seemly now for non-Marxist social scientists to deny the existence of an ideological factor. They have not suffered because of their propriety. I am not aware of any attempt at any American university to establish a Department of Ideology.

Of course if one is reasonably consistent about one's system of classification and if the procedure can be shown to promote rather than retard the advancement of knowledge, there can be no objection to dividing happenings among any number of factors. Up to the moment, there is no evidence that so dividing happenings has advanced knowledge, and there seem to be a good many situations where it has retarded it. At best the result is the mere division among an arbitrarily selected set of factors of the conditions antecedent to an event. In consequence of this unambitious exercise the historian sometimes assumes that his slotting of preconditions has adequately explained the event, although by obscuring the connection between preconditions slotted into different factors it has only made that event less intelligible.

Sometimes this tucking of historical data into homemade pigeonholes (a process that its more pompous practitioners call 'an analysis of historical factors') dangerously darkens counsel about what went on in the past. This happens when the tuckers forget, or are unaware, who made the pigeonholes and who decided into which pigeonhole any particular bit of data was to be tucked. In this state of affairs one ascends with rocket speed from the peaceful plane of history to the noisy region of logomachy. In this region take place long and earnest discussions about whether in bringing on the First World War or the French Revolution or the Reformation the economic, or the ideological, or the political, or the social factor was the basic, or dominant, or most important one. To establish his claim to victory in such battles of words, the champion of each factor quite seriously points to the enormous mass of historical data tucked away in his favorite pigeonhole in his own homemade filing system and at the meagreness of the data in the other pigeonholes. Of course since each participant in this foolish game decides where each bit of data goes in his own system, his favorite pigeonhole is bound to be fuller than the rest. The whole performance is like the Dodo's caucus race: everybody wins; indeed, given the rules, or lack of them, everybody is bound to win. But unlike the participants in the caucus race, the participants in the argument about factors are unwilling to let it go at that and pass out prizes all round; each one hypnotizes himself into believing that his favorite factor is really the sole winner and ought to get all the prizes.

Another futile controversy once raged over whether the political, social, and ideological factors were dependent on or independent of the economic factor, and perhaps it still rages. The terms of the controversy point to a remarkably successful ploy on the part of those addicted to the economic interpretation of history. For those terms *assume* that the economic factor is independent of the other three. So that factor is conceded at least a draw before the contest even starts. Recently a quite intelligent scholar proclaimed with a certain rejoicing the victory of politics—or power—and ideology in their struggle for independence as factors in history. Perhaps if we forthwith declare the independence of lust, laziness, and pride, faith, hope, and charity, as factors in history, we will begin to re-establish the valid claim that in his work the historian should consider the full range of human habits, passions, concerns and actions. Declarations about the independence of various factors do not make sense or nonsense but pure anti-sense. The factors in question owe their existence as concepts to an almost violent act of abstraction. In this act a group of human activities are forcefully ripped out of the historical matrix to which in actuality they were bound. Sometimes they are then investigated in this purely artificial state of disassociation from that matrix. In some sense the investigation may even be instructive; but nothing whatever is gained by making believe that the act of abstraction did not take place, and that the abstracted activities have a historical existence independent of the other activities of the same time, the same place and the same people, from which they were forcefully torn away.[1]

[1] Just as the galleys of this book were being corrected Dr. Henry Kissinger was publicly making some thoughtful observations on the dilemmas of America in the world today. He remarked that one of our most serious difficulties was the result of the American belief that one intricate tangle after another was *really* an

Historians and others use the term 'factor' in another way less noxious than that described above, but no better calculated to promote the advancement of knowledge. Used in this other way 'factor' means 'anything whatever (A) deemed to be of any use whatever for the explanation of some circumstance (B).' For example:

1. Switzerland's lack of a seacoast (A) is a major factor in the size of its navy (B).

2. The rise of the middle class (A) and nationalism (A') are factors in modern history (B).

3. The amount of rainfall (A) is a factor in agriculture (B).

Between the first two examples and the third, however, there is a distinction. In the nineteenth century the word 'cause' in either its noun form or its verb form would have done the work done by 'factor' in Examples 1 and 2. But somehow 'cause' got into trouble with the philosophers and the scientists and was dropped by all the best and some of the less good intellectual clubs. The work the word had been doing had to go on being done, however, since everyone found it necessary to go on talking about the species of relation which 'cause' had formerly designated. So 'factor' was slid into the slot which 'cause' had once filled in the vocabulary of rational discourse, and this made everybody very happy. Thus the human mind progresses—sideways.

In Example 3, 'factor' is not used to spare bashful intellectuals the embarrassment of writing 'cause'; it has a far different function. It is there in order to confer on a vague and banal observation a specious air of precision and consequence and thus to spare its user the unpleasant mental effort of saying something exact, consequential, and worthy of attention. It might be profitable for historians to put the word 'cause' back where it used to be and to stop using 'factor' when they really have not anything very clear in mind.

In the language which historians use a term sometimes gets involved in extraordinary ambiguities and confusion. This has happened to the term 'Renaissance', as it has to the term 'factors'. When such an accident occurs historians face a decision: whether to try to jettison

economic problem, or *really* a political problem, or *really* a social problem; and he suggested that this illusion was preventing America from applying *all* its usable and useful resources in coping with problems far too complex to resolve by means of lopsided measures derived from a dubious system of classification. It was at once gratifying and grisly to learn of the very present and practical relevance of the particular problem with which this section of the 'Retrospect' deals. In general, of course, it was not in the least a surprise to hear that imbecility in thinking ends up sooner or later in futility or incompetence in action.

the term entirely or whether to attempt to restore its utility by·shearing off most of the enmeshing ambiguities and confusions. The decision should be made solely on grounds of expediency. (1) How firmly is the term fixed in historical usage, and how long would it take to get rid of it? (2) How seriously is it involved in ambiguity and confusion, and how much time do historians waste in talking past each other because when they use the term they do not have the same thing or even roughly similar things in mind? (3) Is there any prospect that some rough consensus about the use of the term may be attained within the foreseeable future? (4) Given such a consensus will the term be very useful to historians? With respect to the term Renaissance, for example, the answer to the second question is most unfavorable. At the present moment 'Renaissance' is used in ways and senses that are not only divergent but wholly contradictory. But it is most firmly fixed in historical usage; there is some prospect of a future consensus about its use as a substantive with respect to Italy and as an adjective with respect to lands north of the Alps; and under such conditions the term will be most useful. With 'factors' all the indices of expediency are on the minus side. Having been in common use by serious historians hardly more than half a century, it is not hopelessly frozen into the historian's vocabulary. The present confusion in the use of 'factors' is massive; the vested interests on the side of maintaining the confusion are considerable; and the only consensus to be hoped for is a general agreement that the term is practically unnecessary.

VIII

My own irritation with relativism, economic interpretation, tunnel history and factor analysis is of symptomatic rather than specific interest. During the past two decades historians concerned with various eras and civilizations have shown ever increasing dissatisfaction with the categories and concepts, the terminology and *idées maîtresses*, which traditionally have been used to give shape to the raw data of history. From prehellenic antiquity to the present the need for revision has become apparent. But if a historical revolution comparable in thoroughness to the scientific revolution of the seventeenth century seems desirable (and may indeed be under way), it should not and cannot take the scientific revolution for a model. Many of the difficulties with the categories which historians are in the process of getting rid of arose from an attempt, at once ill considered and unsuccessful, to apply to history the major generalizations of the physical and biological science of the past two centuries. Many fingers were burnt, many heads broken and an inordinate amount of the time of intelligent men was wasted in the attempt to contrive for history universal laws like the law of inertia or to shape and squeeze angular and resistant historical data to fit such laws.

History has been poorest in its vocabulary of *general terms for dealing with limited areas during limited periods of time*. The determination of what general terms are useful is a matter not for amateurs but for experts. In the civilizations of the ancient Near East during the second millennium B.C. are the terms 'mythopoeic thought', 'priest-king', and 'temple-city' useful; are 'warlordship' and 'priestlordship', 'pasture' and 'sown', 'maritime' and 'riverine' convenient antitheses? If so, where and for how long? If these terms are of no use, what terms are? Only scholars who are on a standing of intimacy with the detailed historical data concerning the Near East from 2000 to 1000 B.C. can give adequately informed answers to such questions. And this means that if there should be a historical revolution even remotely comparable in its dimensions to the scientific revolution of three centuries ago, it would be a revolution without Keplers or Galileos or Newtons. Once historians give up the dream of discovering universal laws of historical change—and this seems to me the prime condition of any new departure in the writing of history—they give up with it the hope of the kind of massive breakthrough that has taken place several times in the natural sciences with Newton, Lavoisier, Darwin, Planck, Einstein and Morgan, to cite only the most obvious examples. What we may hope for is piecemeal advances as historian after historian re-examines the place and time with which he is mainly concerned, and seeks to contrive, for telling about what went on in that bounded place and time, a vocabulary of conceptions better suited to bring out its character than the fairly shopworn one now in use. Perhaps this bit-by-bit process of rethinking the very language of historical writing has already gotten under way.

The sense that his own field of investigation offers difficulties of outstanding density and unequalled prickliness is natural to any scholar; for the trouble of cultivating other fields he has only the word of other scholars, but he experiences directly the troubles of cultivating his own field. Quite aware of the danger of bias, nevertheless I believe that at the present time the historical field which has concerned me presents special difficulties. The awkward situation of the historian of the early modern age results from the nearness of that age to the time when the systematic and organized study—the 'scientific' study—of history as an academic discipline began, that is, to the nineteenth century. Over the past two hundred years a considerable and useful vocabulary for dealing with those years—the centuries of the 'isms'—developed. This made the work of writers on recent history relatively easy because the men of the time themselves selected the labels to describe their own purposive doings. Thus, in politics alone, we have conservatism, liberalism, radicalism, individualism, capitalism, socialism, communism, fascism, anarchism, nationalism, colonialism, imperialism. In matters of religion we have Catholicism, Protestantism, theism, agnosticism, atheism, secularism, humanism. And so on. Much of the vocabulary of recent history is ready-made; its terms were used by contemporary men of action as well as later by men of words seeking to render what happened intelligible. To that extent they are relevant, usable, indispensable—they are the rubrics under which the actors sought to state and understand the aims of their own deeds and those of their opponents. Moreover, the Big Thing, the Ineluctable Force of the recent era, that with which all else had to come to terms some way or other, has been identified for more than a century; it is the Industrial Revolution, the Coming of Great Industry, whatever name one chooses to give to that continuous, rapid and systematic transformation of all aspects of production, which distinguishes the past two hundred years from all preceding ages. This is not, of course, to say that historians writing of those two hundred years have solved all or even most of the problems they face. It is to say that they inherited a ready-made vocabulary; and that that vocabulary in the main was suitable for application to a good many of their problems. For the sake of brevity we will call it the vocabulary of recent history.

Since the vocabulary of recent history worked for the age in which systematic historical study itself was established, the initial inclination of many historians to seek to fit the events of every age into the categories provided by that vocabulary is intelligible enough. The result justified much of the argument if not the title of Professor Butterfield's *Whig Interpretation of History*. There was a danger that the whole past would be judged on the basis of the value systems—moral, political, religious, aesthetic—current during the last two centuries. The very diversity of those systems, however, has tended to diminish the danger that alarmed Professor Butterfield. Valuative judgments on the past came from the whole spectrum of recent creeds and therefore tended to neutralize each other. Curiously enough, the most rigid value scheme was the one concerned with aesthetic judgment; there a mainly naturalistic canon of taste for a long while straitened the historians' understanding of the visual arts of other civilizations.

Although moderately sophisticated historians freed themselves from the valuative element in the vocabulary of recent history, to escape from the vocabulary itself was a far more difficult matter. Thus, given a little practice, it became easy enough not to side with Ikhnaton in his violent contest with the priests of Amon Ra. It was more difficult to avoid importing into the investigation of that conflict a way of thinking which might not become explicit, derived from the conflict of Higher Criticism with scriptural literalism or even—God save the mark—the conflict between Mr. Huxley and Bishop Wilberforce. Nevertheless the further into the past and the further afield one goes, the harder it becomes to find times and places to which the vocabulary of recent history has even a specious relevance. One may achieve an illusion of such relevance in dealing with the conflict between Ikhnaton and the priests of Amon Ra. But then, what is one to do with the remaining two millennia or so of ancient Egyptian civilization? To apply the vocabulary of recent history to ancient Egypt is to consign that society to a rarely broken silence. And this of course has been fortunate, since there patently must be sensible things worth saying about so durable a civilization. If no nobler motive, a mere concern to avoid technological unemployment must have impelled Egyptologists to seek a language more appropriate than the vocabulary of recent history for writing about ancient Egyptian civilization.

The nearer historians came to the recent era, however, the less necessary it was—or at least the less necessary it seemed—to seek for a new vocabulary. It was, after all, easier to apply the vocabulary of recent history to the Christian West in 1600 than to any other earlier time or any other place. For as we go back, one by one the terms by means of which in recent times men have indicated their aims and intentions become useless; and the further back we go, the more of them become useless, and the more useless they become. These diminishing returns on the vocabulary of recent history have by now freed most medievalists from its trammels. In Jolliffe's *Angevin Kingship* and Southern's *Making of the Middle Ages* we watch all sorts of men of the West in the eleventh and twelfth centuries using whatever physical, mental, and moral equipment they have in an effort to deal as they think best with the world as they find it. In some of the doings of these men—their partial transformation of brute force into legitimate authority, for example—medievalists may discern the bare possibility of what later actually happened; but they are not thereby tempted to obliterate or neglect the rest of what is knowable about the eleventh and twelfth centuries, or to try to tell about it wholly in terms appropriate to history since the Enlightenment.

The temptation to futurism is far stronger where the future is as near as the nineteenth century is to the seventeenth. Of course there are bits of the vocabulary of recent history that even the most zealous futurist cannot shoehorn into early modern history. To whom in that era can the term anarchist be applied, or the term agnostic? Other bits of the vocabulary may roughly fit a few men or a transient episode. The Levellers were certainly democrats, and one can perhaps get away with describing the Diggers and some of the more hot-eyed religious sectaries of the sixteenth century as socialists; with less violence other parts of the vocabulary of recent history can be stretched to cover some men and events of the early modern age. And several parts—Catholicism, Protestantism, anticlericalism, rationalism, skepticism, mercantilism, capitalism—quite clearly fit the early modern era as well as they do our own. The consequence of all this fitting, and part-fitting, and pseudo-fitting has been most unfortunate. In effect, more than is the case with any other age the vocabulary of early modern history is mainly the result of a series of *subtractions* from the vocabulary of recent history. Just because a considerable part of the vocabulary of recent history could be used in writing about the early modern age, historians of that age felt less driven to find terms fully adequate to the data that they dealt with. When they contrived at all, their contrivance was unimaginative, half-hearted, and feeble. Thus the attempt to give a motor to early modern history equivalent to the Industrial Revolution turned up the Commercial Revolution, a most unfortunate conception. It is not clear in the first place that early modern history needs or can use so powerful a motor: it was not going all that fast. And anyway the commercial revolution does not provide such a motor. On examination it turns out to be an amorphous mess of historical entities feebly wired together by dubious analogies. It stretches back and back with no visible stopping point short of the twelfth century. It spreads over a half dozen or so casually related or entirely unrelated phenomena—the rise of capitalism, merchant banking, the putting-out system, the shift of the economic center of the West to the Atlantic seaboard, mercantilism, the price revolution, the increasing use of money as a means of payment—

and covers them with a single phrase without making them at all coherent as a historical complex.

But at least the Commercial Revolution was an experiment, however unfortunate, in contrivance. In other matters pertaining to early modern history until recently there has been no systematic attempt at contrivance at all. Instead early modern historians tended to use whatever part of the vocabulary of recent history was not hopelessly *mal à propos* for matters which it could be stretched into covering and to disregard or fail to organize whatever that vocabulary could not be forced to cover. Consequently as one moves back toward 1450 more and more of early modern history slips through the interstices in the vocabulary of recent history and lies about overlooked and neglected. Moreover the terms of recent history tend to be maintained at their current value, although as we recede in time their actual and relative consequence undergoes major alteration. In nothing is this clearer than in the importance that historians have long attached to nationalism as an operative agent in determining policy and the outcome of events in the sixteenth century. Consider as a single example the matter of dynastic marriages. The diplomatic correspondence of every European monarchy of the early modern era is crammed full of marriage negotiations and proposals of marital alliances among the ruling houses of Europe. Busy, hard-headed calculating statesmen, whose power, whose fortunes, whose very lives sometimes, depended on how well they weighed the importance of things, spent enormous stores of precious time and energy in working out the marriage arrangements of the family of the prince they served. If the preoccupation of very shrewd and powerful men who had every reason to ponder such matters with particular care is any gauge, the dynastic marriage was one of the most important elements of European political life in the early modern era. Yet although for several decades now analytical history has been all the mode, no historian has systematically analyzed the marriage policies of a single European dynasty during that era. Much less, despite the plethora of materials, has anyone attempted to use the history of marriage negotiations and arrangements as a device for gauging the importance of dynasticism in those days. For every European country, however, essays on national patriotism in the early modern era abound, and such evidence as they present has been taken to justify the position which for a century historians have assigned to nationalism as a force in the affairs of early modern Europe. The assigned position matched as nearly as possible the importance undoubtedly possessed by nationalism in recent history, but it was surely not warranted by the actualities of early modern politics or even of early modern sentiment. This overweighting of the nation in early modern history took place at the expense of the dynasty simply because in recent history, compared to the nation, the dynasty did not matter much. Here, though not here alone, willingness to stammer along with the vocabulary of recent history was stultifying. With respect to dynasticism, it imposed on early modern historians a torpid silence; with respect to nationalism, a foolish babbling.

IX

In what follows I wish quite briefly to offer a few suggestions about what historians of the early modern age might do to provide themselves with means more effective than the ones they at present command for dealing with the data that concern them. But before proceeding, a word of caution. In the first place, the suggestions will here be set down quite barely, with no specific examples of their application to the details of early modern history. But the proper test of any proposed way of dealing with the data of history is precisely to deal with the data of history in that way; and the person who ought to do the dealing first is the one who makes the proposal. It is both my expectation and my hope that other historians will be as skeptical of my untried suggestions as I would be of theirs. My only excuse for proceeding, in a way so unsatisfactory to myself is that the time needed for testing those suggestions may not be available to me. Such, of course, is the human condition; but two recent and rather massive intimations of mortality have made me more than ordinarily aware of that condition.

In the second place, my suggestions are just that. They are not intended to be final, complete, ultimate, or even adequate. There are no doubt many ways of characterizing the past two centuries; in one aspect they have been the centuries of ultimate solutions—gone sour. Especially in what concerns human kind the propounding of such solutions has become a spiritual disorder. We have got so habituated to grandiose claims, that a modest proposal is unlikely to be much heeded; and one achieves the apotheosis implied by the designation 'seminal mind' only by propounding at great length and with excessive elaboration universal solutions demonstrated false in the end only by the wearisome toil of scores of investigators or by the slow anguish of bitter experience. Having provided a little of the toil and witnessed some of the anguish, it is not my wish to add to either. My sole and limited object is to suggest a slightly better way than the one now in use of talking about some two centuries of the history of the Western World.

Talking is a matter of words, and, as I have already suggested, one of the serious problems of early modern history is that of vocabulary. To get rid of bad language which impeded understanding and corrupted communication has been hard work for historians of the early modern age; but a good bit of it has now been done. To find useful words and to use them with the care and latitude required to give them a sufficient precision and density of connotation is even harder work. We historians of the early modern era should not forget, however, that some of the work has already been done for us. Granted that much of the vocabulary of recent history is of no use to us, that it in fact misleads us, there remains a considerable part of it which, carefully reassessed, is appropriate to early modern history. Moreover a whole series of terms of general utility properly apply to almost every period and every place where men have left traces. The powerful and the weak, the rich and the poor, level of employment of labor, population growth and decline, the rate of return on investment, opportunity of investment, habits and customs of consumption, status system and status symbols, personnel, materiel, morale—terms like these help one think in an orderly way about the events of almost any age. They include many terms from the technical vocabularies of other disciplines primarily systematic rather than historical, and the task of rendering them precise and working out their logical (not their historical) implications falls to those disciplines.

The additions to the vocabulary of early modern history that most concern me are those of less than universal relevance, the time-bound terms which emerge from an examination of the actual concerns of early modern men. In Essay 3 I have scantily written about a few polar pairs of terms already sporadically and unsystematically used by historians of the early modern era: Catholic–Protestant, lay–clerical, secular–religious, *gubernaculum–jurisdictio*, town–hinterland, court–country, dynasty – region, realm – province, *Realpolitik* – legitimacy. These pairs, it will be noted, are not all of the same species, so to speak. Secular–religious refers to the spiritual disposition of men, lay–clerical to the orders of society, *Realpolitik*–legitimacy to political outlook and practice, court–country to institutions arraying almost the whole range of an early modern man's activities and loyalties. But although they differ from one another in several respects, they also share common ground. All of the terms stand for phenomena the actuality, the presentness of which would have been evident to active men in the early modern age. Not that those men would have used the terms with the consistency which a present-day historian ought to aim at in using them. In the sixteenth century men often wrote 'secular' instead of 'lay' as the antonym of 'clerical'. Still, they would not have found it difficult to distinguish between 'secular' and 'lay' as we have used those terms in Essay 3, nor to recognize the importance in their own time of both the distinction and the things distinguished. And although a sixteenth-century statesman would find the term *Realpolitik* wholly strange, he would find nothing at all strange about the way of acting that *Realpolitik* is intended to designate. The polar pairs suggested above are, and will be, useful not in so far as by contortion and main force we are able to impose them on the data of early modern history, but in so far as the data of modern history impose them on us, impel us to use them as the means of making sense of what we know.

Despite their diversity our polar terms have in common a valuative character. To sixteenth-century men they presented themselves not only as actualities, but as alternatives, as the objects of choice. Except in the case of the Catholic–Protestant alternative, none of the *general choices* were of an either–or sort. But with respect to each man and each group the general choice is in fact a composite, the historian's estimation of the general tendency of the known particular choices of that man or group. Of course, the choices of some men are so consistent as to render the problem of estimation trivial. No doubt Wolsey throughout his court career indulged in a curiously sentimental country attachment to his home town of Ipswich; and Thomas Cromwell patiently managed rather than commanded or attacked that institutional embodiment of country, the House of Commons. Nevertheless in their individual decisions Wolsey and Thomas Cromwell came down so regularly and so unreservedly on the side of dynasty and court against region and country as to make it quite clear where they stood. Between Wolsey and Cromwell on the one hand and the court-hating impoverished backwoods gentry-henchmen of Percys and Courtenays and Nevilles on the other, were ranged the Englishmen of the age of the Tudors, inclining one way on one particular question, the other way on another. It scarcely needs saying, then, that the tensions in society created by the pulls of each polar pair emerge on the surface of history not always as the conflicts of organized groups but very often as the uncertainties, unresolved dilemmas and inconsistencies of individual men. Thus the Coligny brothers play a hazardous game—both court favorites assisting in the formation of dynastic policy and leaders of a faction as much regional and country as it is Protestant—until for their gamble they pay a very steep reckoning on St. Bartholomew's Day.

The paired terms, or rather the actualities they are intended to point to, do not exist in a historical vacuum, and it is most undesirable to think of a single pair in total isolation from all the other pairs. To do so is to recreate on a new basis the tunnel history which limited the vision of an earlier generation of historians. Thus in France during the Fronde the judges of the Parlements concerned to preserve *jurisdictio* against the ever more drastic encroachments of *gubernaculum* were themselves men of the court; but in their revolt they had to align themselves with the country against the court and even with the region against the dynasty.

Historical knowledge grows in a different way from mathematical-logical knowledge, to choose its extreme opposite. Almost never does it advance in a long straight line of logically unassailable deductions from immediate premises to distant conclusions. (This is not at all, of course, to excuse the slovenliness of much historical thinking on the grounds that history is not logical.) Historical knowledge seems to grow rather like a tree in an expanding series of rings. In the process the particular and the individual define the content and body of the general, while the general helps to illuminate and make sense of the particular. Thus the strange, unhappy, and short career of Sir Francis Bigod, who, although a Protestant courtier, came down on the country side of the northern Catholic revolt known as the Pilgrimage of Grace in 1537, is rendered intelligible by an awareness of the tensions between the region called the North and the Tudor dynasty, between the country habits and customs of the ancient Yorkshire family of the Bigods and Sir Francis's court perspective acquired during a youth spent in the service and the household of Cardinal Wolsey. And at the same time the study of Bigod's peculiar doings when he returned to the North after being reared in Wolsey's household enables us to make more precise and more ample our understanding of the tension between the court and the country, the dynastic and the regional, in Bigod's day in England. More than this: since Bigod, though a married layman, sought to become a preacher of the gospel, his yearnings lead us to a clearer sense of lay-clerical tension in the early sixteenth century, of how that tension grew as worldly priests faced an ever more fervently religious body of laymen. Thus, through a process of mutual illumination we achieve at once a fuller understanding of a man, Sir Francis Bigod, and of the historical context of his time and place. It is well to repeat 'of his time and place', for the point of balance within each polar pair that we use to help us toward understanding is not fixed; it fluctuates from time to time and from place to place, as does the tension between the poles. And this is to say that each pair has a history of its own, a history that lasts as long as the pair itself and ends only when men cease to make serious decisions in terms of the alternatives which the pair presents.

X

Although the vocabulary of early modern history could usefully be expanded to take in the paired terms just discussed, those terms exhaust neither the possibility nor the need for alteration or for shift of emphasis in that vocabulary. There is another set of terms which early modern historians might well deploy more systematically and more boldly than they have done hitherto—corporatism, fiscality, hierarchy, patriarchy, mercantilism. Except for mercantilism these terms have a common characteristic; although some historians have given some attention to them, they are not generally recognized for what they are—common traits of the Western World in the early modern era. Historians have failed to take some of these terms seriously because early modern men took them so much for granted. But because they were taken for granted they provided some of the boundaries of choice, some of the firm framework within which men decided and acted in the early modern age. Another common trait of these terms is that *they have no historical opposite in the early modern age*. This is not to say that they have no syntactical antonyms or even that they have no polar historical opposite outside the early modern age. Mercantilism, for example, has in recent times had such an opposite in free trade—but not before 1650. Whatever free-trading meant in the early modern era it did not mean the *laissez-faire* opposite of mercantilism. The search for terms of this sort that will describe the prepossessions or the purposes of early modern men or of considerable groups of such men is actively under way. Thus quite independently Professor Bouwsma and Professor Trevor-Roper have been moved to look into the movements toward a spiritual-moral rigorism which cropped up in about half a dozen different lands in the early seventeenth century—as Jansenism in France, for example, and Puritanism in England. One may doubt Trevor-Roper's wisdom in baptizing all these movements with the name Puritanism, a name so obdurately Anglo-American in its associations. One can hardly doubt, however, that it would be well to find a common name for this group of independent yet contemporary and related clusters of events or to study those clusters together.

Neither the polar nor the simple terms set down above exhaust the possibilities; others will certainly occur to other historians, emerging from their specific interests and from the exercise of their historical imaginations. Certainly the ones suggested above fail to deal at all with a large area of the historical spectrum. For any serious investigation of the painting, sculpture, architecture, music, and systematic philosophy of the early modern age they are either irrelevant or peripheral. Whether the current words for dealing with such matters are satisfactory, whether they can be brought into any useful relation to the ones I have suggested I do not know, because about these matters my ignorance is abysmal. But surely an effort to discover such relations could not be less fruitful than the attempt (occasionally masquerading as actual achievement) to apply to methods of making money, getting power, waging war, and juggling ideas the categories of *Kulturgeschichte*. The pretense that a Renaissance spirit is discernible in all forms of human conduct during one time span and a Baroque spirit during the succeeding time span has been so sterile as perhaps too readily to discourage rational historians from seeking more than superficial relations between the forms of social action and of aesthetic expression. Possibly with a new start we might fill a conspicuous gap in the language of early modern history and make it easier to talk sensibly about what went on in that age.

The effectiveness of additions to one's vocabulary is limited by the extent to which one acquires the habit and practice of using them. Unless we gradually learn how to employ such new terms, painstakingly exploring their usefulness in conjunction with the viable parts of our old vocabulary and with their relations to each other, they will not become a living addition to the language of early modern history but merely a dead word-list. In using the word 'language' one comes near to defining the limitations of my suggested additions to the vocabulary of early modern history. For language is more than a random string of words; it is the coherent ordering of words in such a way as to make sense; it is not merely vocabulary, it is also syntax. In the syntax of early modern history the terms with which I hope that its vocabulary may be enriched occupy a peculiar place. For almost all of them are directed to men's voluntary actions, to the alternatives men confronted and the choices they made. In this bias they omit many important historical phenomena which were not the direct result of human intention—the Price Revolution, for but one example, in the early modern era. They also omit that range of conduct in which men act without considering or conceiving of an alternative to the course they adopt. This range is very broad indeed. It includes what men did when driven by coercive authority or by powerful impulses they had no inclination to resist. It also includes the innumerable actions undertaken out of custom and habit so deeply imbedded that the actor was not conscious that he might act in any other way. On the whole it seems that the lower men stand on the pyramids of power, of wealth, and of status, the more their acts are governed by impulse, coercive authority, habit and custom. In effect this means that most of the paired and single terms that I have set down would be of more use to explore the doings of the rulers of the early modern era than the sufferings of the ruled.

Granted that this is so, the proposed additions to the vocabulary of early modern history seem to me desirable just because they focus on human decision. It is well to focus on decision because of a peculiarity of historical vocabulary—one which for decades has affected the language of history. This peculiarity has escaped notice because it is hidden behind some very ordinary words and also because for many many years it neatly fit the shape of contemporary thought and sentiment. Fully to describe it is unnecessary; it is sufficiently revealed by the words in which it is imbedded: *tended, grew out of, developed, evolved; trend, development, tendency, evolution, growth.* In the historical writing of the past half-century these simple words have enabled historians to conceal their ignorance from others and from themselves. They make their appearance at those points in the description of change where the historian wants to persuade himself and others that the change in question was at once inevitable and explicable, although in fact he can neither explain it nor demonstrate its inevitability. Such words are like sealed junction boxes on the complex circuits of history. One knows that inside the boxes there are connections which induce the currents of history to change direction; but the boxes conceal rather than reveal how these connections are made. The paired and single terms described earlier may serve to pry open a few of the junction boxes. For they will force early-modern historians to use words like *think, consider, weigh, ponder, judge, choose, select, pick, decide, act, do*. They will thus serve to reveal what those other words concealed: that very often indeed at the junction between the way things were going and the way they went were the thoughts, the decisions, and the deeds of men.

HARPER TORCHBOOKS

HUMANITIES AND SOCIAL SCIENCES

American Studies

JOHN R. ALDEN: The American Revolution, 1775-1783. *Illus.* TB/3011

RAY A. BILLINGTON: The Far Western Frontier, 1830-1860. *Illus.* TB/3012

JOSEPH CHARLES: The Origins of the American Party System TB/1049

C. COCHRAN & WILLIAM MILLER: The Age of Enterprise: *A Social History of Industrial America* TB/1054

FOSTER RHEA DULLES: America's Rise to World Power, 1898-1954. *Illus.* TB/3021

, A. DUNNING: Reconstruction, Political and Economic, 1865-1877 TB/1073

HAROLD U. FAULKNER: Politics, Reform and Expansion, 1890-1900. *Illus.* TB/3020

LOUIS FILLER: The Crusade against Slavery, 1830-1860. *Illus.* TB/3029

EDITORS OF FORTUNE: America in the Sixties: *the Economy and the Society. Two-color charts* TB/1015

LAWRENCE HENRY GIPSON: The Coming of the Revolution, 1763-1775. *Illus.* TB/3007

FRANCIS J. GRUND: Aristocracy in America: *Jacksonian Democracy* TB/1001

MARCUS LEE HANSEN: The Atlantic Migration: 1607-1860. *Edited by Arthur M. Schlesinger; Introduction by Oscar Handlin* TB/1052

JOHN HIGHAM, Ed.: The Reconstruction of American History TB/1068

WILLIAM LEUCHTENBURG: Franklin D. Roosevelt and the New Deal, 1932-1940. *Illus.* TB/3025

ARTHUR S. LINK: Woodrow Wilson and the Progressive Era, 1910-1917. *Illus.* TB/3023

JOHN C. MILLER: The Federalist Era, 1789-1801. *Illus.* TB/3027

PERRY MILLER & T. H. JOHNSON, Editors: The Puritans: *A Sourcebook of Their Writings*
Volume I TB/1093
Volume II TB/1094

GEORGE E. MOWRY: The Era of Theodore Roosevelt and the Birth of Modern America, 1900-1912. *Illus.* TB/3022

WALLACE NOTESTEIN: The English People on the Eve of Colonization, 1603-1630. *Illus.* TB/3006

RUSSEL BLAINE NYE: The Cultural Life of the New Nation, 1776-1801. *Illus.* TB/3026

GEORGE E. PROBST, Ed.: The Happy Republic: *A Reader in Tocqueville's America* TB/1060

TWELVE SOUTHERNERS: I'll Take My Stand: *The South and the Agrarian Tradition. Introduction by Louis D. Rubin, Jr.; Biographical Essays by Virginia Rock* TB/1072

F. TYLER: Freedom's Ferment: *Phases of American Social History from the Revolution to the Outbreak of the Civil War. Illus.* TB/1074

LYNDON G. VAN DEUSEN: The Jacksonian Era, 1828-1848. *Illus.* TB/3028

LOUIS B. WRIGHT: The Cultural Life of the American Colonies, 1607-1763. *Illus.* TB/3005

LOUIS B. WRIGHT: Culture on the Moving Frontier TB/1053

Anthropology & Sociology

W. E. LE GROS CLARK: The Antecedents of Man: *An Introduction to the Evolution of the Primates. Illus.* TB/559

ST. CLAIR DRAKE & HORACE R. CAYTON: Black Metropolis: *A Study of Negro Life in a Northern City. Introduction by Everett C. Hughes. Tables, maps, charts and graphs*
Volume I TB/1086
Volume II TB/1087

CORA DU BOIS: The People of Alor. *New Preface by the author. Illus.*
Volume I TB/1042
Volume II TB/1043

L. S. B. LEAKEY: Adam's Ancestors: *The Evolution of Man and his Culture. Illus.* TB/1019

ROBERT H. LOWIE: Primitive Society. *Introduction by Fred Eggan* TB/1056

TALCOTT PARSONS & EDWARD A. SHILS, Editors: Toward a General Theory of Action: *Theoretical Foundations for the Social Sciences* TB/1083

SIR EDWARD TYLOR: The Origins of Culture. *Part I of "Primitive Culture." Introduction by Paul Radin* TB/33

SIR EDWARD TYLOR: Religion in Primitive Culture. *Part II of "Primitive Culture." Introduction by Paul Radin* TB/34

W. LLOYD WARNER: Social Class in America: *The Evaluation of Status* TB/1013

Art and Art History

EMILE MÂLE: The Gothic Image: *Religious Art in France of the Thirteenth Century. 190 illus.* TB/44

ERWIN PANOFSKY: Studies in Iconology: *Humanistic Themes in the Art of the Renaissance. 180 illustrations* TB/1077

ALEXANDRE PIANKOFF: The Shrines of Tut-Ankh-Amon. *Edited by N. Rambova. 117 illus.* TB/2011

JEAN SEZNEC: The Survival of the Pagan Gods: *The Mythological Tradition and Its Place in Renaissance Humanism and Art. 108 illustrations* TB/2004

HEINRICH ZIMMER: Myths and Symbols in Indian Art and Civilization: *70 illustrations* TB/2005

Business, Economics & Economic History

REINHARD BENDIX: Work and Authority in Industry: *Ideologies of Management in the Course of Industrialization* TB/3035

THOMAS C. COCHRAN: The American Business System: *A Historical Perspective, 1900-1955* TB/1080

PETER F. DRUCKER: The New Society: *The Anatomy of Industrial Order* TB/1082

ROBERT L. HEILBRONER: The Great Ascent: *The Struggle for Economic Development in Our Time* TB/3030

PAUL MANTOUX: The Industrial Revolution in the Eighteenth Century: *The Beginnings of the Modern Factory System in England*   TB/1079

WILLIAM MILLER, Ed.: Men in Business: *Essays on the Historical Role of the Entrepreneur*   TB/1081

PERRIN STRYKER: The Character of the Executive: *Eleven Studies in Managerial Qualities*   TB/1041

Contemporary Culture

JACQUES BARZUN: The House of Intellect   TB/1051

PAUL VALÉRY: The Outlook for Intelligence   TB/2016

History: General

L. CARRINGTON GOODRICH: A Short History of the Chinese People. *Illus.*   TB/3015

DAN N. JACOBS & HANS BAERWALD: Chinese Communism: *Selected Documents*   TB/3031

BERNARD LEWIS: The Arabs in History   TB/1029

SIR PERCY SYKES: A History of Exploration. *Introduction by John K. Wright*   TB/1046

History: Ancient and Medieval

A. ANDREWES: The Greek Tyrants   TB/1103

HELEN CAM: England before Elizabeth   TB/1026

NORMAN COHN: The Pursuit of the Millennium: *Revolutionary Messianism in medieval and Reformation Europe and its bearing on modern totalitarian movements*   TB/1037

G. G. COULTON: Medieval Village, Manor, and Monastery   TB/1022

F. L. GANSHOF: Feudalism   TB/1058

J. M. HUSSEY: The Byzantine World   TB/1057

SAMUEL NOAH KRAMER: Sumerian Mythology   TB/1055

FERDINAND LOT: The End of the Ancient World and the Beginnings of the Middle Ages. *Introduction by Glanville Downey*   TB/1044

J. M. WALLACE-HADRILL: The Barbarian West: *The Early Middle Ages, A.D. 400-1000*   TB/1061

History: Renaissance & Reformation

JACOB BURCKHARDT: The Civilization of the Renaissance in Italy. *Introduction by Benjamin Nelson and Charles Trinkaus. Illus.*   Volume I TB/40   Volume II TB/41

ERNST CASSIRER: The Individual and the Cosmos in Renaissance Philosophy. *Translated with an Introduction by Mario Domandi*   TB/1097

EDWARD P. CHEYNEY: The Dawn of a New Era, *1250-1453. Illus.*   TB/3002

WALLACE K. FERGUSON, et al.: Facets of the Renaissance   TB/1098

WALLACE K. FERGUSON, et al.: The Renaissance: *Six Essays. Illus.*   TB/1084

MYRON P. GILMORE: The World of Humanism, 1453-1517. *Illus.*   TB/3003

JOHAN HUIZINGA: Erasmus and the Age of Reformation. *Illus.*   TB/19

PAUL O. KRISTELLER: Renaissance Thought: *The Classic, Scholastic, and Humanist Strains*   TB/1048

NICCOLÒ MACHIAVELLI: History of Florence and of the Affairs of Italy: *from the earliest times to the death of Lorenzo the Magnificent. Introduction by Felix Gilbert*   TB/1027

ALFRED VON MARTIN: Sociology of the Renaissance. *Introduction by W. K. Ferguson*   TB/1099

J. E. NEALE: The Age of Catherine de Medici   TB/1085

ERWIN PANOFSKY: Studies in Iconology: *Humanistic Themes in the Art of the Renaissance. 180 illus* tions   TB/▮

J. H. PARRY: The Establishment of the European gemony: 1415-1715: *Trade and Exploration in the of the Renaissance*   TB/▮

FERDINAND SCHEVILL: The Medici. *Illus.*   TB/▮

FERDINAND SCHEVILL: Medieval and Renaissa Florence. *Illus.* Volume I: *Medieval Florence* TB/▮ Volume II: *The Coming of Humanism and the Ag the Medici*   TB/▮

History: Modern European

FREDERICK B. ARTZ: Reaction and Revolut 1815-1832. *Illus.*   TB/▮

MAX BELOFF: The Age of Absolutism, 1660-1815   TB/▮

CRANE BRINTON: A Decade of Revolution, 17 1799. *Illus.*   TB/▮

J. BRONOWSKI & BRUCE MAZLISH: The West Intellectual Tradition: *From Leonardo to Hegel*   TB/▮

GEOFFREY BRUUN: Europe and the French Imperi 1799-1814. *Illus.*   TB/▮

WALTER L. DORN: Competition for Empire, 17 1763. *Illus.*   TB/▮

CARL J. FRIEDRICH: The Age of the Baroque, 16 1660. *Illus.*   TB/▮

LEO GERSHOY: From Despotism to Revolution, 17 1789. *Illus.*   TB/▮

ALBERT GOODWIN: The French Revolution   TB/▮

J. H. HEXTER: Reappraisals in History: *New Views History and Society in Early Modern Europe*   TB/▮

A. R. HUMPHREYS: The Augustan World: *Soc Thought, and Letters in Eighteenth Century Engl*   TB/▮

DAN N. JACOBS, Ed.: The New Communist Manif and Related Documents   TB/▮

HANS KOHN, Ed.: The Mind of Modern Russia: *H torical and Political Thought of Russia's Great*   TB/▮

SIR LEWIS NAMIER: Vanished Supremacies: *Essay European History, 1812-1918*   TB/▮

JOHN U. NEF: Cultural Foundations of Industrial C lization   TB/▮

FREDERICK L. NUSSBAUM: The Triumph of Scie and Reason, 1660-1685. *Illus.*   TB/▮

RAYMOND W. POSTGATE, Ed.: Revolution f 1789 to 1906: *Selected Documents*   TB/▮

PENFIELD ROBERTS: The Quest for Security, 17 1740. *Illus.*   TB/▮

PRISCILLA ROBERTSON: Revolutions of 1848: *A cial History*   TB/▮

N. N. SUKHANOV: The Russian Revolution, 1917: *F witness Account. Edited by Joel Carmichael*   Volume I TB/▮   Volume II TB/▮

JOHN B. WOLF: The Emergence of the Great Pow 1685-1715. *Illus.*   TB/▮

JOHN B. WOLF: France: 1814-1919: *The Rise c Liberal-Democratic Society*   TB/▮

Intellectual History

HERSCHEL BAKER: The Image of Man: *A Study the Idea of Human Dignity in Classical Antiquity, Middle Ages, and the Renaissance*   TB/1

J. BRONOWSKI & BRUCE MAZLISH: The West Intellectual Tradition: *From Leonardo to Hegel*   TB/▮

RMAN COHN: The Pursuit of the Millennium: Revolutionary Messianism in medieval and Reformation Europe and its bearing on modern totalitarian movements TB/1037

THUR O. LOVEJOY: The Great Chain of Being: A Study of the History of an Idea TB/1009

BERT PAYNE: Hubris: A Study of Pride. Foreword by Sir Herbert Read TB/1031

UNO SNELL: The Discovery of the Mind: The Greek Origins of European Thought TB/1018

UL VALÉRY: The Outlook for Intelligence TB/2016

erature, Poetry, The Novel & Criticism

MES BAIRD: Ishmael: The Art of Melville in the Contexts of International Primitivism TB/1023

CQUES BARZUN: The House of Intellect TB/1051

J. BATE: From Classic to Romantic: Premises of Taste in Eighteenth Century England TB/1036

CHEL BESPALOFF: On the Iliad TB/2006

P. BLACKMUR, et al.: Lectures in Criticism. Introduction by Huntington Cairns TB/2003

RAHAM CAHAN: The Rise of David Levinsky: a novel. Introduction by John Higham TB/1028

NST R. CURTIUS: European Literature and the Latin Middle Ages TB/2015

ORGE ELIOT: Daniel Deronda: a novel. Introduction by F. R. Leavis TB/1039

IENNE GILSON: Dante and Philosophy TB/1089

FRED HARBAGE: As They Liked It: A Study of Shakespeare's Moral Artistry TB/1035

ANLEY R. HOPPER, Ed.: Spiritual Problems in Contemporary Literature TB/21

R. HUMPHREYS: The Augustan World: Society, Thought, and Letters in Eighteenth Century England TB/1105

NRY JAMES: The Princess Casamassima: a novel. Introduction by Clinton F. Oliver TB/1005

NRY JAMES: Roderick Hudson: a novel. Introduction by Leon Edel TB/1016

NRY JAMES: The Tragic Muse: a novel. Introduction by Leon Edel TB/1017

NOLD KETTLE: An Introduction to the English Novel. Volume I: Defoe to George Eliot TB/1011
Volume II: Henry James to the Present TB/1012

HN STUART MILL: On Bentham and Coleridge. Introduction by F. R. Leavis TB/1070

RRY MILLER & T. H. JOHNSON, Editors: The Puritans: A Sourcebook of Their Writings
Volume I TB/1093
Volume II TB/1094

NNETH B. MURDOCK: Literature and Theology in Colonial New England TB/99

MUEL PEPYS: The Diary of Samuel Pepys. Edited by O. F. Morshead. Illustrations by Ernest Shepard TB/1007

JOHN PERSE: Seamarks TB/2002

ORGE SANTAYANA: Interpretations of Poetry and Religion TB/9

P. SNOW: Time of Hope: a novel TB/1040

ROTHY VAN GHENT: The English Novel: Form and Function TB/1050

ORTON DAUWEN ZABEL, Editor: Literary Opinion in America
Volume I TB/3013
Volume II TB/3014

yth, Symbol & Folklore

SEPH CAMPBELL, Editor: Pagan and Christian Mysteries TB/2013

MIRCEA ELIADE: Cosmos and History: The Myth of the Eternal Return TB/50

C. G. JUNG & C. KERÉNYI: Essays on a Science of Mythology: The Myths of the Divine Child and the Divine Maiden TB/2014

ERWIN PANOFSKY: Studies in Iconology: Humanistic Themes in the Art of the Renaissance. 180 illustrations TB/1077

JEAN SEZNEC: The Survival of the Pagan Gods: The Mythological Tradition and its Place in Renaissance Humanism and Art. 108 illustrations TB/2004

HEINRICH ZIMMER: Myths and Symbols in Indian Art and Civilization. 70 illustrations TB/2005

Philosophy

HENRI BERGSON: Time and Free Will: An Essay on the Immediate Data of Consciousness TB/1021

H. J. BLACKHAM: Six Existentialist Thinkers: Kierkegaard, Nietzsche, Jaspers, Marcel, Heidegger, Sartre TB/1002

ERNST CASSIRER: Rousseau, Kant and Goethe. Introduction by Peter Gay TB/1092

FREDERICK COPLESTON: Medieval Philosophy TB/76

F. M. CORNFORD: From Religion to Philosophy: A Study in the Origins of Western Speculation TB/20

WILFRID DESAN: The Tragic Finale: An Essay on the Philosophy of Jean-Paul Sartre TB/1030

ETIENNE GILSON: Dante and Philosophy TB/1089

WILLIAM CHASE GREENE: Moira: Fate, Good, and Evil in Greek Thought TB/1104

W. K. C. GUTHRIE: The Greek Philosophers: From Thales to Aristotle TB/1008

F. H. HEINEMANN: Existentialism and the Modern Predicament TB/28

IMMANUEL KANT: Lectures on Ethics. Introduction by Lewis W. Beck TB/105

WILLARD VAN ORMAN QUINE: From a Logical Point of View: Logico-Philosophical Essays TB/566

BERTRAND RUSSELL et al.: The Philosophy of Bertrand Russell. Edited by Paul Arthur Schilpp
Volume I TB/1095
Volume II TB/1096

L. S. STEBBING: A Modern Introduction to Logic TB/538

ALFRED NORTH WHITEHEAD: Process and Reality: An Essay in Cosmology TB/1033

WILHELM WINDELBAND: A History of Philosophy I: Greek, Roman, Medieval TB/38

WILHELM WINDELBAND: A History of Philosophy II: Renaissance, Enlightenment, Modern TB/39

Philosophy of History

NICOLAS BERDYAEV: The Beginning and the End TB/14

NICOLAS BERDYAEV: The Destiny of Man TB/61

WILHELM DILTHEY: Pattern and Meaning in History: Thoughts on History and Society. Edited with an Introduction by H. P. Rickman TB/1075

JOSE ORTEGA Y GASSET: The Modern Theme. Introduction by Jose Ferrater Mora TB/1038

W. H. WALSH: Philosophy of History: An Introduction TB/1020

Political Science & Government

JEREMY BENTHAM: The Handbook of Political Fallacies. Introduction by Crane Brinton TB/1069

KENNETH E. BOULDING: Conflict and Defense: *A General Theory*   TB/3024

CRANE BRINTON: English Political Thought in the Nineteenth Century   TB/1071

JOHN NEVILLE FIGGIS: Political Thought from Gerson to Grotius: 1414-1625: *Seven Studies. Introduction by Garrett Mattingly*   TB/1032

F. L. GANSHOF: Feudalism   TB/1058

G. P. GOOCH: English Democratic Ideas in the Seventeenth Century   TB/1006

J. P. MAYER: Alexis de Tocqueville: *A Biographical Study in Political Science*   TB/1014

JOHN STUART MILL: On Bentham and Coleridge. *Introduction by F. R. Leavis*   TB/1070

JOHN B. MORRALL: Political Thought in Medieval Times   TB/1076

KARL R. POPPER: The Open Society and Its Enemies
Volume I: *The Spell of Plato*   TB/1101
Volume II: *The High Tide of Prophecy: Hegel, Marx, and the Aftermath*   TB/1102

JOSEPH A. SCHUMPETER: Capitalism, Socialism and Democracy   TB/3008

Psychology

ANTON T. BOISEN: The Exploration of the Inner World: *A Study of Mental Disorder and Religious Experience*   TB/87

WALTER BROMBERG: The Mind of Man: *A History of Psychotherapy and Psychoanalysis*   TB/1003

SIGMUND FREUD: On Creativity and the Unconscious: *Papers on the Psychology of Art, Literature, Love, Religion. Intro. by Benjamin Nelson*   TB/45

C. JUDSON HERRICK: The Evolution of Human Nature   TB/545

ALDOUS HUXLEY: The Devils of Loudun: *A Study in the Psychology of Power Politics and Mystical Religion in the France of Cardinal Richelieu*   TB/60

WILLIAM JAMES: Psychology: *The Briefer Course. Edited with an Intro. by Gordon Allport*   TB/1034

C. G. JUNG: Psychological Reflections. *Edited by Jolande Jacobi*   TB/2001

C. G. JUNG: Symbols of Transformation: *An Analysis of the Prelude to a Case of Schizophrenia*
Volume I   TB/2009
Volume II   TB/2010

C. G. JUNG & C. KERÉNYI: Essays on a Science of Mythology: *The Myths of the Divine Child and the Divine Maiden*   TB/2014

ERICH NEUMANN: Amor and Psyche: *The Psychic Development of the Feminine*   TB/2012

ERICH NEUMANN: The Origins and History of Consciousness
Volume I *Illus.*   TB/2007
Volume II   TB/2008

RELIGION

Ancient & Classical

J. H. BREASTED: Development of Religion and Thought in Ancient Egypt. *Introduction by John A. Wilson*   TB/57

HENRI FRANKFORT: Ancient Egyptian Religion: *An Interpretation*   TB/77

G. RACHEL LEVY: Religious Conceptions of the Stone Age and their Influence upon European Thought. *Illus. Introduction by Henri Frankfort*   TB/106

MARTIN P. NILSSON: Greek Folk Religion. *Foreword by Arthur Darby Nock*   TB/78

ALEXANDRE PIANKOFF: The Shrines of Tut-Ankh-Amon. *Edited by N. Rambova. 117 illus.*   TB/20

H. J. ROSE: Religion in Greece and Rome   TB/

Biblical Thought & Literature

W. F. ALBRIGHT: The Biblical Period from Abraham to Ezra   TB/

C. K. BARRETT, Ed.: The New Testament Background: *Selected Documents*   TB/

C. H. DODD: The Authority of the Bible   TB/

M. S. ENSLIN: Christian Beginnings   TB/

M. S. ENSLIN: The Literature of the Christian Movement   TB/

H. E. FOSDICK: A Guide to Understanding the Bible   TB/

H. H. ROWLEY: The Growth of the Old Testament   TB/

D. WINTON THOMAS, Ed.: Documents from Old Testament Times   TB/

Christianity: Origins & Early Development

EDWARD GIBBON: The Triumph of Christendom in the Roman Empire (*Chaps. XV-XX of "Decline and Fall," J. B. Bury edition). Illus.*   TB/

MAURICE GOGUEL: Jesus and the Origins of Christianity. *Introduction by C. Leslie Mitton*
Volume I: *Prolegomena to the Life of Jesus*   TB/
Volume II: *The Life of Jesus*   TB/

EDGAR J. GOODSPEED: A Life of Jesus   TB/

ADOLF HARNACK: The Mission and Expansion of Christianity *in the First Three Centuries. Introduction by Jaroslav Pelikan*   TB/

R. K. HARRISON: The Dead Sea Scrolls: *An Introduction*   TB/

EDWIN HATCH: The Influence of Greek Ideas on Christianity. *Introduction and Bibliography by Frederick C. Grant*   TB/

JOHANNES WEISS: Earliest Christianity: *A History of the Period A.D. 30-150. Introduction and Bibliography by Frederick C. Grant*   Volume I   TB/
Volume II   TB/

Christianity: The Middle Ages and After

G. P. FEDOTOV: The Russian Religious Mind: *Kievan Christianity, the tenth to the thirteenth centuries*   TB/

ETIENNE GILSON: Dante and Philosophy   TB/16

WILLIAM HALLER: The Rise of Puritanism   TB/

JOHAN HUIZINGA: Erasmus and the Age of Reformation. *Illus.*   TB/

A. C. McGIFFERT: Protestant Thought Before Kant. *Preface by Jaroslav Pelikan*   TB/

KENNETH B. MURDOCK: Literature and Theology in Colonial New England   TB/

H. O. TAYLOR: The Emergence of Christian Culture in the West: *The Classical Heritage of the Middle Ages. Intro. and biblio. by Kenneth M. Setton*   TB/

Judaic Thought & Literature

MARTIN BUBER: Eclipse of God: *Studies in the Relation Between Religion and Philosophy*   TB/

MARTIN BUBER: Moses: *The Revelation and the Covenant*   TB/

MARTIN BUBER: Pointing the Way. *Introduction by Maurice S. Friedman*   TB/

MARTIN BUBER: The Prophetic Faith   TB/

MARTIN BUBER: Two Types of Faith: *the interpretation of Judaism and Christianity*   TB/

MAURICE S. FRIEDMAN: Martin Buber: *The Life of Dialogue* TB/64

FLAVIUS JOSEPHUS: The Great Roman-Jewish War, with The Life of Josephus. *Introduction by William R. Farmer* TB/74

T. J. MEEK: Hebrew Origins TB/69

Oriental Religions: Far Eastern, Near Eastern

TOR ANDRAE: Mohammed: *The Man and His Faith* TB/62

EDWARD CONZE: Buddhism: *Its Essence and Development. Foreword by Arthur Waley* TB/58

H. G. CREEL: Confucius and the Chinese Way TB/63

Philosophy of Religion

RUDOLF BULTMANN: History and Eschatology: *The Presence of Eternity* TB/91

RUDOLF BULTMANN AND FIVE CRITICS: Kerygma and Myth: *A Theological Debate* TB/80

RUDOLF BULTMANN and KARL KUNDSIN: Form Criticism: *Two Essays on New Testament Research. Translated by Frederick C. Grant* TB/96

MIRCEA ELIADE: The Sacred and the Profane TB/81

LUDWIG FEUERBACH: The Essence of Christianity. *Introduction by Karl Barth. Foreword by H. Richard Niebuhr* TB/11

ADOLF HARNACK: What is Christianity? *Introduction by Rudolf Bultmann* TB/17

FRIEDRICH HEGEL: On Christianity: *Early Theological Writings. Edited by Richard Kroner and T. M. Knox* TB/79

KARL HEIM: Christian Faith and Natural Science TB/16

IMMANUEL KANT: Religion Within the Limits of Reason Alone. *Introduction by Theodore M. Greene and John Silber* TB/67

PIERRE TEILHARD DE CHARDIN: The Phenomenon of Man TB/83

Religion, Culture & Society

C. C. GILLISPIE: Genesis and Geology: *The Decades before Darwin* TB/51

H. RICHARD NIEBUHR: Christ and Culture TB/3

H. RICHARD NIEBUHR: The Kingdom of God in America TB/49

ERNST TROELTSCH: The Social Teaching of the Christian Churches. *Introduction by H. Richard Niebuhr.* Volume I TB/71
Volume II TB/72

Religious Thinkers & Traditions

AUGUSTINE: An Augustine Synthesis. *Edited by Erich Przywara* TB/35

KARL BARTH: Church Dogmatics: *A Selection. Introduction by H. Gollwitzer; Edited by G. W. Bromiley* TB/95

KARL BARTH: Dogmatics in Outline TB/56

KARL BARTH: The Word of God and the Word of Man. TB/13

ADOLF DEISSMANN: Paul: *A Study in Social and Religious History* TB/15

JOHANNES ECKHART: Meister Eckhart: *A Modern Translation by R. B. Blakney* TB/8

WINTHROP HUDSON: The Great Tradition of the American Churches TB/98

SOREN KIERKEGAARD: Edifying Discourses. *Edited with an Introduction by Paul Holmer* TB/32

SOREN KIERKEGAARD: The Journals of Kierkegaard. *Edited with an Intro. by Alexander Dru* TB/52

SOREN KIERKEGAARD: The Point of View for My Work as an Author: *A Report to History. Preface by Benjamin Nelson* TB/88

SOREN KIERKEGAARD: The Present Age. *Translated and edited by Alexander Dru. Introduction by Walter Kaufmann* TB/94

SOREN KIERKEGAARD: Purity of Heart. *Translated by Douglas Steere* TB/4

WALTER LOWRIE: Kierkegaard: *A Life* Volume I TB/89
Volume II TB/90

GABRIEL MARCEL: Homo Viator: *Introduction to a Metaphysic of Hope* TB/97

PERRY MILLER & T. H. JOHNSON, Editors: The Puritans: *A Sourcebook of Their Writings* Volume I TB/1093
Volume II TB/1094

A. D. NOCK: St. Paul TB/104

PAUL PFUETZE: Self, Society, Existence: *Human Nature and Dialogue in the Thought of George Herbert Mead and Martin Buber* TB/1059

F. SCHLEIERMACHER: The Christian Faith. *Introduction by Richard R. Niebuhr* Volume I TB/108
Volume II TB/109

F. SCHLEIERMACHER: On Religion: *Speeches to Its Cultured Despisers. Intro. by Rudolf Otto* TB/36

PAUL TILLICH: Dynamics of Faith TB/42

EVELYN UNDERHILL: Worship TB/10

G. VAN DER LEEUW: Religion in Essence and Manifestation: *A Study in Phenomenology. Appendices by Hans H. Penner* Volume I TB/100
Volume II TB/101

NATURAL SCIENCES AND MATHEMATICS

Biological Sciences

A. BELLAIRS: Reptiles: *Life History, Evolution, and Structure. Illus.* TB/520

LUDWIG VON BERTALANFFY: Modern Theories of Development: *An Introduction to Theoretical Biology* TB/554

LUDWIG VON BERTALANFFY: Problems of Life: *An Evaluation of Modern Biological and Scientific Thought* TB/521

HAROLD F. BLUM: Time's Arrow and Evolution TB/555

A. J. CAIN: Animal Species and their Evolution. *Illus.* TB/519

WALTER B. CANNON: Bodily Changes in Pain, Hunger, Fear and Rage. *Illus.* TB/562

W. E. LE GROS CLARK: The Antecedents of Man: *An Introduction to the Evolution of the Primates. Illus.* TB/559

W. H. DOWDESWELL: Animal Ecology. *Illus.* TB/543

W. H. DOWDESWELL: The Mechanism of Evolution. *Illus.* TB/527

R. W. GERARD: Unresting Cells. *Illus.* TB/541

DAVID LACK: Darwin's Finches. *Illus.* TB/544

J. E. MORTON: Molluscs: *An Introduction to their Form and Functions. Illus.* TB/529

O. W. RICHARDS: The Social Insects. *Illus.* TB/542

P. M. SHEPPARD: Natural Selection and Heredity. *Illus.* TB/528

EDMUND W. SINNOTT: Cell and Psyche: *The Biology of Purpose* TB/546

C. H. WADDINGTON: How Animals Develop. *Illus.* TB/553

Chemistry

A. FINDLAY: Chemistry in the Service of Man. *Illus.*
TB/524
J. R. PARTINGTON: A Short History of Chemistry.
Illus. TB/522
J. READ: A Direct Entry to Organic Chemistry. *Illus.*
TB/523
J. READ: Through Alchemy to Chemistry. *Illus.* TB/561

Geography

R. E. COKER: This Great and Wide Sea: *An Introduction to Oceanography and Marine Biology. Illus.*
TB/551
F. K. HARE: The Restless Atmosphere TB/560

History of Science

W. DAMPIER, Ed.: Readings in the Literature of Science. *Illus.* TB/512
ALEXANDRE KOYRÉ: From the Closed World to the Infinite Universe: *Copernicus, Kepler, Galileo, Newton, etc.* TB/31
A. G. VAN MELSEN: From Atomos to Atom: *A History of the Concept Atom* TB/517
O. NEUGEBAUER: The Exact Sciences in Antiquity
TB/552
H. T. PLEDGE: Science Since 1500: *A Short History of Mathematics, Physics, Chemistry and Biology. Illus.*
TB/506
GEORGE SARTON: Ancient Science and Modern Civilization TB/501
HANS THIRRING: Energy for Man: *From Windmills to Nuclear Power* TB/556
WILLIAM LAW WHYTE: Essay on Atomism: *From Democritus to 1960* TB/565
A. WOLF: A History of Science, Technology and Philosophy in the 16th and 17th Centuries. *Illus.*
Volume I TB/508
Volume II TB/509
A. WOLF: A History of Science, Technology, and Philosophy in the Eighteenth Century. *Illus.*
Volume I TB/539
Volume II TB/540

Mathematics

H. DAVENPORT: The Higher Arithmetic: *An Introduction to the Theory of Numbers* TB/526
H. G. FORDER: Geometry: *An Introduction* TB/548
GOTTLOB FREGE: The Foundations of Arithmetic: *A Logico-Mathematical Enquiry into the Concept of Number* TB/534
S. KÖRNER: The Philosophy of Mathematics: *An Introduction* TB/547
D. E. LITTLEWOOD: Skeleton Key of Mathematics: *A Simple Account of Complex Algebraic Problems*
TB/525

WILLARD VAN ORMAN QUINE: Mathematical
TB
O. G. SUTTON: Mathematics in Action. *Forewor James R. Newman. Illus.* TB
FREDERICK WAISMANN: Introduction to Mathecal Thinking. *Foreword by Karl Menger* TB

Philosophy of Science

R. B. BRAITHWAITE: Scientific Explanation T
J. BRONOWSKI: Science and Human Values. *Il.*
A
ALBERT EINSTEIN: Philosopher-Scientist. *Edite Paul A. Schilpp* Volume I T
Volume II TI
WERNER HEISENBERG: Physics and Philosophy *Revolution in Modern Science. Introduction by C. Northrop* T
JOHN MAYNARD KEYNES: A Treatise on Probab *Introduction by N. R. Hanson* T
STEPHEN TOULMIN: Foresight and Understan *An Enquiry into the Aims of Science. Forewor Jacques Barzun* TI
STEPHEN TOULMIN: The Philosophy of Science *Introduction* TI
W. H. WATSON: On Understanding Physics. *I duction by Ernest Nagel* TI
G. J. WHITROW: The Natural Philosophy of Ti TI

Physics and Cosmology

DAVID BOHM: Causality and Chance in Mo Physics. *Foreword by Louis de Broglie* TB
P. W. BRIDGMAN: The Nature of Thermodynam
TB
LOUIS DE BROGLIE: Physics and Microphysics. *word by Albert Einstein* TI
T. G. COWLING: Molecules in Motion: *An Intro tion to the Kinetic Theory of Gases. Illus.* TB
A. C. CROMBIE, Ed.: Turning Point in Physics TE
C. V. DURELL: Readable Relativity. *Foreword by man J. Dyson* TB
ARTHUR EDDINGTON: Space, Time and Gravita *An outline of the General Relativity Theory* TB
MAX JAMMER: Concepts of Force: *A Study in Foundation of Dynamics* TB
MAX JAMMER: Concepts of Space: *The Histor Theories of Space in Physics. Foreword by A Einstein* TB
EDMUND WHITTAKER: History of the Theorie Aether and Electricity
Volume I: *The Classical Theories* TB
Volume II: *The Modern Theories* TB
G. J. WHITROW: The Structure and Evolution of Universe: *An Introduction to Cosmology. Ill*
TB

Code to Torchbook Libraries:	
TB/1+	: The Cloister Library
TB/501+	: The Science Library
TB/1001+	: The Academy Library
TB/2001+	: The Bollingen Library
TB/3001+	: The University Library

AURICE S. FRIEDMAN: Martin Buber: *The Life of Dialogue* TB/64

AVIUS JOSEPHUS: The Great Roman-Jewish War, *with The Life of Josephus. Introduction by William R. Farmer* TB/74

J. MEEK: Hebrew Origins TB/69

riental Religions: Far Eastern, Near Eastern

)R ANDRAE: Mohammed: *The Man and His Faith* TB/62

)WARD CONZE: Buddhism: *Its Essence and Development. Foreword by Arthur Waley* TB/58

G. CREEL: Confucius and the Chinese Way TB/63

hilosophy of Religion

UDOLF BULTMANN: History and Eschatology: *The Presence of Eternity* TB/91

UDOLF BULTMANN AND FIVE CRITICS: Kerygma and Myth: *A Theological Debate* TB/80

UDOLF BULTMANN and KARL KUNDSIN: Form Criticism: *Two Essays on New Testament Research. Translated by Frederick C. Grant* TB/96

IIRCEA ELIADE: The Sacred and the Profane TB/81

UDWIG FEUERBACH: The Essence of Christianity. *Introduction by Karl Barth. Foreword by H. Richard Niebuhr* TB/11

)OLF HARNACK: What is Christianity? *Introduction by Rudolf Bultmann* TB/17

RIEDRICH HEGEL: On Christianity: *Early Theological Writings. Edited by Richard Kroner and T. M. Knox* TB/79

ARL HEIM: Christian Faith and Natural Science TB/16

MMANUEL KANT: Religion Within the Limits of Reason Alone. *Introduction by Theodore M. Greene and John Silber* TB/67

IERRE TEILHARD DE CHARDIN: The Phenomenon of Man TB/83

eligion, Culture & Society

. C. GILLISPIE: Genesis and Geology: *The Decades before Darwin* TB/51

I. RICHARD NIEBUHR: Christ and Culture TB/3

I. RICHARD NIEBUHR: The Kingdom of God in America TB/49

RNST TROELTSCH: The Social Teaching of the Christian Churches. *Introduction by H. Richard Niebuhr.* Volume I TB/71
Volume II TB/72

Religious Thinkers & Traditions

AUGUSTINE: An Augustine Synthesis. *Edited by Erich Przywara* TB/35

CARL BARTH: Church Dogmatics: *A Selection. Introduction by H. Gollwitzer; Edited by G. W. Bromiley* TB/95

CARL BARTH: Dogmatics in Outline TB/56

CARL BARTH: The Word of God and the Word of Man. TB/13

ADOLF DEISSMANN: Paul: *A Study in Social and Religious History* TB/15

IOHANNES ECKHART: Meister Eckhart: *A Modern Translation by R. B. Blakney* TB/8

WINTHROP HUDSON: The Great Tradition of the American Churches TB/98

SOREN KIERKEGAARD: Edifying Discourses. *Edited with an Introduction by Paul Holmer* TB/32

SOREN KIERKEGAARD: The Journals of Kierkegaard. *Edited with an Intro. by Alexander Dru* TB/52

SOREN KIERKEGAARD: The Point of View for My Work as an Author: *A Report to History. Preface by Benjamin Nelson* TB/88

SOREN KIERKEGAARD: The Present Age. *Translated and edited by Alexander Dru. Introduction by Walter Kaufmann* TB/94

SOREN KIERKEGAARD: Purity of Heart. *Translated by Douglas Steere* TB/4

WALTER LOWRIE: Kierkegaard: *A Life*
Volume I TB/89
Volume II TB/90

GABRIEL MARCEL: Homo Viator: *Introduction to a Metaphysic of Hope* TB/97

PERRY MILLER & T. H. JOHNSON, Editors: The Puritans: *A Sourcebook of Their Writings*
Volume I TB/1093
Volume II TB/1094

A. D. NOCK: St. Paul TB/104

PAUL PFUETZE: Self, Society, Existence: *Human Nature and Dialogue in the Thought of George Herbert Mead and Martin Buber* TB/1059

F. SCHLEIERMACHER: The Christian Faith. *Introduction by Richard R. Niebuhr* Volume I TB/108
Volume II TB/109

F. SCHLEIERMACHER: On Religion: *Speeches to Its Cultured Despisers. Intro. by Rudolf Otto* TB/36

PAUL TILLICH: Dynamics of Faith TB/42

EVELYN UNDERHILL: Worship TB/10

G. VAN DER LEEUW: Religion in Essence and Manifestation: *A Study in Phenomenology. Appendices by Hans H. Penner* Volume I TB/100
Volume II TB/101

NATURAL SCIENCES AND MATHEMATICS

Biological Sciences

A. BELLAIRS: Reptiles: *Life History, Evolution, and Structure. Illus.* TB/520

LUDWIG VON BERTALANFFY: Modern Theories of Development: *An Introduction to Theoretical Biology* TB/554

LUDWIG VON BERTALANFFY: Problems of Life: *An Evaluation of Modern Biological and Scientific Thought* TB/521

HAROLD F. BLUM: Time's Arrow and Evolution TB/555

A. J. CAIN: Animal Species and their Evolution. *Illus.* TB/519

WALTER B. CANNON: Bodily Changes in Pain, Hunger, Fear and Rage. *Illus.* TB/562

W. E. LE GROS CLARK: The Antecedents of Man: *An Introduction to the Evolution of the Primates. Illus.* TB/559

W. H. DOWDESWELL: Animal Ecology. *Illus.* TB/543

W. H. DOWDESWELL: The Mechanism of Evolution. *Illus.* TB/527

R. W. GERARD: Unresting Cells. *Illus.* TB/541

DAVID LACK: Darwin's Finches. *Illus.* TB/544

J. E. MORTON: Molluscs: *An Introduction to their Form and Functions. Illus.* TB/529

O. W. RICHARDS: The Social Insects. *Illus.* TB/542

P. M: SHEPPARD: Natural Selection and Heredity. *Illus.* TB/528

EDMUND W. SINNOTT: Cell and Psyche: *The Biology of Purpose* TB/546

C. H. WADDINGTON: How Animals Develop. *Illus.* TB/553

Chemistry

A. FINDLAY: Chemistry in the Service of Man. *Illus.*
TB/524

J. R. PARTINGTON: A Short History of Chemistry. *Illus.*
TB/522

J. READ: A Direct Entry to Organic Chemistry. *Illus.*
TB/523

J. READ: Through Alchemy to Chemistry. *Illus.* TB/561

Geography

R. E. COKER: This Great and Wide Sea: *An Introduction to Oceanography and Marine Biology. Illus.*
TB/551

F. K. HARE: The Restless Atmosphere   TB/560

History of Science

W. DAMPIER, Ed.: Readings in the Literature of Science. *Illus.*   TB/512

ALEXANDRE KOYRÉ: From the Closed World to the Infinite Universe: *Copernicus, Kepler, Galileo, Newton, etc.*   TB/31

A. G. VAN MELSEN: From Atomos to Atom: *A History of the Concept Atom*   TB/517

O. NEUGEBAUER: The Exact Sciences in Antiquity
TB/552

H. T. PLEDGE: Science Since 1500: *A Short History of Mathematics, Physics, Chemistry and Biology. Illus.*
TB/506

GEORGE SARTON: Ancient Science and Modern Civilization   TB/501

HANS THIRRING: Energy for Man: *From Windmills to Nuclear Power*   TB/556

WILLIAM LAW WHYTE: Essay on Atomism: *From Democritus to 1960*   TB/565

A. WOLF: A History of Science, Technology and Philosophy in the 16th and 17th Centuries. *Illus.*
Volume I TB/508
Volume II TB/509

A. WOLF: A History of Science, Technology, and Philosophy in the Eighteenth Century. *Illus.*
Volume I TB/539
Volume II TB/540

Mathematics

H. DAVENPORT: The Higher Arithmetic: *An Introduction to the Theory of Numbers*   TB/526

H. G. FORDER: Geometry: *An Introduction*   TB/548

GOTTLOB FREGE: The Foundations of Arithmetic: *A Logico-Mathematical Enquiry into the Concept of Number*   TB/534

S. KÖRNER: The Philosophy of Mathematics: *An Introduction*   TB/547

D. E. LITTLEWOOD: Skeleton Key of Mathematics: *A Simple Account of Complex Algebraic Problems*
TB/525

WILLARD VAN ORMAN QUINE: Mathematical
T

O. G. SUTTON: Mathematics in Action. *Foreword* *James R. Newman. Illus.*   T

FREDERICK WAISMANN: Introduction to Mathematical Thinking. *Foreword by Karl Menger*   T

Philosophy of Science

R. B. BRAITHWAITE: Scientific Explanation   T

J. BRONOWSKI: Science and Human Values. *Il* T

ALBERT EINSTEIN: Philosopher-Scientist. *Edit* *Paul A. Schilpp*   Volume I T
Volume II T

WERNER HEISENBERG: Physics and Philosophy *Revolution in Modern Science. Introduction by* *C. Northrop*   T

JOHN MAYNARD KEYNES: A Treatise on Proba *Introduction by N. R. Hanson*   T

STEPHEN TOULMIN: Foresight and Understand *An Enquiry into the Aims of Science. Foreword* *Jacques Barzun*   T

STEPHEN TOULMIN: The Philosophy of Science *Introduction*   T

W. H. WATSON: On Understanding Physics. *A* *duction by Ernest Nagel*   T

G. J. WHITROW: The Natural Philosophy of Ti
T

Physics and Cosmology

DAVID BOHM: Causality and Chance in Mc Physics. *Foreword by Louis de Broglie*   T

P. W. BRIDGMAN: The Nature of Thermodynam
T

LOUIS DE BROGLIE: Physics and Microphysics. *word by Albert Einstein*   T

T. G. COWLING: Molecules in Motion: *An Intr* *tion to the Kinetic Theory of Gases. Illus.*   T

A. C. CROMBIE, Ed.: Turning Point in Physics   T

C. V. DURELL: Readable Relativity. *Foreword by* *man J. Dyson*   T

ARTHUR EDDINGTON: Space, Time and Gravita *An outline of the General Relativity Theory*   T

MAX JAMMER: Concepts of Force: *A Study in* *Foundation of Dynamics*   TB

MAX JAMMER: Concepts of Space: *The Histor* *Theories of Space in Physics. Foreword by A* *Einstein*   TB

EDMUND WHITTAKER: History of the Theorie Aether and Electricity
Volume I: *The Classical Theories* T
Volume II: *The Modern Theories* T

G. J. WHITROW: The Structure and Evolution o Universe: *An Introduction to Cosmology. Ill*
TB

8352 1422